CARDIOVASCULAR DISABILITY

Updating the Social Security Listings

Committee on Social Security Cardiovascular Disability Criteria

Board on the Health of Select Populations

INSTITUTE OF MEDICINE
OF THE NATIONAL ACADEMIES

THE NATIONAL ACADEMIES PRESS
Washington, D.C.
www.nap.edu

THE NATIONAL ACADEMIES PRESS 500 Fifth Street, N.W. Washington, DC 20001

NOTICE: The project that is the subject of this report was approved by the Governing Board of the National Research Council, whose members are drawn from the councils of the National Academy of Sciences, the National Academy of Engineering, and the Institute of Medicine. The members of the committee responsible for the report were chosen for their special competences and with regard for appropriate balance.

This study was supported by Contract No. SS-00-08-60149 between the National Academy of Sciences and the Social Security Administration. Any opinions, findings, conclusions, or recommendations expressed in this publication are those of the author(s) and do not necessarily reflect the view of the organizations or agencies that provided support for this project.

International Standard Book Number-13: 978-0-309-15698-1
International Standard Book Number-10: 0-309-15698-X

Additional copies of this report are available from The National Academies Press, 500 Fifth Street, N.W., Lockbox 285, Washington, DC 20055; (800) 624-6242 or (202) 334-3313 (in the Washington metropolitan area); Internet, http://www.nap.edu.

For more information about the Institute of Medicine, visit the IOM home page at: **www.iom.edu.**

Printed in the United States of America

The serpent has been a symbol of long life, healing, and knowledge among almost all cultures and religions since the beginning of recorded history. The serpent adopted as a logotype by the Institute of Medicine is a relief carving from ancient Greece, now held by the Staatliche Museen in Berlin.

Suggested citation: IOM (Institute of Medicine). 2010. *Cardiovascular disability: Updating the Social Security listings*. Washington, DC: The National Academies Press.

"Knowing is not enough; we must apply.
Willing is not enough; we must do."
—Goethe

INSTITUTE OF MEDICINE
OF THE NATIONAL ACADEMIES

Advising the Nation. Improving Health.

THE NATIONAL ACADEMIES

Advisers to the Nation on Science, Engineering, and Medicine

The **National Academy of Sciences** is a private, nonprofit, self-perpetuating society of distinguished scholars engaged in scientific and engineering research, dedicated to the furtherance of science and technology and to their use for the general welfare. Upon the authority of the charter granted to it by the Congress in 1863, the Academy has a mandate that requires it to advise the federal government on scientific and technical matters. Dr. Ralph J. Cicerone is president of the National Academy of Sciences.

The **National Academy of Engineering** was established in 1964, under the charter of the National Academy of Sciences, as a parallel organization of outstanding engineers. It is autonomous in its administration and in the selection of its members, sharing with the National Academy of Sciences the responsibility for advising the federal government. The National Academy of Engineering also sponsors engineering programs aimed at meeting national needs, encourages education and research, and recognizes the superior achievements of engineers. Dr. Charles M. Vest is president of the National Academy of Engineering.

The **Institute of Medicine** was established in 1970 by the National Academy of Sciences to secure the services of eminent members of appropriate professions in the examination of policy matters pertaining to the health of the public. The Institute acts under the responsibility given to the National Academy of Sciences by its congressional charter to be an adviser to the federal government and, upon its own initiative, to identify issues of medical care, research, and education. Dr. Harvey V. Fineberg is president of the Institute of Medicine.

The **National Research Council** was organized by the National Academy of Sciences in 1916 to associate the broad community of science and technology with the Academy's purposes of furthering knowledge and advising the federal government. Functioning in accordance with general policies determined by the Academy, the Council has become the principal operating agency of both the National Academy of Sciences and the National Academy of Engineering in providing services to the government, the public, and the scientific and engineering communities. The Council is administered jointly by both Academies and the Institute of Medicine. Dr. Ralph J. Cicerone and Dr. Charles M. Vest are chair and vice chair, respectively, of the National Research Council.

www.national-academies.org

COMMITTEE ON SOCIAL SECURITY CARDIOVASCULAR DISABILITY CRITERIA

NANETTE K. WENGER (*Chair*), Emory University School of Medicine and Grady Memorial Hospital, Atlanta, Georgia
WILLIAM E. BODEN, University at Buffalo Schools of Medicine and Public Health and Kaleida Health, New York
BLASE A. CARABELLO, Michael E. DeBakey Veterans Affairs Medical Center, Houston, Texas
ROBERT M. CARNEY, Washington University School of Medicine, St. Louis, Missouri
MANUEL D. CERQUEIRA, Cleveland Clinic Lerner College of Medicine of Case Western Reserve University, Ohio
MICHAEL H. CRIQUI, University of California, San Diego
ANDREW E. EPSTEIN, University of Pennsylvania and Philadelphia Veterans Affairs Medical Center
ERIKA S. FROELICHER, University of California, San Francisco
GARY H. GIBBONS, Morehouse School of Medicine, Atlanta, Georgia
MARK A. HLATKY, Stanford University, California
ALICE K. JACOBS, Boston University School of Medicine and Boston Medical Center, Massachusetts
KAREN S. KUEHL, George Washington University, Children's National Medical Center, and Washington Hospital Center, Washington, DC
TODD D. MILLER, Mayo Clinic, Rochester, Minnesota
LYNNE W. STEVENSON, Harvard Medical School and Brigham and Women's Hospital, Boston, Massachusetts

Consultant

HOWARD H. GOLDMAN, University of Maryland School of Medicine, Baltimore

Study Staff

FREDERICK (RICK) ERDTMANN, Director, Board on the Health of Select Populations
MICHAEL McGEARY, Study Director
SUSAN R. McCUTCHEN, Senior Program Associate
ERIN E. WILHELM, Research Associate
LAVITA D. COATES-FOGLE, Senior Program Assistant
PAMELA RAMEY-McCRAY, Administrative Assistant
SAMANTHA CHAO, Program Officer
JOI WASHINGTON, Senior Program Assistant
ANDREA COHEN, Financial Associate
WILLIAM McLEOD, Senior Librarian

Reviewers

This report has been reviewed in draft form by individuals chosen for their diverse perspectives and technical expertise, in accordance with procedures approved by the National Research Council's Report Review Committee. The purpose of this independent review is to provide candid and critical comments that will assist the institution in making its published report as sound as possible and to ensure that the report meets institutional standards for objectivity, evidence, and responsiveness to the study charge. The review comments and draft manuscript remain confidential to protect the integrity of the deliberative process. We wish to thank the following individuals for their review of this report:

James A. Blumenthal, Duke University Medical Center, Durham, North Carolina
Robert O. Bonow, Northwestern University Feinberg School of Medicine and Northwestern Memorial Hospital, Chicago, Illinois
Deborah Chyun, New York University
David P. Faxon, Brigham and Women's Hospital, Boston, Massachusetts
Gary S. Francis, Cleveland Clinic and Case Western Reserve University, Minneapolis, Minnesota
William L. Henrich, University of Texas Health Science at San Antonio
William R. Hiatt, University of Colorado, Denver
Stuart Rich, University of Chicago Medical Center, Illinois
Roberta G. Williams, University of Southern California and Childrens Hospital, Los Angeles

Although the reviewers listed above have provided many constructive comments and suggestions, they were not asked to endorse the conclusions or recommendations nor did they see the final draft of the report before its release. The review of this report was overseen by **Harlan M. Krumholz,** Yale University, and **Johanna T. Dwyer,** Tufts University. Appointed by the National Research Council and Institute of Medicine, they were responsible for making certain that an independent examination of this report was carried out in accordance with institutional procedures and that all review comments were carefully considered. Responsibility for the final content of this report rests entirely with the authoring committee and the institution.

Preface

The Committee on Social Security Cardiovascular Disability Criteria, an ad hoc committee of medical experts appointed by the Institute of Medicine (IOM), was charged to conduct a study to assist the Social Security Administration (SSA) with revising its criteria for cardiovascular disability in its Listing of Impairments ("the Listings"). The committee reviewed the current cardiovascular disability criteria in the Listings and identified areas in which the committee believed the cardiovascular listings should be revised and updated based on current medical knowledge and practice. Specifically, the committee (1) conducted a comprehensive review of the relevant research literature and current professional practice guidelines developed jointly by the American Heart Association and the American College of Cardiology; (2) assessed the current cardiovascular listings in light of current research knowledge and evidence-based medical practice; and (3) produced a concise report with specific recommendations for revision of the cardiovascular listings based on evidence (to the extent possible) and on professional judgment (where evidence was lacking). SSA uses the Listings to expedite the approval of claims from individuals who are so obviously disabled that they have a high probability of being found disabled if SSA went through the full disability determination process. The primary purpose of the consensus committee was to make concrete recommendations designed to improve the utility of the cardiovascular listings for evaluating disability claims by improving the sensitivity and specificity of the listing criteria to identify individuals who meet SSA's definition of disability, that is, those who are no longer able to engage in substantial work activities.

The contemporary approach to patient-centered care is designed to achieve optimal outcomes, including disease outcomes. This is the approach that the committee extended to tailor a process for disability evaluation that would ensure optimal outcomes.

The committee is grateful for the contributions of many individuals who expanded our knowledge and understanding of cardiovascular disability and suggested improvements in the disability evaluation process. They are listed in the Acknowledgments section of this report. The committee acknowledges with deepest appreciation the expert support and collegial relationship of the IOM staff. They are Michael McGeary (study director), Susan McCutchen (senior program associate), Erin Wilhelm (research associate), LaVita Coates-Fogle (senior program assistant), and Frederick (Rick) Erdtmann (director, Board on the Health of Select Populations).

The cardiovascular community has a tradition of evidence-based clinical practice guidelines that address a number of cardiovascular disease states. These guidelines are updated periodically to reflect current knowledge. A specific and uniform grading system identifies the level of evidence and the robustness of the database supporting this evidence. However, a review of the currently applicable clinical practice guidelines, although with abundant recommendations for diagnostic and prognostic testing, clinical management, and resultant outcomes, clearly shows (as viewed by the committee) an unmet need for a research base for the evaluation of cardiovascular disability.

The approach of the committee is its unique contribution. Careful review of the scientific literature from both primary and secondary sources was undertaken to identify tests or procedures that would quantify functional capacity and, furthermore, be generally available either in the claimants' medical records or for purchase in the assessment of potential claimants. With this in mind, we sought to apply the best available knowledge and to recommend new practices and perspectives to ensure the optimal outcomes for disability claimants who meet SSA's definition of disability.

Highlighted in the committee deliberations was that a large number of recently available cardiovascular test procedures precisely delineate anatomy or pathoanatomy, but that there is no consistent relationship between anatomy and functional capacity. The committee therefore concluded that the tests delineating anatomy should be used to define the presence and severity of disease, but that the disability process usually requires additional information on the functional limitations imposed by the disease. The committee recommended revisions in most of the current listings and suggested new listings for certain cardiovascular problems, including hypertrophic cardiomyopathy, right heart failure, and pulmonary hypertension. We developed flowcharts for decision making for most of the cardiovascular listings to assist the adjudicator in the definition of disease and levels of functional limitations required to meet those listings. We also reviewed important comorbidities that the adjudicator should consider in assessing whether a claimant's cardiovascular condition equals a listing. Finally, we delineated four areas of research that SSA could pursue to improve the disability decision process, including the listings.

The committee first met in December 2009, with three subsequent formal sessions in February, April, and June 2010 (and numerous conference calls), during which we categorized and evaluated cardiovascular medically determinable physical and mental impairments that could be expected to result in death or that have lasted or can be expected to last for a continuous period of not less than 12 months.

I would like to express my personal gratitude for the skills and dedication of the individual committee members and for their expertise, enthusiasm, and energy. On behalf of the committee, I would also like to thank Howard Goldman, who chairs IOM's standing committee of medical experts to assist SSA, for his participation and advice.

The intellectual content is evidence based and objective. The conclusions were reached by consensus and are the combined judgment of the committee. Our emphasis in this report is on consistency, quality, and appropriateness criteria.

Future covariables that should influence disability determination and guide its research agenda include the impact of changes in the national and regional economy, changes in health insurance and access to health care and disease evaluation, and the expansion of the evidence base enabled by open government, among others. All are likely to alter cardiovascular disease outcomes and inform consequent cardiovascular disability determinations.

Nanette K. Wenger
Chair, Committee on Social Security
Cardiovascular Disability Criteria

Acknowledgments

Many individuals and organizations contributed to the study. In particular, the committee and staff would like to thank:

ROBYN BARST, Columbia University College of Physicians and Surgeons
AMY BASKEN, National Congenital Heart Association
MARGARET BEARDSWORTH, Pulmonary Hypertension Association
WILLIAM R. DAVIDSON, JR., Penn State Milton S. Hershey Medical Center
CHRISTINE DEHAAN, Social Security Administration
LAURENCE DESI, SR., Social Security Administration
ROBIN DOYLE, Social Security Administration
SHEILA EVERETT, Social Security Administration
HARRISON FARBER, Boston University
JAMES W. FASULES, American College of Cardiology
JOSEPHINE GRIMA, National Marfan Foundation
LARRY F. HAMM, American Association of Cardiovascular and Pulmonary Rehabilitation
MONTE HETLAND, Social Security Administration
JAMILLAH JACKSON, Social Security Administration
KATHERINE KRONER, Pulmonary Hypertension Association
VANESSA LEVINE, Alliance of Community Health Plans
GAVIN LINDBERG, Health and Medicine Council of Washington
JOANNA MARASHLIAN, Social Security Administration

PATRICK E. McBRIDE, American Association of Cardiovascular and Pulmonary Rehabilitation
GREGORY L. MONETA, Oregon Health and Science University
MICHELLE J. NICKOLAUS, Penn State Milton S. Hershey Medical Center
MIKE O'CONNOR, Social Security Administration
RONALD J. OUDIZ, University of California, Los Angeles
KEVIN PARMER, Social Security Administration
JEFFREY PRICE, National Association of Disability Examiners (NADE) and North Carolina Disability Determination Services
J. SCOTT PRITCHARD, NADE and Oregon Disability Determination Services
FRANK SCHUSTER, Social Security Administration
PAUL SCOTT, Social Security Administration
ARTHUR R. SPENCER, Social Security Administration
SHIRLEETA STANTON, Social Security Administration
STEVEN STEINBERG, Social Security Administration
JANET TRUHE, Social Security Administration
AMY VERSTAPPEN, Adult Congenital Heart Association
CHERYL WILLIAMS, Social Security Administration
ROBERTA G. WILLIAMS, University of Southern California

In addition, the committee would like to thank those at the Social Security Administration headquarters and regional offices who helped arrange the visits of committee members to state disability determination services (DDS) offices and the staff in the DDSs who took the time to explain the disability determination process and how the Listings are used in that process, and to discuss practical problems encountered in using them.

Contents

APPENDIXES

Tables, Figures, and Boxes

TABLES

FIGURES

BOXES

Abbreviations and Acronyms

AAA	abdominal aortic aneurysm
ABI	ankle-brachial index
ACC	American College of Cardiology
ACE	angiotensin-converting enzyme
ACS	acute coronary syndrome
ADLs	activities of daily living
AHA	American Heart Association
ALJ	administrative law judge
AR	aortic regurgitation
AVNRT	atrioventricular nodal reentrant tachycardia
AVRT	atrioventricular reentrant tachycardia
BMI	body mass index
BMS	bare metal stents
BNP	brain natriuretic peptide
BP	blood pressure
BRFSS	Behavioral Risk Factor Surveillance System
CABG	coronary artery bypass graft
CAD	coronary artery disease
CCB	calcium channel blocker
CCS	Canadian Cardiovascular Society
CDC	Centers for Disease Control and Prevention
CDR	continuing disability review
CE	consultative examination

CHD	chronic heart disease
cm	centimeter
COPD	chronic obstructive pulmonary disease
CPX	cardiopulmonary exercise
CT	computed tomography
CTA	computed tomography angiography
CVD	cardiovascular disease; chronic venous disease
CVI	chronic venous insufficiency
CXR	chest x-ray
DDS	disability determination services
DES	drug-eluting stent
DM	diabetes mellitus
Dx	diagnosis
ECG	electrocardiogram
EECP	enhanced external counterpulsation
EF	ejection fraction
ESV	end systolic volume
ETT	exercise tolerance test
EVAR	endovascular aneurysm repair
FDA	Food and Drug Administration
HDL	high-density lipoprotein cholesterol
HF	heart failure
HFpEF	heart failure with preserved ejection fraction
IADLs	instrumental activities of daily living
ICD	implantable cardioverter-defibrillator
ICD	International Classification of Diseases
IHD	ischemic heart disease
IOM	Institute of Medicine
kg	kilogram
LA	left atrial/atrium
LDL	low-density lipoprotein cholesterol
LED	lower extremity disease
LV	left ventricle
LVDD	left ventricular diastolic dysfunction
LVEF	left ventricular ejection fraction
LVOT	left ventricular outflow tract

m	meter
MER	medical evidence of record
MESA	Multi-Ethnic Study of Atherosclerosis
METs	metabolic equivalents of task
MI	myocardial infarction
MIE	medical improvement expected
min	minute
MINE	medical improvement not expected
MIP	medical improvement possible
ml	milliliter
mm	millimeter
mm Hg	millimeters of mercury
mph	miles per hour
MR	mitral regurgitation
MRA	magnetic resonance angiography
MRI	magnetic resonance imaging
NHANES	National Health and Nutrition Examination Survey
NHLBI	National Heart, Lung, and Blood Institute
NPRM	Notice of Proposed Rulemaking
NRC	National Research Council
NT-proBNP	N-terminal prohormone brain natriuretic peptide
O_2	oxygen
PAD	peripheral artery disease
PCI	percutaneous coronary intervention
PET	positron emission tomography
PO_2	partial pressure of oxygen
POMS	Program Operations Manual System
proBNP	prohormone brain natriuretic peptide
PVC	premature ventricular contraction
PVD	peripheral vascular disease
RER	respiratory exchange ratio
RFC	residual functional capacity
SD	standard deviation
sec	second
SGA	substantial gainful activity
SIP	Sickness Impact Profile
SPECT	single-photon emission computerized tomography
SRS	summed reversibility score

SSA	Social Security Administration
SSDI	Social Security Disability Insurance
SSI	Supplemental Security Income
SSS	summed stress score
TA	thoracic aorta
TBI	toe-brachial index
TG	triglycerides
TID	transient ischemic dilatation
Torr	Torricelli
U.S.	United States
VHD	valvular heart disease
VO_2	oxygen consumption
WHO	World Health Organization
WMA	wall motion abnormality
WMI	wall motion index

Executive Summary

In 2010, more than 3.3 million individuals are expected to apply to the Social Security Administration (SSA) for disability benefits. SSA uses a five-step evaluation process to determine disability. This sequential decision process is both time and resource intensive, because determining whether applicants (referred to as claimants in this report) qualify for benefits is a complex process.

To streamline the process, SSA uses a screening tool called the Listing of Impairments (known as the Listings) to identify claimants who are the most severely impaired, that is, disabled to such a degree that they do not need to go through the full sequential decision process. These individuals, if evidence in their medical records indicates that they cannot work or that their illness is likely to be terminal within a relatively short period of time, are found to be disabled immediately. Claimants whose medical conditions do not meet SSA's criteria at the Listings step are not necessarily denied; rather, they are further evaluated based on their functional capacity, work history, education, and age. There are different, non-work-based criteria for children under age 18 in the Supplemental Security Income program. However, as for adults, the Listings for children are meant to identify the most severely impaired claimants so that SSA does not have to go through the entire disability evaluation process. The Listings also apply to beneficiaries (i.e., people who are already receiving disability benefits) who must undergo a periodic review of their continuing disability. The purpose of the Listings is to provide a more rapid decision for individuals, whether claimants or beneficiaries, who clearly would qualify based on the severity of their medical condition, at the same time saving SSA the substantial administrative costs of an in-depth vocational evaluation.

SSA currently organizes the Listings under 15 body systems, including the cardiovascular system. Because of the key role the Listings play in the disability determination process, they should reflect advances in medical treatment and diagnostic methods, be cognizant of the changing nature of employment in the United States, and be administratively practical to apply. SSA asked the Institute of Medicine (IOM) to convene an expert committee to recommend improvements in the cardiovascular system listings. Last revised in 2006, the cardiovascular system comprises eight adult and five child categories of impairments. In response to its charge, the IOM committee concluded that the functional performance of individuals with cardiovascular conditions, or with multiple conditions across body systems, deserves greater emphasis in determining disability under the listings. In considering changes that SSA could make to the listings, the committee concluded that relying solely on objective anatomical measures of impairment to assess an individual's disability status without considering function would be insufficient, as such measures generally correlate only weakly with degree of disability. Incorporating measures of functional assessment allows for a more effective evaluation of the work capacity of the whole person.

The committee's approach to developing listing-level criteria was first to determine if a test result (e.g., reduced left ventricular ejection fraction) or set of test results is sufficient to ensure that virtually all individuals with such results are unable to work. Second, if anatomical measures are insufficient to evaluate work disability, as is the case for most cardiovascular conditions, the committee recommended that evidence-based functional assessments, if not already required in the listing, should also be applied to meet a listing.

Exercise tests on a treadmill or bicycle provide an objective measure of a person's maximal aerobic capacity and are commonly used to provide diagnostic and prognostic information. The information can also be compared with the aerobic demands of various jobs, usually expressed as metabolic equivalents (METs). SSA currently uses inability to achieve five METs as a listing-level criterion for ischemic heart disease, heart failure, and congenital heart disease in adults, and will pay to have such tests performed if they are necessary for adjudication and considered safe for the claimant.

The committee determined that the current state of medical evidence shows that exercise tests are generally safe for patients with cardiovascular conditions such as ischemic heart disease, heart failure, and congenital heart disease, and found that SSA's criteria for determining whether it is safe to order an exercise test are too strict. The committee urges SSA to update the safety criteria to allow broader use of exercise testing in the disability evaluation process. In cases in which exercise testing is not useful or safe for the claimant, the committee recommends that SSA use alternative procedures such as the 6-minute walk or heel rise tests. SSA should also use validated instruments to assess a claimant's capacity to perform everyday activities, such as activities of daily living (ADLs) and instrumental ADLs, where exercise is not possible or contraindicated (e.g., in cases of severe peripheral vascular disease, valve disease, or arrhythmias).

This report provides 24 recommendations, most of which offer detailed advice for revising the current listings. The committee also recommends establishing new listings in the cardiovascular system for pulmonary hypertension with vascular causes and for severe symptomatic aortic stenosis, and adding more criteria for heart failure caused by cardiomyopathy or right heart failure. Suggested criteria for these new listings are provided.

The report also addresses some common comorbidities associated with cardiovascular diseases. Unfortunately, there is no validated method for quantifying the combined effects of comorbidities, such as major depression and cardiovascular impairments. However, the report provides information on the impact of comorbidities on individuals with cardiovascular diseases and urges SSA to provide such information to its adjudicators and maintain its currency.

During the course of its work, the committee encountered several critical knowledge gaps (for example, the relationship of anatomical severity measures and functional limitation and the effect of comorbidities), and recommends that SSA pursue research opportunities, both within the organization and externally, to improve the quality of the Listings and to better inform future revisions of the cardiovascular and other body systems. In the final chapter, the committee suggests several ways to approach this research.

Overview

The Social Security Administration (SSA) asked the Institute of Medicine (IOM) to conduct a 1-year study and make recommendations for improving the cardiovascular disability criteria in the SSA Listing of Impairments. The Listings, as they are known, contain criteria for determining incapacity to work due to the effects of more than 120 adult and 90 childhood diseases and conditions that cause disability. SSA uses the Listings as a screening tool early in the disability determination process to identify applicants (referred to as claimants in this report) for benefits who are so severely impaired that further information about their vocational capacity or other factors, such as age, educational attainment, and work history, is not needed to rule favorably on their claims for disability benefits. This screening device shortens the decision process, which gives claimants a more rapid decision and saves SSA substantial administrative costs.

There are different criteria that are not based on work for children under age 18 in the Supplemental Security Income program. However, as for adults, the Listings for children are meant to identify the most severely impaired claimants, so that SSA does not have to go through the entire disability evaluation process.

Given the role of the Listings in expediting decisions and reducing administrative workload, it is important that they conform to advances in treatment and diagnostic methods as well as to the changing nature of employment in the United States. The Listings should also be consistent, correct, and as easy to use as possible. Accordingly, SSA periodically revises them. To assist in the process of revising the cardiovascular system listings, SSA asked the IOM to form an expert committee to "review the medical literature to determine the latest standards of care, the latest technology for the understanding of disease processes, and the latest science demonstrating the effect of cardiovascular disorders on patients' health and functional capacity" and "to make concrete recommendations that are designed to improve the utility of the cardiovascular listings for evaluating cardiovascular disability claims by improving the sensitivity and specificity of the listing criteria to identify individuals who meet SSA's definition of disability" (see Box 1-1 in Chapter 1 for relevant excerpts from the contractual statement of work).

The IOM formed a committee of cardiovascular experts (see Appendix A for their biographies). The committee met four times in plenary session. Much of the work was performed by groups of committee members assigned to address specific cardiovascular conditions. Committee members heard presentations and received position statements from clinical experts and advocacy groups and considered their comments. They reviewed the relevant scientific literature, based their recommendations on existing evidence, and drew on the clinical practice guidelines of the American College of Cardiology (ACC) and American Heart Association (AHA). The body of this report contains the committee's consensus conclusions and recommendations concerning the cardiovascular system listings (Chapters 5 through 14). A description of the literature search methodology and an analysis of the ACC/AHA guidelines are found in Appendixes B and C, respectively.

SOCIAL SECURITY DISABILITY

The Social Security Act defines disability as "the inability to engage in any substantial gainful activity by reason of any medically determinable physical or mental impairment(s) which can be expected to result in death or which has lasted or can be expected to last for a continuous period of not less than 12 months." Under the Supplemental Security Income (SSI) program, a child is "considered disabled if he or she has a medically determinable physical or mental impairment or combination of impairments that causes marked and severe functional limitations, and that can be expected to cause death or that has lasted or can be expected to last for a continuous period of not less than 12 months."

The SSA disability standard is not based on a diagnosis or on degree of anatomical impairment alone. Rather, it focuses on the functional limitations imposed by one or more impairments and how they affect an individual's capacity to work given the limitations caused by the medical impairment or impairments and his or her age, education, and work history, or in the case of children, how the impairment or impairments limit age-appropriate activities at home, at school, and in the community. Deciding if someone meets the SSA disability standard by considering these factors is time and resource intensive. The Listings are a means for SSA to quickly identify claims that would be approved by the full evaluation process without having to go through the full process.[1]

THE LISTINGS AND THE DISABILITY DECISION PROCESS

Initially, SSA uses a five-step decision process to determine whether adults are disabled (Figure O-1).[2] The steps are followed in a set order, and the analysis stops at any step at which a decision about disability is made. The Listings are applied at the third step.

Step 1

The SSA field office determines whether the claimant is engaging in substantial gainful activity.[3] If yes, the claimant is found not disabled. If no, the claim is forwarded to the disability determination services (DDS) for evaluation.

Step 2

In most states, a DDS team comprising a lay "disability examiner" and a "medical consultant" or "psychological consultant" determines if there is evidence of a severe, medically determinable impairment or combination of impairments.[4] If no, the claimant is found not disabled. If a severe impairment or impairments are indicated, the analysis proceeds to Step 3.

---

[1] SSA has three additional ways to expedite decisions: (1) flagging TERI (TERminal Illness) cases for expedited processing; (2) using a predictive model to identify QDD (Quick Disability Determination) cases that are highly likely to be allowed and processing them within 20 days; and (3) using CAL (Compassionate ALlowances) to approve cases with certain diagnoses—either terminal (e.g., gallbladder cancer) or permanently disabling (e.g., mixed dementia).

[2] If denied benefits, a claimant may appeal. SSA has several levels of appeal, and the claimant also has the right to appeal in federal court (described in Chapter 2). Although the Listings are used at each level of appeal, for simplicity, this report focuses on the initial determinations made by state agencies called disability determination services (DDSs) that, by law, make the initial determinations for SSA.

[3] Substantial gainful activity is generally defined as earning more than a certain monthly amount, which is $1,640 for statutorily blind individuals and $1,000 for nonblind individuals in 2010.

[4] In some DDSs, disability examiners are permitted to make certain disability determinations alone under a pilot program that SSA is conducting.

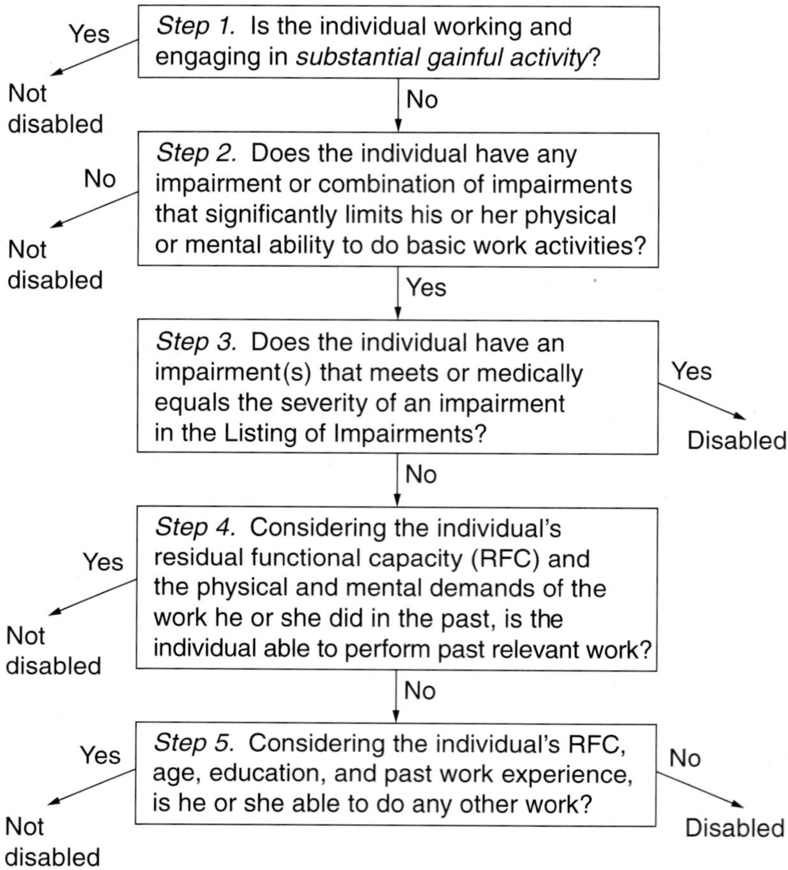

FIGURE O-1 Five-step sequential evaluation process for adults.
SOURCES: 20 CFR §§ 404.1520 and 416.920.

Step 3

The DDS team compares the information in the case file with the Listings. If the impairment or set of impairments meets all of the requirements of a specific listing, or equals one in severity, the claimant is generally found disabled.[5] If not, the analysis proceeds to Step 4.

[5] The law also includes a "duration requirement." The impairment must be expected to result in death or the disability must have lasted or be expected to last for a continuous period of at least 12 consecutive months.

Step 4

The DDS team assesses the claimant's residual functional capacity (RFC)[6] and compares it with the physical and mental demands of work he or she did in the past 15 years. If the claimant is judged able to do past relevant work, he or she is found not disabled. Otherwise, the analysis proceeds to Step 5.

Step 5

The DDS team decides whether the claimant is able to do any other work, given his or her RFC, age, education, and past work experience. If the claimant can do other work, he or she is found not disabled. If not, and if the impairment or impairments meet the duration requirement, he or she is found disabled.

SSI Children's Claims

Claims of children under SSI go through the first three steps of the decision process. Because the law provides a stricter standard of disability for SSI children based on listing-level severity, there are no steps for children beyond Step 3. However, if a child's impairment or impairments do not meet or medically equal a listing, the child may still be found disabled at Step 3 based on a finding that the impairment or impairments "functionally equal the listings." Unlike the policies of meeting and medically equaling listings, functional equivalence does not refer to any specific listings. Rather, the finding is based on limitations of age-appropriate abilities in several functional domains, such as task completion and social interaction (see Chapter 2 for further explanation). This policy is unique to children under the SSI rules.

CARDIOVASCULAR DISABILITY TRENDS

Currently, there are eight adult cardiovascular system listings and five child-specific listings (Table O-1).[7] (If a child has a condition not included in the child-specific cardiovascular listings, e.g., an aortic aneurysm, he or

[6] In general, RFC is what the individual can still do in a work setting despite the limitations from all of his or her medical impairments, including any impairments that are not severe.

[7] Unless otherwise indicated, the Listings referred to in this summary are contained in the SSA document, *Disability Evaluation Under Social Security*, issued in September 2008 (SSA, 2008a,b). This document contains the current cardiovascular listings and is also available online for adults at http://www.ssa.gov/disability/professionals/bluebook/AdultListings.htm and for children at http://www.ssa.gov/disability/professionals/bluebook/ChildhoodListings.htm.

TABLE O-1 Current Adult and Child Cardiovascular Listings

Adult		Child	
4.02	Chronic heart failure	104.02	Chronic heart failure
4.04	Ischemic heart disease		
4.05	Recurrent arrhythmias	104.05	Recurrent arrhythmias
4.06	Congenital heart disease	104.06	Congenital heart disease
4.09	Heart transplant	104.09	Heart transplant
4.10	Aneurysm of aorta or major branches		
4.11	Chronic venous insufficiency		
4.12	Peripheral arterial disease		
		104.13	Rheumatic heart disease

SOURCES: SSA, 2008a (for adults), 2008b (for children).

she is evaluated using the adult Listings criteria.) The cardiovascular listings were last updated in 2006.

In calendar year 2009, SSA allowed approximately 64,000 adult claims for cardiovascular disability. Of these, 15,000 (24 percent) were allowed based on impairments that met or medically equaled listings. Chronic heart failure (CHF) accounted for 42 percent of the listings-based allowances in 2009, followed by chronic venous insufficiency (21 percent) and ischemic heart disease (17 percent).

In 2009, SSA also allowed approximately 3,500 child claims for cardiovascular disability; most (82 percent) were for meeting or medically equaling a listing and the remainder (18 percent) were for functionally equaling a listing. Most of the child allowances (93 percent) were for a congenital heart condition or conditions.

APPROACHES TO REVISING THE CARDIOVASCULAR LISTINGS

Before summarizing the major conclusions and recommendations regarding each of the cardiovascular listings, it is helpful to review issues that apply generally to all listings and that explain some commonalities in the recommendations. These include the criteria for evaluating the specific listings, the trade-offs between sensitivity and specificity inherent in designing a screening tool like the Listings, the limited predictive capacity of most clinical factors, and the safety of exercise tests.

The general approach taken by the committee was to use the following algorithm to arrive at listing-level criteria that are the most objective and the easiest to administer, while maintaining a reasonable degree of accuracy.

For each type of cardiovascular impairment:

1. Determine if there is a diagnosis that by itself indicates either (A) a terminal illness of short duration or (B) a condition so severely incapacitating that it is nearly always work disabling. If one exists, make it a sufficient requirement for a listing-level allowance (also consider recommending it as a compassionate allowance if it is not already designated as one).
2. If the diagnosis is not sufficient by itself to be a listing-level criterion, determine if there is an accepted measure of impairment severity shown to have a high degree of association with incapacity to work or with very serious functional limitations that would seem to preclude work. If there is, make that degree of impairment severity a sufficient requirement (given the diagnosis) for a listing-level allowance.
3. If the diagnosis and/or severity measure or measures are insufficient to accurately differentiate disabled from nondisabled claimants, require evidence that the claimant is seriously functionally limited.

Limitations of the Listings as a Screening Tool

The Listings are used to determine if a claimant is able to engage in any gainful activity, that is, perform any work for pay or profit. In fact, the work capacity of a population of claimants with a given impairment will vary on a continuum from no work to high work capacity. Along this continuum, the line between having no work capacity and some work capacity can be difficult to draw. This uncertainty results in classification errors, that is, false negatives (claimants denied who should be allowed) and false positives (claimants allowed who should have been denied). As with other diagnostic screening tools, tightening the criteria reduces false positives (thus increasing specificity), but it also increases the likelihood of false negatives (thus reducing sensitivity). Loosening the criteria will reduce false negatives (thus allowing a larger percentage of true positives to be allowed quickly), but it will also increase the number of false positives.

SSA wants to keep the false-positive rate low, while maintaining the sensitivity of the Listings. The greater the sensitivity of a listing, the greater the percentage of Step 3 allowances that is made for those truly unable to work. Therefore, in formulating recommendations to improve the Listings, the committee focused on the trade-off between sensitivity and specificity and sought ways to increase sensitivity without unduly reducing specificity. The only way to increase both sensitivity and specificity is to find or develop a better discriminator between true positives and true negatives, which is a research goal discussed below.

Limited Predictive Ability of Clinical Factors

Objective clinical factors are limited in their ability to predict the functional capacity of an individual with an impairment or impairments. These limitations make it challenging to balance the sensitivity and specificity of the Listings criteria. For example, few individuals with a left ventricular ejection fraction (LVEF) of 30 percent or less are able to engage in usual daily activities, including working in an office, but some could. The latter would be false positives using the 30 percent criterion. Meanwhile, some individuals with an ejection fraction greater than 30 percent are totally incapacitated in the same circumstances. They would be the false negatives using this criterion.

This imprecision of clinical measures of impairment in determining disability led the committee to recommend that evidence of functional limitations be required in addition to clinical criteria to meet most of the cardiovascular listings.

Maximizing the Use of Exercise Testing

The introductory section of the cardiovascular system listings highlights the extensive use of exercise tests to determine functional capacity in patients with ischemic heart disease, CHF, and peripheral artery disease. The text also indicates that SSA might purchase an exercise test if needed to determine whether a claimant's impairment or impairments meet or equal a cardiovascular listing; however, the current Listings are based on an overly strict assessment of the risk associated with the performance of these tests. In fact, an extensive body of research shows that exercise testing is safe in most cases and much safer than is assumed in the current Listings.

The committee encourages SSA to revise the cardiovascular listings to conform to the current understanding of the safety of exercise tests. Chapters 4, 5, 7, and 8 provide further detail on the relevant medical literature on the safety of exercise testing.

SUMMARY OF CONCLUSIONS AND RECOMMENDATIONS

Most of this report consists of detailed chapters on specific cardiovascular conditions that are already in the Listings or should be added. The chapters are summarized below, each followed by the committee's full recommendations.

Heart Failure, Cardiomyopathy, and Right Heart Failure

Heart failure (HF) occurs when the heart is unable to supply sufficient oxygenated blood to body tissues to meet systemic aerobic requirements or when the heart can only do so with elevated pressures that eventually damage it. The primary manifestations of HF are fatigue, dyspnea, and peripheral fluid retention, which alone or in combination may limit a patient's ability to perform activities and potentially lead to disability.

Most patients do not detect any functional limitation until their ejection fraction is less than 40 percent. A few patients can live virtually normal lives with an ejection fraction as low as 20 percent, but most with disease this advanced have major limitation of activity.

The most direct assessment of ability to work is the ability to perform physical exertion. A patient's ability to perform activities of daily living, work, and vigorous exertion requires the integration of cardiovascular, pulmonary, and circulatory systems. Since the current cardiovascular listings were issued in 2006, exercise testing has been consistently demonstrated and widely accepted to be practical and safe for most patients with chronic HF. The committee also recommends revising the chronic HF listing to include separate evaluation criteria for three related conditions: chronic HF, hypertrophic cardiomyopathy, and right HF. The current listing requires both an objective cardiac abnormality *and* a functional limitation, a construct that should be retained. In addition, the committee recommends adding a listing that can be met by having a left ventricular ejection fraction of 20 percent or less without having to demonstrate a functional limitation.

RECOMMENDATION 5-1. Retain the current framework of listing 4.02 chronic heart failure, requiring both (A) an objective cardiac abnormality, and (B) a functional limitation. This framework would apply to each of the following: systolic heart failure, diastolic heart failure, hypertrophic cardiomyopathy, and right heart failure.

Systolic Heart Failure

The criteria for systolic heart failure should include:

A. An objective cardiac abnormality demonstrated by a left ventricular ejection fraction of 30 percent or less (or an ejection fraction of a systemic ventricle in congenital heart disease without an anatomic, systemic left ventricle), or a left ventricular diameter of 7 cm or greater,

AND

B. A functional abnormality demonstrated by one of three criteria:

1. Exercise testing (see Recommendation 5-2); or
2. Cardiologist-assessed excessive risk of exercise testing and cardiac limit to activities of daily living; or
3. Three hospitalization-equivalent events in the past 12 months.

Diastolic Heart Failure

The criteria for diastolic heart failure should include:

A. An objective cardiac abnormality demonstrated by moderate or severe diastolic dysfunction, usually indicated by echocardiography,

AND

B. A functional abnormality can be demonstrated by one of three criteria:

1. Exercise testing (see Recommendation 5-2); or
2. Cardiologist-assessed excessive risk of exercise testing and cardiac limit to activities of daily living; or
3. Three hospitalization-equivalent events in the past 12 months.

Hypertrophic Cardiomyopathy

The criteria for hypertrophic cardiomyopathy should include:

A. An objective cardiac abnormality demonstrated by a left ventricular or septal wall thickness greater than 15 mm in the absence of another known cause for left ventricular hypertrophy (e.g., hypertension, aortic valve disease),

AND

B. A functional abnormality demonstrated by one of three criteria:

1. Exercise testing (see Recommendation 5-2); or
2. Cardiologist-assessed excessive risk of exercise testing and cardiac limit to activities of daily living; or
3. Three hospitalization-equivalent events in the past 12 months.

Right Heart Failure

The criteria for right heart failure should require both an objective cardiac diagnosis implicated as a cause of right heart failure and clinical evidence of functional limitation manifest as severe systemic venous congestion:

A. An objective cardiac abnormality demonstrated by one of the following:

1. Congenital heart disease; or
2. Pulmonary hypertension; or
3. Right ventricular enlargement or dysfunction.

AND

B. Functional abnormalities meeting criteria for right heart failure:

1. Systemic venous congestion despite chronic diuretic therapy, assessed twice with at least 3 months in between, causing either

   - Peripheral edema to the knee or above; or
   - Severe ascites documented by abdominal imaging study.

RECOMMENDATION 5-2. Revise the exercise criteria to reflect the current acceptability of exercise testing as safe in heart failure and the objective measurements that can now be performed during exercise testing. Limitation is defined as a standard treadmill test (or bicycle test) performed at a workload equivalent to one of the following criteria:

- Less than 15 ml/kg/min peak VO_2/(oxygen consumption) on cardiopulmonary exercise test; or
- Less than 5 metabolic equivalents of task if using standard treadmill test without gas exchange.

RECOMMENDATION 5-3. Add an additional listing route in which the objective cardiac abnormality of a left ventricular ejection fraction of 20 percent or less, documented twice with at least 3 months intervening, is sufficiently severe that demonstration of functional limitation is not needed to meet the listing.

Heart Transplantation

A heart transplant is an option for some individuals for whom medical therapy alone does not successfully treat the symptoms associated with heart failure. However, heart transplant recipients require a period of time to recover after the transplant operation during the period of highest risk for complications such as infection, rejection of the donor heart, or other complications that may occur in the pre- or post-operative period. Based on contemporary practice, the committee concludes that patients who have undergone cardiac transplantation should receive at least a 6-month period to adequately recover.

For individuals who have undergone heart transplantation, SSA currently grants disability for the year after transplantation. After a year, the recipient is reevaluated under other, appropriate listings to determine if there is residual impairment that meets the SSA definition of disability, or whether the claimant is disabled based on RFC. The committee concludes that the current listing evaluation criteria for heart transplant recipients are appropriate and recommends that individuals granted disability for a year after their procedure be reevaluated beginning after 9 months to ensure that those who are still disabled do not experience a gap in benefits.

RECOMMENDATION 6-1. Maintain the current listing criterion for heart transplant recipients, meaning the claimant meets the listing (4.09) for 1 year after transplantation surgery.

RECOMMENDATION 6-2. Reevaluate heart transplant recipients for disability 9 months after surgery to avoid a potential gap in benefits should the claimant continue to be disabled because of residual impairment from transplantation or other cardiac or noncardiac causes.

Ischemic Heart Disease

Ischemia is defined as inadequate blood supply (circulation) to a local area due to blockage of the blood vessels supplying the area. Ischemic means that an organ is not getting adequate blood and oxygen. Ischemic heart disease, also called coronary artery disease or coronary heart disease (CHD), is the term given to heart problems caused by narrowed heart (coronary) arteries that supply blood to the heart muscle. Although the narrowing can be caused by a blood clot or by constriction of the blood vessel, most often it is caused by buildup of plaque, called atherosclerosis. When the blood flow to the heart muscle is completely blocked, the heart muscle cells die, which is termed a heart attack or myocardial infarction (MI). Most people with early (less than 50 percent narrowing) CHD do not experience symptoms or limitation of blood flow. However, as the atherosclerosis progresses, especially if left untreated, symptoms may occur. They are most likely to occur during exercise or emotional stress, when the demand for the oxygen carried by the blood increases.

The discomfort experienced when the heart muscle is deprived of adequate oxygen is called angina pectoris. This is a clinical syndrome characterized by discomfort in the chest, jaw, shoulder, back, or arms that is typically aggravated by exertion or emotional stress and relieved promptly with rest or by taking nitroglycerin. Angina usually occurs in patients with CHD, but it can also occur in individuals with valvular disease, hypertrophic cardiomyopathy, uncontrolled hypertension, and other, rarer causes.

Angina is classified using the Canadian Cardiovascular Society (CCS) scheme, which grades angina or an anginal equivalent (e.g., exertional dyspnea) based on the level of activity that causes symptoms. As many as 3 to 4 million Americans may have silent ischemia, or ischemia without pain, or a heart attack without prior warning. People with angina may also have undiagnosed episodes of silent ischemia. Furthermore, those who have had heart attacks or individuals with diabetes are at risk for developing silent ischemia.

CHD is the leading cause of death in both men and women. It caused one of every six U.S. deaths in 2006; CHD mortality was 425,425, and MI mortality was 141,462. Approximately every 25 seconds, an American will experience a coronary event, and approximately every minute a death will be attributed to a coronary event. Approximately every 34 seconds, an American has an MI, and in 15 percent of the cases it is fatal. In addition, in 2006, 1,115,000 inpatient diagnostic cardiac catheterizations were performed as well as 661,000 inpatient percutaneous coronary interventions (PCIs) and 253,000 coronary artery bypass surgery (CABG) procedures. The estimated direct and indirect cost of coronary heart disease for 2010 is $177.1 billion.

Because the extent of coronary disease alone as assessed by angiography does not reliably correlate with functional status, there is no anatomic diagnosis (in the absence of symptoms) that would render an applicant disabled at the Listings level. Therefore, the committee recommends that the definitive diagnosis of CHD in patients with CCS Class III or IV angina, or anginal-equivalent symptoms, be coupled with a functional limitation to meet a listing.

RECOMMENDATION 7-1. The committee recommends that the definitive diagnosis of coronary heart disease (diagnosed by documented prior myocardial infarction OR prior coronary revascularization OR specific criteria on exercise or stress-imaging tests OR coronary angiography) in patients with Canadian Cardiovascular Society Class III or

IV angina or anginal-equivalent symptoms be coupled with a functional limitation to meet a listing.

RECOMMENDATION 7-2. The committee recommends that one of four functional limitations be present to meet a listing:

1. Clinical: Documentation of three separate ischemic episodes requiring unplanned hospitalization (inpatient or observation status), each requiring revascularization (three separate percutaneous coronary intervention [PCI] procedures or two PCI and one coronary artery bypass graft [CABG] procedure) if amenable to revascularization, within a consecutive 12-month period;

OR

2. Exercise stress test (with or without imaging): Ischemic response defined by ST-segment depression of greater than or equal to 1 mm measured 0.08 seconds after the J-point that is horizontal or downsloping in configuration or ST-segment elevation greater than or equal to 1 mm in leads without Q waves or fall in systolic blood pressure greater than or equal to 10 mm Hg below resting systolic blood pressure at a workload of less than or equal to 5 metabolic equivalents of tasks;

OR

3. Stress-imaging test: Ischemic response with either exercise or pharmacologic vasodilator stress indicated by greater than or equal to two reversible and/or fixed regional myocardial perfusion defects during nuclear testing and transient ischemic dilation *or* resting left ventricular ejection fraction (LVEF) less than 50 percent, OR greater than or equal to two reversible and/or fixed regional wall motion abnormalities and either a fall in LVEF OR resting LVEF less than 50 percent;

OR

4. Among patients who have not had prior CABG, severe coronary heart disease with either 50 percent stenosis in the left main artery or greater than or equal to 70 percent stenosis in the proximal or midportion of greater than or equal to two major coronary arteries and a LVEF less than 50 percent.

RECOMMENDATION 7-3. The committee recommends that patients with prior coronary artery bypass graft and either severe disease in native coronary arteries that have not been bypassed (greater than or equal to 50 percent stenosis in the left main artery or greater than or equal to 70 percent stenosis in the proximal or midportion of greater than or equal to two major native coronary arteries) and/or greater than or equal to 70 percent stenosis in greater than or equal to two bypass grafts and with Canadian Cardiovascular Society Class III or IV angina (or angina-equivalent symptoms) meet a listing.

RECOMMENDATION 7-4. The committee recommends that children who are disabled prior to interventions are considered as disabled until 6 months following surgery and then reevaluated. The table of pharmacologic interventions for ischemia in adults cannot be applied to children as necessarily appropriate therapies.

Peripheral Artery Disease

Peripheral artery disease (PAD) occurs when arteries outside the heart and brain become narrowed or obstructed. Most people with early PAD do not experience symptoms. If left untreated, PAD may progress to the point that the leg muscles are deprived of adequate oxygen when a person uses them to walk or climb stairs. In severe cases of PAD, the person may experience pain even when at rest, or leg or foot wounds may not heal normally or at all. In the most severe instances, the muscles may die and the lower leg or foot must be amputated. The resulting limitations of mobility may become severe enough to prevent an individual with PAD from engaging in work.

The most common method to establish or rule out a diagnosis of lower extremity PAD is the ankle-brachial index (ABI) because it is reasonably accurate with good sensitivity and excellent specificity, easy to perform, inexpensive, and noninvasive. ABI values of 0.41 to 0.90 are considered to represent mild to moderate PAD. Values of 0.40 or less indicate severe PAD and a high risk of amputation due to critical limb ischemia. When the ABI is greater than or equal to 1.4, indicating calcified medial arteries, the toe-brachial index (TBI) should be used, because arteries in the toes are much less likely to be calcified.

Exercise treadmill tests are used to provide objective evidence of the degree of the functional limitations of PAD, identify any non-PAD exercise limitations, and determine the safety of prescribing an exercise program, as well as to measure the response to therapy. Treadmill testing is not suitable for patients who, due to age or other reasons, are not able to exercise enough to allow reliable results. In such cases, a 6-minute walk test may be used to obtain an objective assessment of functional limitation and response to therapy. Another useful exercise test is the heel-rise test.

The recommendation for improving the PAD listing as an early screening tool is to supplement the medical diagnostic and severity requirements with evidence of severe functional limitations. Because the path to disability for PAD is functional limitation to mobility, the committee recommends using the same criteria for lower extremity disability used in the musculoskeletal listings. The committee also recommends retaining the current objective criterion, but expanding the list of other tests that can diagnose and determine the severity of PAD (e.g., TBI, Doppler waveforms, duplex ultrasonography, magnetic resonance angiography, computed tomography angiography, contrast angiography).

RECOMMENDATION 8-1. The requirement for diagnostic evidence of peripheral artery disease (PAD) should be based on appropriate medically acceptable testing, and evidence of listing-level PAD should be based on an ankle-brachial index (ABI) of less than 0.50 or other test results consistent with severe PAD, combined with a requirement that, despite prescribed treatment, (1) leg pain interferes with mobility consistent with the musculoskeletal system listings, or (2) there have been three hospitalizations due to PAD within a 12-month period. Specifically,

Recommendation 8-1a. The word *imaging* in the phrase "appropriate medically acceptable imaging" currently in 4.12 should be replaced by the word *testing* or other term broader than *imaging*, because nonimaging tests such as Doppler techniques are commonly used to diagnose PAD and also to assess its severity.

Recommendation 8-1b. The current requirement in listing 4.12 for the presence of *intermittent claudication* should be changed to require that "leg pain" caused by PAD be present because the definition of intermittent claudication excludes too many individuals with disabling leg symptoms.

Recommendation 8-1c. Listing 4.12 should require that the applicant be on a regimen of prescribed treatment because therapies exist that can improve functional capacity.

Recommendation 8-1d. Criterion A in listing 4.12—an ABI of less than 0.50—should be retained, coupled with a new requirement for evidence of a severe limitation, such as an extreme functional

limitation on effective mobility or three hospitalizations for PAD within a 12-month period (see Recommendation 8-1f).

Recommendation 8-1e. Current criteria B, C, and D in listing 4.12 should be replaced by a new criterion B that an appropriate test or tests be consistent with severe PAD, when the ABI is 0.50 or greater or there is evidence of medial calcification of the ankle arteries. These tests should include the toe-brachial index, Doppler waveforms, duplex ultrasonography, magnetic resonance angiography, computed tomography angiography, contrast angiography, and graded treadmill tests. These test results should be coupled with a new requirement for evidence of a severe functional limitation on mobility or a history of three hospitalizations due to PAD within a 12-month period (see Recommendation 8-1f).

Recommendation 8-1f. Criterion A or new criterion B should be necessary but not sufficient to establish listing-level impairment unless there is also evidence of a severe limitation on mobility, for example, as defined in the musculoskeletal system listings (i.e., "inability to ambulate effectively") or there is a history of three hospitalizations due to PAD within a 12-month period.

Chronic Venous Insufficiency

Chronic venous insufficiency (CVI) is widespread and a common cause of disability in the United States. It results from reflux of blood due to incompetent venous valves or from obstruction in the leg veins. The resulting venous hypertension causes symptoms such as a feeling of heaviness of the legs, edema, pain while standing, and restless legs. In severe cases, it causes skin ulcers that do not heal well despite treatment. The main treatments are the use of compression stockings and continuous elevation of the legs to prevent blood pooling and pain, and diligent skin care to prevent and heal ulcers. CVI is associated with pain, physical function and mobility limitations, and depression and social isolation, which affect functional capacity to work.

The committee recommends that the current structure of the CVI listing be maintained, but that revisions for updating and clarifying the language of the current listing be made.

RECOMMENDATION 9-1. Listing 4.11 should be revised to require symptoms attributed to chronic venous insufficiency (CVI) as well as reflux or obstruction in the venous system, documented by duplex ultrasound or comparable technique. The documented symptomatic

venous reflux or obstruction should be coupled with a requirement of the following:

- **Trophic changes of skin below the knee consistent with severe chronic venous insufficiency (e.g., hyperpigmentation, lipodermatosclerosis, brawny edema) and unresponsive to compression therapy;**

OR

- **Recurrent or persistent venous ulceration that has not been responsive to prescribed treatment for at least 6 months;**

OR

- **Three hospitalizations for CVI during a 12-month period.**

Congenital Heart Disease

Congenital heart disease is an umbrella term that includes all heart defects present at birth, including dozens of defects that may occur singly or in combination. The abnormal structure of the cardiac chambers, valves, or great vessels in patients with congenital heart disease alters the normal pattern of blood flow. Individuals with congenital heart disease may develop cardiac complications such as arrhythmias, heart failure, or valve insufficiency, even after surgical correction of the structural abnormalities. Surgery is the mainstay of treatment for congenital heart disease. The expected results can be classified as (1) curative, with rare long-term sequelae; (2) reparative, with lifelong sequelae and sometimes significant late impairment; or (3) palliative, with significant lifelong impairment of function.

With improvements in infant surgery and palliation of more complex lesions, the number of survivors of congenital heart disease has increased and the population of children and adults with congenital heart disease in the United States has grown. In addition, congenital heart patients are more likely to have developmental abnormalities, mental retardation, growth retardation, somatic abnormalities (e.g., auditory, dental, facial, musculoskeletal), central nervous system abnormalities, seizures, visual abnormalities, and medical disorders (e.g., renal insufficiency or liver cirrhosis). As a result, adults with complex congenital heart disease are substantially less likely to be employed or have medical insurance.

Even after surgery, some children are impaired. At school age, for example, 11 to 17 percent of children with operated congenital heart disease have significant limitations in adaptive behavior, socialization, communication skills, and daily living skills. Children who have had only palliative surgery typically have severe lifelong functional limitations. The functional status of patients should be relatively stable by age 12, however, when children can cooperate sufficiently to undergo exercise testing. Reevaluation of patients with congenital heart disease at this age can establish their longer-term capacities and facilitate educational and vocational planning. Functional limitations may develop at any age, however, due to the development of arrhythmia, heart failure, endocarditis, or pulmonary hypertension, among other problems.

The committee's recommendations for improving the congenital heart disease listings for adults and children (4.06 and 104.06) are extensive, both because of the differences in consequences as individuals advance in age and because of the variety of congenital conditions. The recommendations include different criteria for children in three age groups: Group A: birth (from 6 months after heart surgery) to age 12; Group B: birth to age 12, no surgery indicated; and Group C: children ages 12 to 18. The committee also recommends consideration of comorbidities—such as learning disabilities, cognitive impairment, and associated noncardiac congenital anomalies—in evaluating congenital heart disease.

RECOMMENDATION 10-1. **Learning disabilities, cognitive impairment, and associated noncardiac congenital anomalies are frequent comorbidities for individuals with congenital heart disease. Disability evaluators should be trained to understand the effects of these comorbidities to better evaluate if a combination of impairments, no one of which meets a listing, equals a listing.**

RECOMMENDATION 10-2. **Assessment of disability in children should account for the natural history of congenital heart disease and patterns of development by dividing children into three age/treatment groups:**

***Group A*: Infants prior to and for 6 months after definitive cardiac surgery;**
***Group B*: Children from 6 months after definitive surgery until age 12 and children from birth onward for whom surgery is not indicated; and**
***Group C*: Children age 12 and older.**

RECOMMENDATION 10-3. **Infants with a medically confirmed diagnosis of cardiac malformation requiring open-heart surgery should be considered disabled until 6 months after definitive corrective surgery. A diagnosis of significant cardiac disease and documentation of a surgical plan or surgical event should be sufficient evidence of disability.**

RECOMMENDATION 10-4. Children from 6 months after definitive cardiac surgery until their 12th birthday and children from birth onward for whom surgery is not indicated, with congenital heart disease documented by appropriate medically acceptable imaging or cardiac catheterization, with one of the following criteria should be considered disabled:

A. Cyanotic heart disease, with persistent, chronic hypoxemia as manifested by:

1. Hematocrit of 55 percent or greater; or
2. Arterial O_2 saturation of less than 90 percent in room air, or resting arterial PO_2 of 60 Torricelli or less; or
3. Hypercyanotic spells, syncope, characteristic squatting, or other incapacitating symptoms directly related to documented cyanotic heart disease; or
4. Exercise intolerance with increased hypoxemia on exertion measured by pulse oximetry.

OR

B. Secondary pulmonary vascular obstructive disease with pulmonary arterial systolic pressure elevated to at least 70 percent of the systemic arterial systolic pressure determined by echocardiography or right heart catheterization;

OR

C. Symptomatic acyanotic heart disease interfering seriously with the ability to independently initiate, sustain, or complete activities;

OR

D. Chronic heart failure manifested by:

1. Persistent tachycardia at rest (see Table I[8]); or

[8] See Table 1, Section 104.02, Chronic Heart Failure. For tachycardia at rest, apical heart rate: under age 1, 150 beats per minute; ages 1 through 3, 130 beats per minute; ages 4 through 9, 120 beats per minute; ages 10 through 15, 110 beats per minute; and over age 15, 100 beats per minute (SSA, 2008b).

2. Persistent tachypnea at rest (see Table II[9]); or
3. Markedly decreased exercise tolerance; or
4. Growth disturbance with:

    a. An involuntary weight loss or failure to gain weight at an appropriate rate for age, resulting in a fall of 15 percentiles from an established growth curve (on the current Centers for Disease Control and Prevention [CDC] growth chart), which is currently present (see 104.00A3f) and has persisted for 2 months or longer; or
    b. An involuntary weight loss or failure to gain weight at an appropriate rate for age, resulting in a fall to below the third percentile from an established growth curve (on the current CDC growth chart), which is currently present (see 104.00A3f) and has persisted for 2 months or longer.

RECOMMENDATION 10-5. Children age 12 and older should be considered disabled if they have congenital heart disease documented by appropriate medically acceptable imaging or cardiac catheterization, with one of the following criteria:

A. Cyanosis at rest, and:

    1. Hematocrit of 55 percent or greater; or
    2. Arterial O_2 saturation of less than 90 percent in room air, or resting arterial PO_2 of 60 Torricelli (Torr) or less.

OR

B. Intermittent right-to-left shunting resulting in cyanosis on exertion (e.g., Eisenmenger's physiology) as determined by pulse oximetry and with arterial PO_2 of 60 Torr or less or pulse oximetry 85 percent or less at a workload equivalent to 5 metabolic equivalents of task (METs) or less;

OR

[9] See Table II, Tachypnea at Rest, Section 104.02, Chronic Heart Failure. For tachypnea at rest, respiratory rate, under age 1, over 40 breaths per minute; ages 1 through 5, over 35 breaths per minute; ages 6 through 9, over 30 breaths per minute; and over age 9, over 25 breaths per minute (SSA, 2008b).

C. Secondary pulmonary vascular obstructive disease with pulmonary arterial systolic pressure elevated to at least 70 percent of the systemic arterial systolic pressure determined by echocardiography or cardiac catheterization;

OR

D. Single ventricle, including hypoplastic left heart syndrome, double inlet left ventricle, and Fontan operation for single ventricle;

OR

E. Chronic heart failure manifested by:

1. Exercise capacity with maximal oxygen consumption less than 15 ml/kg/min or work load less than 5 METs; or
2. Three hospitalizations or emergency room visits with use of intravenous medications for heart failure management in 1 year; or
3. Evidence of right heart failure manifested by:

   a. Symptoms of dyspnea, edema, or exercise intolerance; and
   b. Jugular venous distension, hepatomegaly, ascites, and/or dependent edema on three clinic visits in 1 year.

RECOMMENDATION 10-6. Adults with a medically confirmed diagnosis of congenital heart disease should be considered disabled if they also demonstrate one of the following:

A. Cyanosis at rest, and:

   1. Hematocrit of 55 percent or greater; or
   2. Arterial O_2 saturation of less than 90 percent in room air, or resting arterial PO_2 of 60 Torricelli (Torr) or less;

OR

B. Intermittent right-to-left shunting resulting in cyanosis on exertion (e.g., Eisenmenger's physiology) as determined by pulse oximetry and with arterial PO_2 of 60 Torr or less or pulse oximetry 85 percent or less at a workload equivalent to 5 metabolic equivalents of task (METs) or less;

OR

C. Secondary pulmonary vascular obstructive disease with pulmonary arterial systolic pressure elevated to at least 70 percent of the systemic arterial systolic pressure determined by echocardiography or right heart catheterization;

OR

D. Single ventricle including hypoplastic left heart syndrome, double inlet left ventricle, and Fontan operation for single ventricle;

OR

E. Diagnosis of congenital heart disease and chronic heart failure manifested by:

1. Exercise capacity with maximal oxygen consumption less than 15 ml/kg/min or work load less than 5 METs; or
2. Three hospitalizations or emergency room visits with intravenous medication administration for heart failure management in 1 year; or
3. Evidence of right heart failure manifested by:

    a. Symptoms of dyspnea, edema, or exercise intolerance; and
    b. Jugular venous distension, hepatomegaly, ascites, and dependent edema on three clinic visits in 1 year.

Pulmonary Hypertension

Pulmonary hypertension (PH) is present when the pulmonary artery pressures are elevated above normal. The term applies particularly to diseases that affect the small pulmonary arteries and markedly increase their resistance to blood flow. PH may be of unknown cause (idiopathic PH) or secondary to conditions such as connective tissue disease, sarcoidosis, an autoimmune disorder, congenital heart disease, and other inherited conditions. PH may also develop secondary to lung disease or hypoxemia, such as chronic obstructive pulmonary disease, interstitial lung disease, and obstructive sleep apnea. Pulmonary embolism and left-sided heart disease are common causes of PH.

PH is associated with high mortality and marked functional limitations.

The condition is often quite advanced at the time of diagnosis, largely because PH symptoms are nonspecific and the diagnosis is difficult to make.

Patients with PH show marked limitations on standard functional status measures and show evidence of reduced functional capacity on standard HF measures. PH patients with pulmonary artery hypertension are advised to avoid heavy physical exertion or isometric exercise, which may lead to loss of consciousness. Patients with PH may be unable to work either because of functional limitations or their use of continuous intravenous treatment.

There is no current cardiovascular listing for PH. There is a listing for one type of PH, cor pulmonale, in the respiratory system listings. The committee recommends that SSA establish a new listing for PH in the cardiovascular system listings.

RECOMMENDATION 11-1. The Social Security Administration should establish a new listing in the cardiovascular system for pulmonary hypertension. The new listing should allow claimants with pulmonary hypertension documented by right heart catheterization to meet the listing if (A) there is evidence of severe pulmonary hypertension OR (B) there is evidence of moderate pulmonary hypertension AND of marked functional limitations.

A. Evidence of severe pulmonary hypertension, which is associated with severe functional limitation, includes any of the following:

- **Mean pulmonary artery pressure of 40 mm Hg or greater; or**
- **Pulmonary vascular resistance of 6 Wood units (mm Hg per liter per minute) or greater; or**
- **Continuous parenteral therapy with prostacyclin analogs.**

OR

B. Evidence of moderate pulmonary hypertension, which imposes severe functional limitation on many but not all individuals, includes any of the following:

- **Recurrent syncope secondary to pulmonary hypertension; or**
- **Right heart failure (same criteria as for heart failure listing); or**
- **Mean pulmonary artery pressure between 25 and 39 mm Hg; or**

- **Pulmonary vascular resistance above 3 and below 6 Wood units.**

AND

Evidence of marked functional disability provided by either of the following:

- **An exercise capacity of less than 5 metabolic equivalents of task; or**
- **Three or more hospital admissions within a consecutive 12-month period to treat right heart failure or pulmonary hypertension.**

Valvular Heart Disease

Valvular heart disease (VHD) is characterized by damage to or a congenital defect in one or more heart valves. Damaged or defective valves can cause two types of problems: either they fail to open properly (a condition called stenosis), impeding blood flow, or they leak (a condition called regurgitation), permitting backward blood flow.

Valve conditions may be congenital, arise from inflammation, or occur due to complications from infections. Mild or moderate valve disease is usually asymptomatic at first but, due to the progressive and degenerative nature of the disease, may eventually become severe and may lead to heart failure and death if left untreated. Symptoms of VHD in decreasing frequency include shortness of breath or dyspnea, chest pain and palpitations, syncope, or near syncope.

The committee recommends establishing a listing for severe symptomatic aortic stenosis, which is usually fatal within 5 years unless the valve is replaced and could cause sudden death from the exertion of manual labor. Determining disability using measurements of functional criteria is not advised for individuals with severe symptomatic aortic stenosis, because there is great risk to the patient in performing exercise tests. Severe symptomatic mitral stenosis, aortic regurgitation, or mitral regurgitation may also warrant disability at the listing level, but these patients must demonstrate functional limitation in addition to an objective diagnosis of severity.

RECOMMENDATION 12-1. Provide a listing-level pathway to disability for symptomatic claimants with objective evidence via echocardiogram or other appropriate medically acceptable imaging of severe aortic stenosis, characterized by mean gradient greater than 40 mm Hg,

jet velocity greater than 4.0 m/sec, valve area less than 1.0 cm^2, and valve area index less than 0.6 cm^2/m^2.

RECOMMENDATION 12-2. Provide a listing-level pathway to disability for symptomatic claimants with objective evidence via echocardiogram or other appropriate medically acceptable imaging of severe mitral stenosis, aortic regurgitation, or mitral regurgitation and demonstrated functional limitation. Objective evidence is measured by one of the following:

- Severe mitral stenosis characterized by mean gradient greater than 10 mm Hg, pulmonary artery systolic pressure greater than 50 mm Hg, and valve area less than 1.0 cm^2; or
- Severe aortic regurgitation characterized by regurgitant volume greater than or equal to 60 ml/beat, and regurgitant orifice area greater than or equal to 50 cm^2, and increased left ventricular size; or
- Severe mitral regurgitation characterized by regurgitant volume greater than or equal to 60 ml/beat or regurgitant fraction greater than or equal to 50 percent, and regurgitant orifice area greater than or equal to 0.40 cm^2, and enlarged left atrial size and enlarged left ventricular size.

Functional limitation(s) from severe mitral stenosis, aortic regurgitation, or mitral regurgitation would be demonstrated by one of the following:

- Three hospitalizations with heart failure in 12 months; or
- Inability to achieve 5 metabolic equivalents of task on an exercise test; or
- Objective evidence of right heart failure.

Arrhythmias

The current listing for arrhythmia is met if the claimant has recurrent arrhythmias that cause syncope or near syncope that is not reversible and does not respond to prescribed treatment. The link between arrhythmia and syncope or near syncope must be documented on an electrocardiogram.

The committee recommends that the listing define listing-level arrhythmias as tachycardia or bradycardia, because these are the arrhythmias that are potentially incapacitating and should be documented in the medical record. Furthermore, because episodes of near syncope due to arrhythmia are difficult to document and because there can be other severe and disabling symptoms of arrhythmia, the committee recommends that the listing be met if the symptoms of arrhythmia seriously limit the ability of the claimant to independently initiate, sustain, or complete activities of daily living.

RECOMMENDATION 13-1. Revise listing 4.05 to define arrhythmias as recurrent episodes of tachycardia or bradycardia documented by electrocardiography or other appropriate medically acceptable testing; that cause cardiac syncope, near syncope, or other debilitating symptoms; are not due to a reversible cause; do not respond to prescribed treatment; and very seriously limit the ability to independently initiate, sustain, or complete activities of daily living or instrumental activities of daily living.

Aneurysm or Dissection of the Aorta and Peripheral Arteries

Aneurysms can impinge on adjacent body structures as they enlarge, causing symptoms such as breathlessness, wheezing, cough, tracheal deviation, or pain. Aortic dissections can impede the flow of blood to an adjacent branch peripheral artery and cause ischemia in affected organs or other tissues. According to the ACC/AHA guidelines for thoracic aortic disease: "For patients with a current thoracic aortic aneurysm or dissection, or previously repaired aortic dissection, employment and lifestyle restrictions are reasonable, including the avoidance of strenuous lifting, pushing, or straining," although aerobic (but not isometric) exercise is considered to be reasonably safe.

The current listing for aneurysm is met if a clamant has an aneurysm from any cause with dissection that cannot be controlled by treatment. SSA considers the dissection uncontrolled if there is persistent chest pain due to progression of the dissection; an increase in the size of the aneurysm; or compression of one or more branches of the aorta supplying the heart, kidneys, brain, or other organs.

The committee recommends that the listing distinguish between aneurysm and dissection because one may occur without the other. In place of the requirement for dissection that is not controlled by treatment, the listing should require that the aneurysm or dissection cause chronic debilitating symptoms as a result of its effects on the function of the heart, brain, peripheral nerves, or limbs despite treatment. In patients with a genetic predisposition to aneurysm formation or aortic dissection, such as Marfan syndrome, the listing should accept that standard medical management may prescribe substantial restrictions in physical activity in adults and children with asymptomatic aortic aneurysms or dissections, which may affect employment possibilities.

RECOMMENDATION 14-1. Revise listing (4.10) to require the presence of chronic disabling symptoms due to the aneurysm or dissection. Disabling symptoms may be the result of the functional impairment to the heart, brain, peripheral nerves, or limbs due to the aneurysm or dissection. Claimants should be evaluated under the appropriate related cardiovascular listings or listings for other body systems if necessary.

RECOMMENDATION 14-2. Revise the introductory text to the cardiovascular system to account for the following changes:

- Include the term *dissection* in the primary description of the condition (i.e., aneurysm or dissection);
- Develop the definitions for aneurysm and dissection to include: An aneurysm is a bulge in the aorta or a peripheral artery. A dissection of the aorta or its branches occurs when the inner lining of the artery is "torn" and begins to separate from the rest of the arterial wall. An aneurysm or dissection may compromise organ function and produce symptoms by the compression of other structures in the tissue or body compartment or induce ischemia by compromising the flow of blood to the heart, kidneys, brain, or other organs;
- Revise the effects of aneurysm or dissection to include: An aneurysm or dissection can cause heart failure, renal (kidney) failure, or neurological complications. If an aneurysm or dissection is present, there must be one or more of these associated symptomatic conditions; the condition(s) are evaluated using the appropriate associated listings; and
- Revise the diagnostic criteria of Marfan syndrome to include: There is no specific laboratory test to diagnose Marfan syndrome, although the mutation in the gene that causes it has been defined. The diagnosis is generally made by medical history, including family history and physical examination including an evaluation of the musculoskeletal features, a slit-lamp eye examination, and a heart test(s), such as an echocardiogram. In some cases, a genetic analysis may be useful, but such analyses may not provide any additional helpful information. Include a description of Loeys-Dietz syndrome as another example of a genetic disorder with increased risk of aortic aneurysm and/or dissection affecting both children and adults.

COMORBIDITIES

Many individuals with a severe cardiovascular impairment, such as heart failure, coronary artery disease, and peripheral vascular disease, have comorbid conditions that further reduce their capacity to work. For example, major depressive disorders often affect individuals with cardiovascular conditions, with depression present in up to 20 percent of patients with cardiac conditions. Depression has a significant, negative impact on the overall functional capacity of affected individuals and increases morbidity and mortality. Other prevalent conditions that combine with cardiovascular disease to increase functional limitations include diabetes mellitus, chronic obstructive pulmonary disease and other respiratory diseases, and obesity.

The committee has no recommendations for changing SSA's current policies for dealing with multiple impairments, none of which meets a cardiovascular listing by itself, but which might combine in such a way that the claimant equals the Listings. How to evaluate the effect of comorbidities in applying the cardiovascular listings is based on judgment of the adjudicators that cannot be reduced to a formula. The committee intends the information in this chapter to underline the effect of comorbidities and to better inform those decisions.

FUTURE DIRECTIONS FOR IMPROVING THE LISTINGS

In the course of its work, the committee encountered a number of knowledge gaps in evaluating the effectiveness of the cardiovascular listings, such as the relationship of anatomical severity measures and functional limitation and the effect of comorbidities. Additional research would reduce information gaps and improve listing quality. To better inform the next revisions of any body system within the Listings, the committee encourages SSA to support a full and balanced program of in-house and external research in four areas: policy implications, programmatic issues, correlation of impairments with functional limitations, and the underlying prevalence of impairments and disability in the population.

RECOMMENDATION 16-1. SSA should plan and sponsor a balanced program of research to improve the reliability, validity, and utility of the Listings in four areas: policy implications, programmatic issues, correlation of impairments and impairment severity with functional limitations related to work capacity, and the underlying prevalence of and trends in impairments in the population. This program would also enable SSA to enhance the other steps of the disability determination process.

REFERENCES

SSA (Social Security Administration). 2008a. *Listing of impairments—Adult listings (Part A). Disability evaluation under Social Security (Blue Book).* http://www.socialsecurity.gov/disability/professionals/bluebook/AdultListings.htm (accessed July 22, 2010).

SSA. 2008b. *Listing of impairments—Childhood listings (Part B). Disability evaluation under Social Security (Blue Book).* http://www.socialsecurity.gov/disability/professionals/bluebook/ChildhoodListings.htm (accessed July 22, 2010).

1

Introduction

In 2010, the Social Security Administration (SSA) expects more than 3.3 million individuals to apply for disability benefits on the basis that they have a physical or mental impairment that prevents them from engaging in "any substantial gainful activity," or if children, from engaging in age-appropriate activities at home, at school, or in the community. Determining whether claimants (i.e., applicants) have an impairment that meets SSA's definition of disability can entail an intensive and lengthy individualized evaluation of their medical condition. The full evaluation requires a consideration of the effects of the medical condition or conditions on the claimant's ability to function and consideration of the claimant's age, education, and work history. Under the Supplemental Security Income (SSI) program, claimants also include children under age 18 who have a physical or mental impairment or combination of impairments that cause "marked and severe functional limitations." The full evaluation of these claimants requires consideration of, and judgments about, functional limitations in six domains of functioning.

To reduce the administrative burden of evaluating the disability of millions of claimants each year, SSA uses a screening tool called the Listing of Impairments, also known as the Listings, to quickly identify claimants with medical conditions so severe that they can be allowed benefits without going through the full evaluation process. This expedites the approval process for the claimants and saves SSA substantial administrative and economic resources.

The Listings describe physical and mental impairments so severe that anyone who has such an impairment cannot be expected to work at all regardless of age, education, or work experience, or in the case of a child, has marked and severe functional limitations. Although strict, the Listings account for nearly half of the disability approvals granted each year. In part because of advances in medical treatment, SSA updates and revises the Listings periodically. The Listings are organized by body system (e.g., neurological, musculoskeletal, cardiovascular, immune) and, at any given time, SSA is revising several of the body systems (there are 14 adult and 15 child body systems).

In August 2009, SSA commissioned the Institute of Medicine (IOM) to convene a committee to conduct a 1-year study of the Listings and to make concrete recommendations that are designed to improve the usefulness of the cardiovascular listings for evaluating cardiovascular disability claims by improving the sensitivity and specificity of the listing criteria to identify claimants who have impairments that meet SSA's definition of disability. (See Box 1-1 for relevant excerpts from the contractual statement of work.) The information and recommendations in the report will be part of the input to its formal process for developing a Notice of Proposed Rulemaking and, subsequently, final rules that will be published in the *Federal Register* to update the cardiovascular listings.

In response to this assignment, the IOM formed a committee of cardiovascular medical experts to review the cardiovascular listings, medical literature, and advances in technology, and to recommend improvements. The committee's membership includes a wide range of expertise able to evaluate cardiovascular disability criteria, including coronary artery disease, valvular heart disease, heart failure, congenital heart disease (including adult), peripheral vascular disease, cardiac rehabilitation and stress testing, interventional cardiology, arrhythmia, pulmonary arterial hypertension, nursing, and psychiatric comorbidities. Short biographies of the committee members are in Appendix A.

To address its charge, the committee and staff conducted an intensive review of the relevant medical research literature, current clinical practice guidelines, and program data from SSA, and received briefings from knowledgeable stakeholders. Over the course of the 12-month study, the committee met four times (December 2009, and February, April, and June 2010). The public was invited to meet with the committee (December 2009) and to participate in three public webinars (held in April 2010).[1] The committee received oral and written statements from various stakeholders (see the Acknowledgments section at the beginning of this report). Committee members also conducted site visits at seven disability determination offices

[1] The webinars addressed congenital heart disease (April 5), pulmonary hypertension (April 7), and chronic venous insufficiency and aneurysm (April 14).

BOX 1-1
Cardiovascular Committee's Statement of Work

IOM shall form a Consensus Committee to perform a focused review of the medical literature to determine the latest standards of care, the latest technology for the understanding of disease processes, and the latest science demonstrating the effect of cardiovascular disorders on patients' health and functional capacity . . .

The primary purpose of the Consensus Committee is to make concrete recommendations that are designed to improve the utility of the Cardiovascular Listings for evaluating cardiovascular disability claims by improving the sensitivity and specificity of the listing criteria to identify individuals who meet SSA's definition of disability . . .

The IOM shall form a Consensus Committee composed of approximately 8–12 members having clinical expertise in the cardiovascular system. The responsible committee shall hold meetings to gather and analyze data and information that addresses the following tasks.

1. The Consensus Committee shall review, in a written report for the use of SSA, the most current medical literature to determine the latest standards of care, the latest technology for the understanding of disease processes, and the latest science demonstrating the impact of cardiovascular disorders on patients' health and functional capacity.
2. The Consensus Committee shall produce a written report for the use of SSA analyzing documents received in response to SSA's Cardiovascular ANPRM request for public comments, including the AHA and ACC guidelines to determine which, if any, guidelines have the potential to become indicators of disability as defined by SSA (that is, to assess which, if any, of the comments or guidelines would be useful in developing listing criteria for determining disability).
3. The Consensus Committee shall produce a written report for the use of SSA that compares and contrasts findings in the most current medical literature and ANPRM public comments with SSA's current cardiovascular listings, as well as the key concepts included in the introduction of the cardiovascular listings.
4. The Consensus Committee shall recommend guidance that, if incorporated into the cardiovascular listings, would improve their utility for evaluating disability claims based on the cardiovascular listings. The Committee will take into account considerations regarding the applicability of their recommendations in the SSA disability program. Examples of such considerations are: (1) consistency with standard medical practice, (2) cost and nationwide availability of any recommended tests, and (3) minimal risk and inconvenience to the claimant.
5. The Consensus Committee shall produce a written report indicating what evidence, laboratory findings, signs and symptoms within the medical evidence of record (MER) may improve the sensitivity and specificity of the listing criteria to identify individuals who meet SSA's definition of disability.
6. The Consensus Committee will produce a written report for SSA with all of its findings. The report may be made available to the interested public only after the Task Order has ended.

in different parts of the United States,[2] where they spoke with experienced disability examiners and medical consultants who apply the cardiovascular listings. This helped committee members to better understand the disability determination process and the challenges encountered in evaluating cardiovascular disability.

REPORT STRUCTURE

This report consists of 16 chapters, of which this introduction is the first. Chapter 2 provides the reader an overview of SSA's disability determination process. Chapter 3 provides statistics on cardiovascular disease prevalence and incidence as well as trends in cardiovascular claims for Social Security disability benefits. Chapter 4 describes the committee's approach to evaluating the current Social Security cardiovascular listings disability criteria and designing recommendations to improve them. Chapters 5 through 14 address specific cardiovascular conditions: heart failure, cardiomyopathy, and right heart failure (Chapter 5); heart transplantation (Chapter 6); ischemic heart disease (Chapter 7); peripheral artery disease (Chapter 8); chronic venous insufficiency (Chapter 9); congenital heart disease (Chapter 10); pulmonary hypertension (Chapter 11); valvular heart disease (Chapter 12); arrhythmias (Chapter 13); and aneurysm or dissection of the aorta and peripheral arteries (Chapter 14). Chapter 15 addresses the impact of comorbidities. Chapter 16 identifies research that SSA could undertake and support to improve the Listings in the future.

[2] Oakland, California; San Diego/La Jolla, California; Stone Mountain, Georgia; Boston, Massachusetts; St. Paul, Minnesota; Buffalo, New York; and Washington, DC.

2

Social Security Disability Programs and Procedures

This chapter contains a brief summary of the Social Security Administration's (SSA's) disability programs and procedures. Readers familiar with Social Security disability may wish to proceed directly to the next chapter. However, it may be useful to review some key features of the programs that the committee considered and treated as givens in their approach to evaluating and recommending changes in the cardiovascular listings, as follows:

- The statutory definition of disability used to decide if a claimant should receive disability benefits is strict—essentially, it requires an adult claimant to have a medically determinable impairment or impairments that prevent the ability to work for a continuous period of not less than 12 months or is expected to result in death. An individual with partial or short-term disability is not entitled to Social Security disability benefits. Therefore, many individuals with severe impairments that limit, or even prevent, their ability to perform their usual work will not be entitled.
- One example of why a claimant with a severe cardiovascular impairment may not be disabled is that the effects of treatment may improve his or her functional status. Treatment may include medical, surgical, or a prescribed program of progressive physical activity, among others. When a claimant with a cardiovascular impairment is on a prescribed treatment program, SSA may defer evaluation of the impairment or impairments for up to 3 months from the beginning of the treatment cycle to gauge net benefit on the individual's functional status.

- By law, the disability must result from a "medically determinable impairment," defined as an impairment that results from anatomical, physiological, or psychological abnormalities that can be shown by medically acceptable clinical and laboratory diagnostic techniques. Therefore, diagnostic techniques and measures of medical severity of cardiovascular impairments in SSA's Listing of Impairments (the Listings) should be as current as possible.
- The Listings are the third step in the five-step sequential evaluation process for adults (see Figure 2-1), where they serve as an administrative expedient to quickly identify allowances, that is, cases in which the impairment is considered severe enough to prevent the claimant from doing any work. Thus the Listings help SSA avoid subjecting obviously disabled claimants to a time- and resource-intensive, in-depth assessment of their residual functional capacity and vocational issues that must be performed at later steps of the sequential evaluation process.
- The use of the Listings as an administrative expedient has declined over time. Currently, nearly half of the allowances made annually are based on the Listings, compared with approximately 70 percent in the 1980s.
- The adult Listings are based on a standard stricter than the statutory definition of disability, that is, the inability to engage in "any *gainful* activity" rather than the inability to engage in "any *substantial gainful* activity." The Listings standard is stricter because the purpose of the Listings is to describe impairments that are severe enough to prevent an individual from doing any work without even considering his or her age, education, or work experience.
- Claimants who are not allowed at the Listings step are not necessarily denied. Those with severe impairments may be allowed at Step 5 of the sequential evaluation process based on an assessment of their residual functional capacity and considering their age, education, and work history.
- SSA has Listings for children under age 18 with criteria that are used to assess a child's impairment or impairments. If the criteria in the Listings for children do not apply, or if there is no equivalent child listing, SSA may use the criteria in an appropriate adult listing. In addition to meeting or *medically equaling* a listing, a child may *functionally equal* the Listings by having "marked and severe functional limitations."
- After nonmedical eligibility is confirmed by an SSA field office, the claim is sent to one of the SSA state agencies, usually called disability determination services (DDS), in the state where the claimant lives. DDSs, funded by SSA, are responsible for case de-

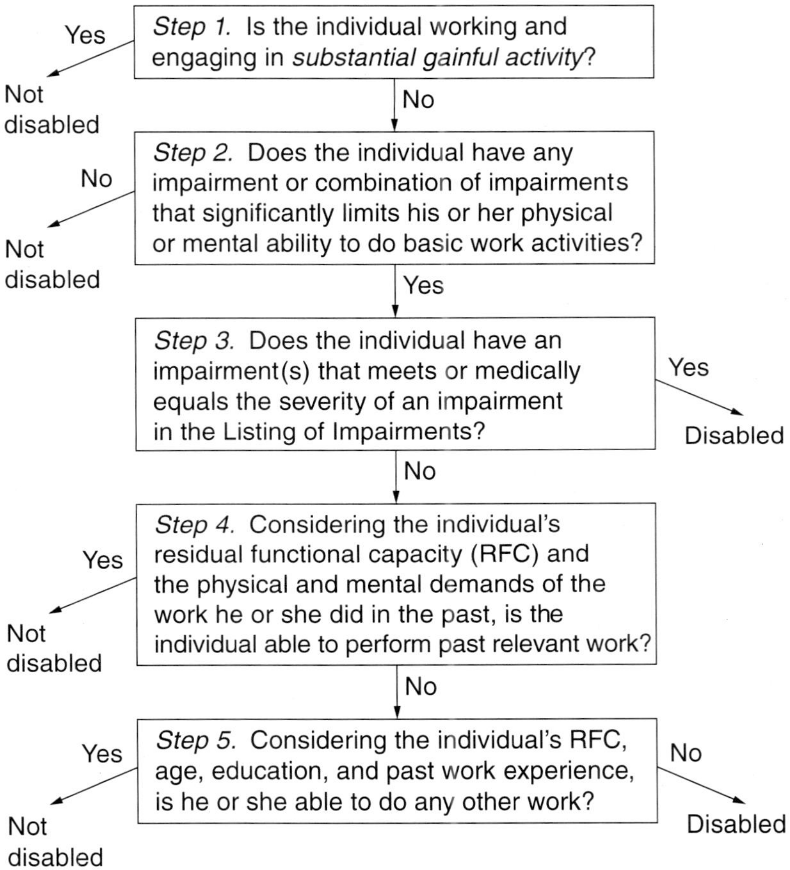

FIGURE 2-1 Five-step sequential evaluation process for adults.
SOURCES: 20 CFR §§ 404.1520 and 416.920.

velopment, the initial decision to allow or deny the claim, and the first level of appeal.

- In most states, the decisions in DDSs are usually made by an adjudicative team composed of a medical consultant (e.g., a licensed physician) or a psychological consultant (a licensed or certified psychologist) and a lay disability examiner. The adjudicative team determines whether a claimant is disabled based on medical and other evidence in the case record, but does not see the claimant in person.
- Most claims involving cardiovascular impairments involve medical consultants who are generalists (i.e., internists or family practice

doctors), except that: (1) claims for children under the Supplemental Security Income (SSI) program must involve a pediatrician or another appropriate specialist, and (2) claims for adults or children in which there is an indication of a mental impairment and that are unfavorable to the claimant must generally involve a psychiatrist or psychologist. Few subspecialists, such as cardiologists, are in the DDSs (IOM, 2007).

- SSA will not pay for expensive, invasive, or risky procedures that would otherwise be useful in diagnosis and assessing impairment severity, such as coronary angiography. Therefore, some claimants who have not undergone such procedures privately (because, for example, they lack health insurance or geographic access to care) may not be able to show an impairment that meets a listing.
- SSA prefers that the requirements for meeting a listing rely on tests, examinations, or other kinds of information that are likely to be available in the medical record. If the Listings rely solely or primarily on cutting-edge tests that are better technically, but not generally available in doctors' offices or health facilities nationally, or that are very expensive, few claimants would be able to show an impairment that meets a listing, which would defeat the purpose of the Listings.
- By law, SSA cannot interfere with the patient–doctor relationship, so the most it will require, and only to meet some listings, is adherence to "prescribed therapy," which may or may not be optimum therapy as defined by the latest clinical guidelines. Willful refusal to follow prescribed therapy that is clearly expected to restore the capacity to work may be grounds for denial, but SSA does not require disabled claimants to stop smoking, lose excess weight, or take other evidence-based steps to reduce or end disability.

SSA DISABILITY PROGRAMS

SSA pays disability benefits through two programs: Social Security Disability Insurance (SSDI) and SSI. In 2008, more than 12 million people received Social Security disability benefits (see Table 2-1). SSA expects to receive more than 3.3 million applications for disability benefits in fiscal year 2010, about 300,000 more than in fiscal year 2009 and 700,000 more than in fiscal year 2008 (SSA, 2010).

DEFINITION OF DISABILITY

To be found disabled, a claimant's impairment or impairments must meet SSA's statutory definition of disability. Adult disability is based on the

TABLE 2-1 Numbers of Disability Program Beneficiaries and Benefit Amounts, 2008

	Number of Beneficiaries	Average Monthly Benefit
Adults		
SSDI only	6.6 million	$1,129
SSI only	3.0 million	$608
SSDI and SSI	1.3 million	$747
Children		
SSI only	1.2 million	$561
Total	12.1 million	

NOTES: SSDI: Social Security Disability Insurance; SSI: Supplemental Security Income. The numbers do not include dependents of disabled beneficiaries who receive benefits.
SOURCES: SSA, 2009a (for adults), 2009b (for children).

inability to work. Childhood disability under SSI is based on functional limitations. The definitions are as follows:

- Adult disability is "the inability to engage in any substantial gainful activity by reason of any medically determinable physical or mental impairment(s) which can be expected to result in death or which has lasted or can be expected to last for a continuous period of not less than 12 months."
- A child under the age of 18 is considered disabled if he or she has "a medically determinable physical or mental impairment, which results in marked and severe functional limitations, and which can be expected to result in death or which has lasted or can be expected to last for a continuous period of not less than 12 months."

DISABILITY EVALUATION DECISION PROCESS

SSA uses a sequential evaluation process to determine whether a claimant is disabled. The evaluation stops at any step in the sequence at which a decision about disability is made. The steps are different for adults and children, although the Listings are applied at the third step in each case.

Adult Disability Decision Process

At Step 1 of the adult evaluation (Figure 2-1), SSA determines whether the claimant is engaging in substantial gainful activity (SGA). If not, the claim is forwarded to the DDS and proceeds to Step 2 to determine whether the claimant has a severe medically determinable impairment or impairments that significantly limit the claimant's ability to perform basic work activities (e.g., standing, sitting). If the claimant is found to have a severe impairment, then SSA determines, at Step 3, whether the impairment satisfies the criteria describing a medical condition found in the Listings. The Listings serve as an administrative expedient to quickly identify allowances.

Step 3 is the first point at which the claimant may be found disabled, but if the claimant's impairment or impairments do not meet or medically equal a listing, the claim is *not* denied. Rather, adult claims not allowed at the Listings step proceed to Step 4, which consider the claimant's ability to perform past relevant work, and if necessary, to Step 5, which considers the claimant's ability to do other work that exists in significant numbers in the national economy. At Step 4, SSA assesses the claimant's residual functional capacity (RFC), which is the claimant's remaining ability to do physical and mental work-related activities despite limitations from all of his or her impairment or impairments, including any impairments that are not "severe." Assessing RFC is a time- and resource-intensive process based on an analysis of all relevant medical and other evidence in the case record and requires a more detailed assessment of functioning than under listings that also include functional criteria.

At Step 4, SSA uses the RFC assessment to determine the claimant's capacity to do past relevant work (defined in part as jobs held during the previous 15 years). If SSA determines that the claimant is unable to perform past relevant work, the claim progresses to Step 5.

At Step 5, SSA evaluates the claimant's capacity to adjust to any other kind of work, taking into consideration his or her age, educational attainment, work experience, and RFC. Generally, the greater the age of the individual, the lower his or her educational attainment, and the lower the skill level of previous jobs held, the more likely it will be that SSA will find the claimant disabled. If the claimant is found capable of performing other work, he or she is not considered disabled. If he or she cannot perform other work, he or she is considered disabled based on medical and vocational factors.

Child Disability Determination Process

For children under age 18 applying for SSI benefits, Steps 1 and 2 of the evaluation process are essentially the same (Figure 2-2). At Step 3, the considerations are whether a child's impairment meets or medically equals *a* listing, as in the adult evaluation process, or "functionally equals *the* Listings." Unlike meets and medical equivalence, functional equivalence is not based on specific listings but on a standard of "listing-level severity"; that is, an impairment or impairments must result in "marked" limitations

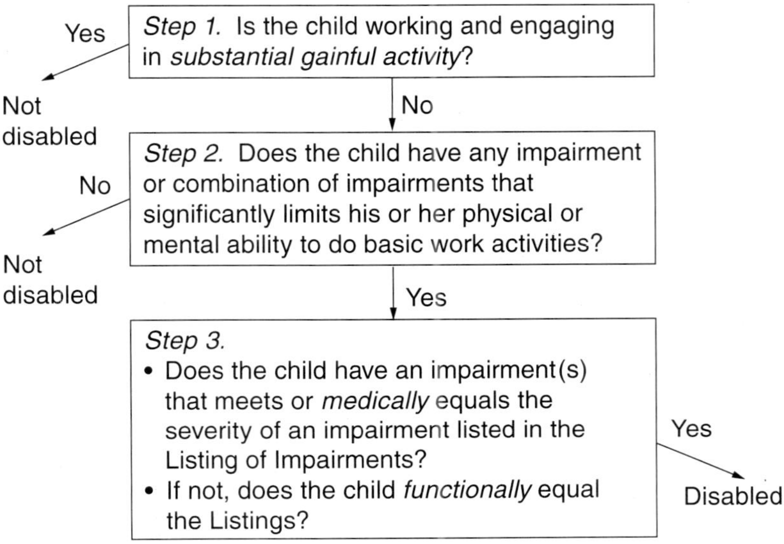

FIGURE 2-2 Disability evaluation process for Supplemental Security Income children.
SOURCE: 20 CFR § 416.924.

in two domains of functioning or an "extreme" limitation in one domain. Domains are broad areas of functioning intended to capture all of what a child can or cannot do in activities at home, at school, and in the community compared with other children of the same age who do not have impairments. The domains are as follows:

- Acquiring and using information;
- Attending and completing tasks;
- Interacting and relating with others;
- Moving about and manipulating objects;
- Caring for yourself; and
- Health and physical well-being.

For each of the first five domains, a "marked" limitation is found when a child's impairment or impairments interfere seriously with his or her ability to independently initiate, sustain, or complete activities. A "marked" limitation also means one that is "more than moderate" but "less than extreme." It is the equivalent of the functioning one would expect to find on standardized testing with scores that are at least two, but less than three, standard deviations below the mean.

An "extreme" limitation is found when a child's impairment or impairments interfere very seriously with his or her ability to independently initiate, sustain, or complete activities. An "extreme" limitation also means a limitation that is "more than marked," and is the rating given to the worst limitation. It is the equivalent of the functioning one would expect to find on standardized testing with scores that are at least three standard deviations below the mean. Limitation in the sixth domain, "health and physical well-being," is also assessed on the frequency of impairment-related illnesses or exacerbations that result in significant documented symptoms or signs.

THE LISTING OF IMPAIRMENTS

History and Purpose

SSA has used a listing of impairments to ease the administrative burden of determining the functional capacity of each claimant since the disability freeze program, the immediate predecessor to the SSDI program, began in 1955.[1] The Listings were, and are, a set of serious medical conditions used to identify claimants with medical conditions of such severity that they could be considered disabled without further evaluation. SSA updates the Listings periodically. Every adult claim that can be allowed based on the Listings is one that does not have to undergo the lengthy RFC assessment or the vocational analyses required at Steps 4 and 5. Thus, the Listings are an administrative expedient that allows SSA to process many cases more quickly and efficiently, which saves time and resources.

In applying the Listings, SSA's concern is that the criteria in the Listings describe impairments that are severe enough to prevent an individual from doing any gainful activity, regardless of his or her age, education, or work experience. This Listings severity standard is stricter than the statutory standard for disability in adults because, under the Listings, claimants have to be unable to engage in "any *gainful* activity" rather than in "any *substantial gainful* activity" as required by the statute. Although the Listings standard is stricter, SSA also wants a reasonable threshold of severity for the criteria in the Listings in order to allow as many claimants as appropriate under the Listings. Further, SSA wants the criteria in the Listings to be clear and easy to apply so that their adjudicators can allow claims quickly under Listings.

Over time, however, the Listings have become much less effective in expediting allowances. The percentage of claims initially allowed based on the Listings has been declining steadily, from 70 percent in the 1980s to

[1] The 1954 Social Security amendments allowed a "freeze" of a worker's earnings record while unable to work because of a disability, so that the time period during which there were no earnings was not counted in computing retirement and survivors benefits.

about 50 percent now (IOM, 2007). At the same time, the percentage of claims allowed initially has remained about the same, raising the question of whether the Listings could be revised to allow more claims at Step 3, thus reducing the number of claims to decide at Steps 4 and 5.

Structure

The Listings consist of Part A (primarily for adults) and Part B (for children only). They are organized into 14 body systems for adults and 15 for children.[2] For each body system, the Listings are preceded by a narrative introductory text that defines key concepts, terms, and procedures used in that body system to document the diagnosis and severity of an impairment. For ease of use, the Listings are numbered according to body system and disease or condition. For example, 4.00, the cardiovascular system, has eight separate adult listings, as follows:

- Chronic heart failure (4.02);
- Ischemic heart disease (4.04);
- Recurrent arrhythmias (4.05);
- Symptomatic congenital heart disease (4.06);
- Heart transplant (4.09);
- Aneurysm of aorta or major branches (4.10);
- Chronic venous insufficiency (4.11); and
- Peripheral arterial disease (4.12).

Updating the Listings

SSA has periodically revised the Listings since first publishing them as regulations in 1968. The last comprehensive revision was in 1985. Since then, SSA has focused on updates that address single body systems or sometimes specific listings. In recent years, SSA has been systematically updating all the body systems on a continual basis.

Over time, SSA has added steps to the revision process to expand input from knowledgeable sources outside SSA. Rather than beginning the revision process by proposing new or revised rules in a Notice of Proposed Rulemaking (NPRM) in the *Federal Register*, SSA first issues an Advance Notice of Proposed Rulemaking, which announces its intention to update a

[2] The 14 body systems are as follows: musculoskeletal system, special senses and speech, respiratory system, cardiovascular system, digestive system, genitourinary impairments, hematological disorders, skin disorders, endocrine system, impairments that affect multiple body systems, neurological, mental disorders, malignant neoplastic diseases, and immune system disorders. The additional body system for children is growth impairment.

specific body system or a specific listing or listings and asks for suggestions from the public. SSA may also hold one or more outreach meetings at which researchers, clinicians, patients, and patient representatives give presentations commenting on the existing listings and offering suggestions on how to revise them. After these additional steps in the process, SSA drafts proposed rules and publishes an NPRM for public comment before issuing final rules.

INITIAL DECISIONS

Social Security disability claims are initially processed through a network of local SSA field offices and DDSs. Field offices make determinations that claimants are not entitled based on non-disability criteria and generally make the determination when a claimant is doing SGA. In most cases, however, DDSs develop and evaluate medical and other evidence of disability and make the initial disability determination.

The DDS first attempts to obtain evidence from the claimant's treating physicians and medical sources. If that evidence is unavailable or insufficient to make a determination, the DDS will arrange for a consultative examination (CE) to obtain the necessary additional medical information. The claimant's treating physician is the preferred source for the CE, but the DDS also may obtain it from an independent source.

Based on all the medical and other information, the DDS makes the initial disability determination. Disability determinations are most often made by an adjudicative team composed of a medical consultant (e.g., a licensed physician) or a psychological consultant (a licensed or certified psychologist) and a lay disability examiner. Reasonable efforts are made to ensure that an appropriate specialist evaluates cases involving mental disorders (e.g., a psychologist or psychiatrist) or those involving children (e.g., a pediatrician or speech-language pathologist). Most claims involving physical impairments are evaluated by medical consultants who are generalists (e.g., internists and family medicine physicians); relatively few subspecialists work for DDSs except in a few large states.

In fiscal year 2009, DDSs adjudicated 2.8 million disability claims in an average time of 101 days (SSA, 2009c).

APPEALS PROCESS

After the initial decision, claimants have the opportunity to appeal the determination. The appeals process generally consists of four levels: the first three are reconsideration, administrative law judge hearing, and appeals council review. If the claimant is still dissatisfied with SSA's final decision, he or she may ask for judicial review by filing a civil lawsuit in federal district court. The appeals process levels are described below:

- *Reconsideration*—If the claimant is dissatisfied with the determination, he or she may request reconsideration. A different adjudicative team in the DDS then makes a new determination, following the same procedures described for initial determinations above. In fiscal year 2009, DDSs conducted 598,000 reconsiderations (SSA, 2009c).
- *Administrative law judge (ALJ) hearing*—If the claimant is dissatisfied with the reconsideration determination, he or she may appeal to SSA's Office of Disability Adjudication and Review for a de novo hearing before an ALJ. Claimants usually appear before the ALJ in person. Most claimants have an attorney or other representative, although representation is not required. The ALJ may ask for testimony from a medical or vocational expert, or both. Most ALJ decisions are based on the claimant's RFC rather than the first three steps of sequential evaluation, including the Listings. In fiscal year 2009, ALJs held 661,000 hearings (SSA, 2009c).
- *Appeals Council*—If the claimant is dissatisfied with the ALJ decision, the claimant may ask for review by SSA's Appeals Council. The Appeals Council will review the ALJ decision and will not usually make its own decision. Thus, the Appeals Council may deny or dismiss the request for review without making a decision. The Appeals Council may also issue its own decision affirming, modifying, or reversing the ALJ decision or remand the case to an ALJ for more proceedings at the hearing level. There were 89,000 Appeals Council reviews in fiscal year 2009 (SSA, 2009c).
- *Federal court*—If the claimant is dissatisfied with the Appeals Council's action, the claimant may appeal to the federal courts, up to and including the Supreme Court.

REVIEW OF CONTINUING DISABILITY

SSA is required by law to determine if there is continuing disability in every case allowed. At the time of the initial allowance, cases are classified as follows:

- Medical improvement expected (MIE);
- Medical improvement possible (MIP); or
- Medical improvement not expected (MINE).

In MIE cases, a continuing disability review (CDR) is conducted 6 to 18 months after the most recent decision that the individual is disabled. Cases that involve medical interventions, such as bypass surgery, angioplasty, or pacemaker implantation, may be classified as MIE and reviewed after a year or similar time period.[3] For organ transplantation, including heart transplantation, a 1-year period of disability is specified in the applicable listings. After the year, the beneficiary is reevaluated to determine if a residual impairment exists that still prevents SGA.

MIP cases, in which improvement is possible but not predictable, are subject to a CDR at least every 3 years. MINE cases involve extremely severe conditions that SSA expects from experience to remain static or be progressively disabling.[4] The law still requires SSA to review them, but they are reviewed every 5 to 7 years.

SSA confirms that many beneficiaries are still disabled through the use of a "mailer"—a form sent to the claimant to determine whether there has been a change in the claimant's medical or other status. When SSA conducts a full CDR, it develops medical and other evidence on the beneficiary's current condition, including health status, work status, education and vocational training, and activities of daily living. If the evidence shows that there has been medical improvement in the beneficiary's impairment or impairments and the person has the ability to engage in SGA, his or her benefits may be terminated. SSA completed 317,000 CDRs in fiscal year 2009 (SSA, 2009c).

DEVELOPMENT OF MEDICAL EVIDENCE

The DDS is responsible for developing a person's complete medical history for at least the previous 12 months in most claims. "Every reasonable effort" is made to obtain medical reports from the claimant's treating physician and other medical sources. DDS medical and psychological consultants (hereafter both referred to as medical consultants) are involved in evaluating the medical and other evidence by reviewing information in existing records, assessing it for completeness and consistency, requesting additional information as needed, and clarifying any concerns that the disability examiner may have about the medical and other evidence in the case record. Evidence includes objective medical information (i.e., signs and laboratory findings) and other evidence, including statements or reports from the claimant, the treating or examining physician, psychologist, or other source, and others about the claimant's medical history, diagnosis, prescribed treatment, daily activities, efforts to work, and any other infor-

[3] Program Operations Manual System (POMS), SSA's procedural manual, cites fractures, burns, and gunshot wounds as examples of MIE impairments (Program Operations Manual System, Section DI 13005.055).

[4] POMS gives total deafness, total blindness, amputation of more than one limb, amputation of a leg at the hip, amputation as a consequence of diabetes, and any longstanding condition that has resulted in bed confinement or the need for a wheelchair, walker, or crutches as examples of MINE impairments (Program Operations Manual System, Section DI 13005.022).

mation about the impact of the claimant's impairment or impairments and related symptoms on the ability to work.

REFERENCES

IOM (Institute of Medicine). 2007. *Improving the Social Security disability decision process,* edited by J. D. Stobo, M. McGeary, and D. K. Barnes. Washington, DC: The National Academies Press. http://www.nap.edu/catalog.php?record_id=11859 (accessed June 29, 2010).

SSA (Social Security Administration). 2009a. *Annual statistical report on the Social Security Disability Insurance Program, 2008.* http://www.ssa.gov/policy/docs/statcomps/di_asr/2008/index.html (accessed June 2, 2010).

SSA. 2009b. *SSI annual statistical report, 2008.* http://www.ssa.gov/policy/docs/statcomps/ssi_asr/index.html (accessed June 2, 2010).

SSA. 2009c. *FY 2009 performance and accountability report.* Baltimore, MD: SSA. http://www.ssa.gov/finance/2009/Full%20FY%202009%20PAR.pdf (accessed June 28, 2010).

SSA. 2010. Social Security helps states with mounting disability claims. http://www.ssa.gov/pressoffice/pr/est-pr.htm (accessed May 10, 2010).

3

Cardiovascular Disability Trends

IMPACT OF CARDIOVASCULAR DISEASES

Although the mortality rate from cardiovascular disease has declined by 65 percent over the past 4 decades, it remains the leading cause of death for men and women in the United States (NHLBI, 2009). In 2006, 831,000 Americans died of cardiovascular diseases, compared with 560,000 deaths from cancer, 125,000 from chronic obstructive pulmonary disease and other respiratory conditions, and 122,000 from accidents, which were the next most common causes of death (Lloyd-Jones et al., 2010; NHLBI, 2009).

Prevalence

Approximately 81 million American adults (more than one in three) have cardiovascular disease, and more than half of them (53 percent) are under age 60 (Lloyd-Jones et al., 2010). Specifically, of the 81 million

- 74.5 million have high blood pressure that, if uncontrolled, will eventually result in substantial morbidity and death;
- 17.6 million have coronary heart disease, of whom 10.2 million will suffer from angina pectoris (chest pain) and 8.5 million will experience a myocardial infarction (heart attack);
- 5.8 million have heart failure;
- 6.4 million have had a stroke; and
- Between 650,000 and 1.3 million have congenital cardiovascular defects.

Prevalence increases with age, but cardiovascular disease is not just a disease of the aged. Although only about 10 percent of adults ages 20 to 39 have a cardiovascular condition, that percentage rises to nearly 40 percent among those ages 40 to 59 (Lloyd-Jones et al., 2010).

Incidence

According to the Framingham Heart Study, the incidence of cardiovascular disease also increases with age, up to 74 cases per thousand person-years among men ages 85 to 94. However, among working-age persons, the incidence among men ages 45 to 54 and ages 55 to 65 is 10 and 24 cases per thousand person-years, respectively (NHLBI, 2006).[1]

Morbidity and Disability

Cardiovascular diseases also cause substantial morbidity and disability. Cardiovascular conditions are a major cause of sick leave, and diseases of the circulatory system are estimated to be the fourth most common basis for long-term disability insurance claims (Leopold, 2003).

Since at least 1990, cardiovascular diseases have accounted for the highest number of inpatient hospital days (followed by respiratory diseases, mental disorders, and injuries) and for the highest health care expenditures (NHLBI, 2009). In 2007, heart disease was the third leading cause of activity limitation, after arthritis and back/neck conditions, and hypertension was sixth (NHLBI, 2009).

SOCIAL SECURITY CARDIOVASCULAR DISABILITY TRENDS

Total Beneficiaries and New Awardees in 2008

In December 2008, 758,324 adults ages 18 to 64 whose primary impairment was a disease of the circulatory system were receiving Social Security Disability Insurance (SSDI) or Supplemental Security Income (SSI) benefits (SSA, 2009a). They constituted 6.9 percent of the adult disability beneficiaries. Diseases of the circulatory system are the fourth most prevalent diagnostic category among adult beneficiaries after mental disorders (43.1 percent), diseases of the musculoskeletal system and connective tissue (20.3 percent), and diseases of the nervous system and sense organs (9.1 percent). In December 2008, 5,862 children under age 18 were receiving SSI

[1] Rates among women under age 65 are less than half those of men in the same age range. The conditions included are coronary heart disease, heart failure, cerebrovascular accident, and intermittent claudication.

disability benefits for diseases of the circulatory system, and an additional 60,466 were receiving benefits for congenital anomalies, some of which may be cardiovascular related, but the exact number cannot be known without further research (SSA, 2009b).

During 2008, 95,445 adults with a disease of the circulatory system were awarded SSDI benefits, which was nearly 10 percent of the SSDI allowances awarded that year and the third highest number of allowances after those for adults with diseases of the musculoskeletal system and connective tissue, and with mental disorders (SSA, 2009a). In 2008, 915 children under age 18 with diseases of the circulatory system were awarded SSI benefits, and 8,625 with congenital anomalies, some of which may be cardiovascular-related, were awarded SSI benefits (SSA, 2009b).

Disposition of Adult Cardiovascular Disability Claims, 1989–2008

For the past 20 years, the Social Security Administration (SSA) has decided about 145,000 adult claims a year for SSDI or SSI benefits, or both, for adults with a cardiovascular condition as the primary impairment (Figure 3-1).[2]

Over the same period, the initial allowance rate for adult cardiovascular claims averaged about 40 percent each year (Figure 3-2), but the share of allowances based on meeting or medically equaling the Listings—thus avoiding the time- and resource-intensive Steps 4 and 5 of the sequential evaluation process—dropped substantially, a trend that is discussed in the next section.

Use of the Adult Cardiovascular Listings

Body System-Level Trends

Closer inspection of the share of initial adult allowances made at Step 3 (based on the cardiovascular listings) rather than at Step 5 (based on residual functional capacity, age, education, and work experience) shows a substantial decrease in the share of allowances made at Step 3 for adult cardiovascular claims, from 60 percent in 1990 to 26 percent in 2008 (Figure 3-3). The shift from the majority of initial adult cardiovascular allowances being made at Step 3 to the majority of allowances being made at Step 5 was fairly steady except for a substantial decrease in the share of listings-based allowances in 1994 that continued through 1995.

---

[2] The increase in claims in the early 1990s was due in part to the July 1990 to March 1991 recession (Lewin-VHI, 1995).

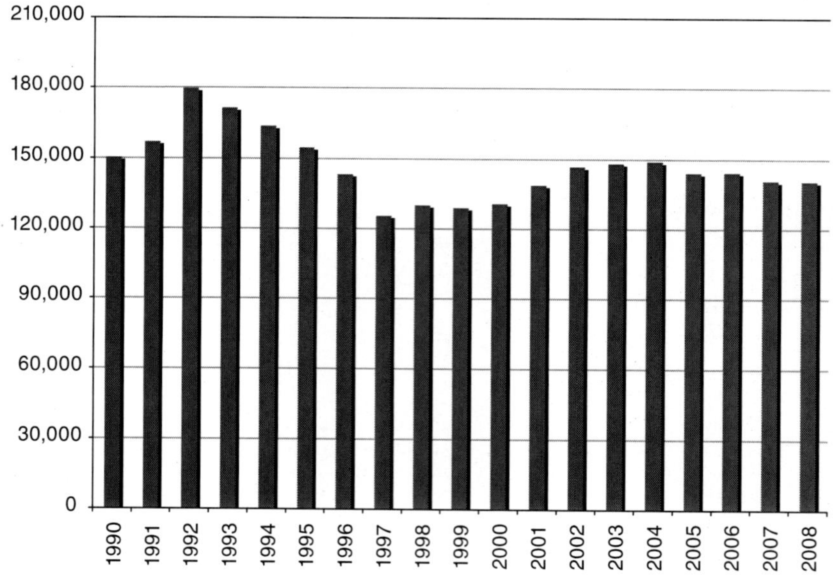

FIGURE 3-1 Annual number of initial adult cardiovascular claims, 1990–2008.
SOURCE: IOM staff, using data from a dataset provided by SSA. This dataset records the number of initial and reconsideration decisions made by the state disability determination services by primary impairment code and calendar year, which can be aggregated at the body system level, as has been done in this figure.

Part of the transition from Step 3 to Step 5 allowances during the period 1994 to 1995 may be attributed to the types of claims received during and after the 1990 to 1992 recession (Lewin-VHI, 1995). In recessions, some workers with impairments who have been able to find employment in an expanding economy are laid off. They may apply for disability, but they may be less likely to have impairments that meet the listing-level severity standard of inability to engage in any gainful work, or even SSA's less strict disability standard of inability to engage in any *substantial* gainful activity. (The overall allowance rate was also depressed during the same years [Figure 3-2]).

The decrease in the share of allowances made at Step 3 during the period 1994 to 1995 also coincided with a substantial revision of the cardiovascular listings that took effect in February 1994. The committee heard anecdotally from various SSA and disability determination services (DDS) employees that the 1994 revision made the listings criteria very technical and thus more difficult for adjudicators to understand and apply. If true, this outcome underlines the value of simplicity in listings criteria, as long as they remain medically appropriate.

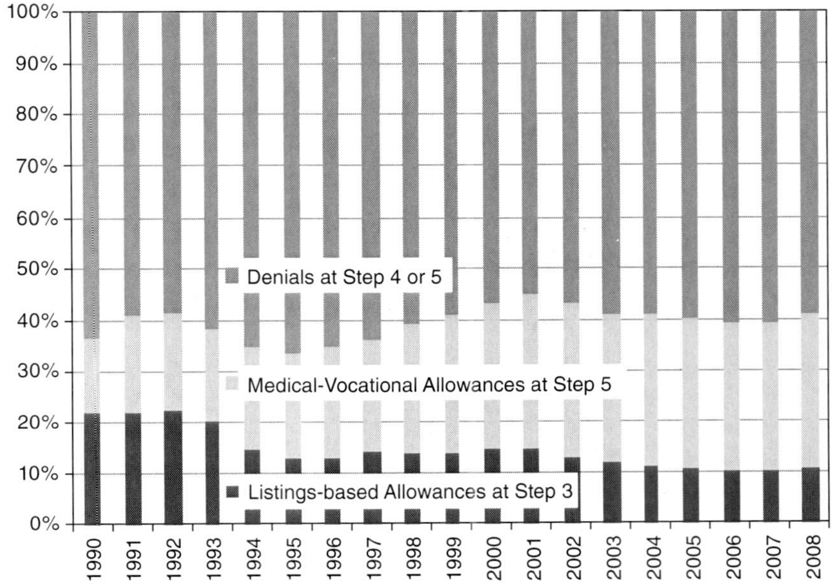

FIGURE 3-2 Annual allowance rate for initial adult cardiovascular claims, 1990–2008.
SOURCE: IOM staff, using data from a dataset provided by SSA. This dataset records the number of initial and reconsideration decisions made by the state disability determination services by primary impairment code and calendar year, which can be aggregated at the body system level, as has been done in this figure.

The next comprehensive revision of the adult cardiovascular listings took effect in April 2006 and had a lesser impact on the shares of allowances made at Steps 3 and 5. The percentage of adult allowances made on the basis of these listings stayed about the same in 2007 and 2008 rather than continuing to gradually transition from Step 3 to Step 5 allowances, as it had each of the previous 9 years.

Listing-Level Trends

SSA data can provide the number of allowances made at Step 3 by listing (Figure 3-4). However, because the Listings are a screen-in step, SSA data cannot classify Step 5 allowances by any specific listing that a claimant may have failed to meet or medically equal at Step 3. Therefore, it is not possible to report trends in Step 5 allowances or denials at Steps 4 or 5 in terms of the cardiovascular listings.

During the past decade, almost all (95 percent) of the adult allowances that SSA made using the cardiovascular listings were allowed under four

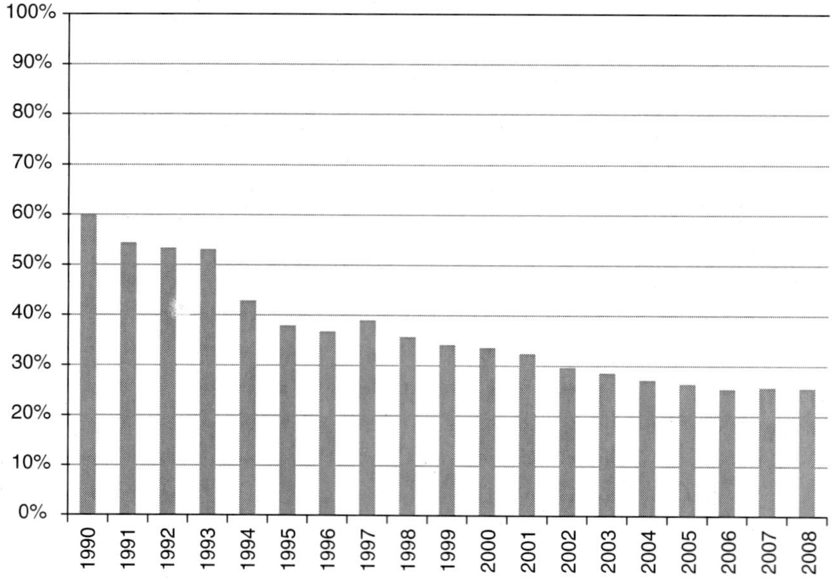

FIGURE 3-3 Annual percentage of initial adult allowances made on the basis of the cardiovascular listings, 1990–2008.
SOURCE: IOM staff, using data from a dataset provided by SSA. This dataset records the number of initial and reconsideration decisions made by the state disability determination services by primary impairment code and calendar year, which can be aggregated at the body system level, as has been done in this figure.

of these listings (Figure 3-4).[3] The number of listings allowances peaked in 2001 at nearly 19,000, declined to less than 14,000 in 2006 and 2007, and began increasing again, reaching 15,000 in 2009. The upward trend after 2007 may have resulted from the 2006 cardiovascular listings revisions. The main reason for the upward trend may be the revisions SSA made to the listings for chronic heart failure and, to a lesser extent, chronic venous insufficiency.[4] Over the same time period, though, Step 3 allowances based on the listing for ischemic heart disease continued to decline.

[3] Each of the remaining four cardiovascular listings accounts for less than 200 allowances each year.

[4] The cardiomyopathy listing was removed in 2006 because it was a reference listing, which may have slightly increased the number of allowances based on the chronic heart failure listing. (A reference listing, such as the pre-2006 listing for cardiomyopathy, is one that refers the adjudicator to another listing that should be used to evaluate the case, e.g., chronic heart failure, ischemic heart disease, recurrent arrhythmias, or central nervous system vascular accident. Reference listings for hypertensive cardiovascular disease and valvular heart disease were also eliminated in 2006.)

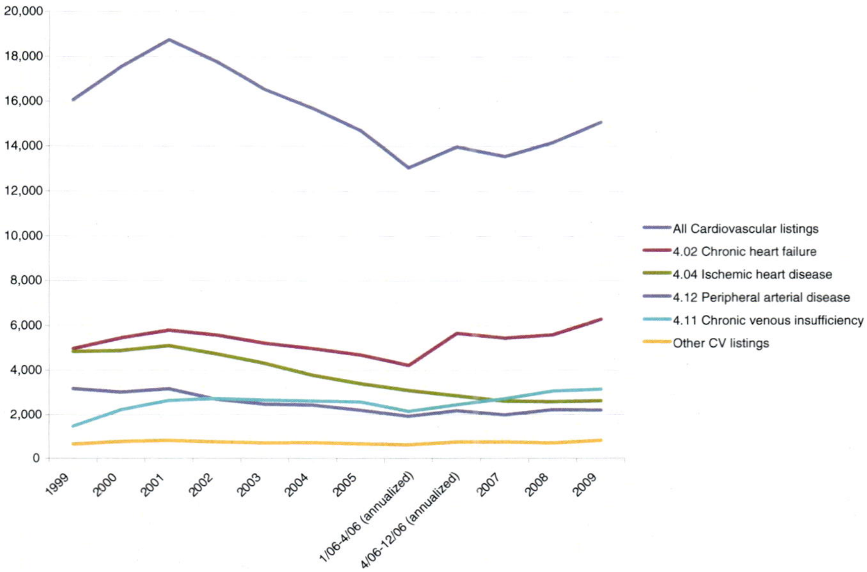

FIGURE 3-4 Annual number of initial adult allowances based on the cardiovascular listings, 1999–2009.
SOURCE: IOM staff, using data from a dataset provided by SSA. This dataset records the number of initial allowances based on meeting or equaling the cardiovascular listings made by the state disability determination services by listing and calendar year.

Impairment-Level Trends

SSA assigns a primary impairment code to each claim that receives a medical determination and can report, by impairment code, if the impairment in each claim met or medically equaled a listing, if the claim was allowed at Step 5, or if it was denied. SSA currently uses 24 cardiovascular impairment codes. These data are helpful in understanding general trends in claims involving cardiovascular impairments because there is substantial, although not absolute, consistency between each listing and its related impairment code. For example, 87 percent of the allowances under 4.02 (chronic heart failure) in 2009 were coded as either chronic heart failure or cardiomyopathy, and 75 percent of the allowances under 4.04 (ischemic heart disease) were coded as chronic ischemic heart disease.[5]

[5] Other codes may be used as the primary impairment in cases where the claimant's condition equals the listing.

As expected, there was variation in the impairment codes used for Step 3 allowances based on meeting or medically equaling an adult cardiovascular listing during the period 1990 to 2009. Figure 3-5 includes some impairment codes mentioned in the following bulleted text:

- The percentage of listing-level allowances for phlebitis/thrombophlebitis allowances based on the listings *increased* from 14 to 26 percent.
- The percentage of listing-level allowances *stayed about the same* for some impairment codes, for example, heart transplantation (80 percent), chronic pulmonary heart disease (60 percent), and varicose veins of the lower extremities (55 percent).
- The most-used cardiovascular impairment codes saw a *steady downward trend* in the number of listing-level allowances from 1990 to 2009. Listing-level allowances of claims coded as acute myocardial infarction declined from 39 to 12 percent, angina pectoris from 31 to 6 percent, and peripheral arterial disease from 68 to 41 percent.
- The use of two other cardiovascular impairment codes also declined over the period, but with *a distinct drop* in 1994 and 1995.

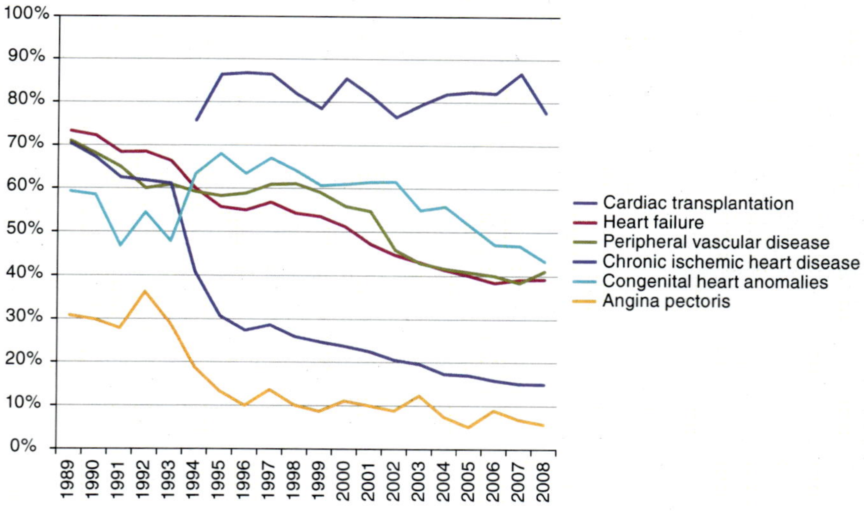

FIGURE 3-5 Percentage of adult initial allowances based on the cardiovascular listings, by selected impairment code, 1989–2008.
SOURCE: IOM staff, using data from a dataset provided by SSA. This dataset records the number of initial and reconsideration decisions made by the state disability determination services by primary impairment code and calendar year.

Ischemic heart disease allowances based on the listings decreased from 67 to 15 percent, but 20 of those percentage point losses occurred from 1993 to 1994 and another 10 percentage points from 1994 to 1995. This decrease accounts for much of the overall decrease shown in Figure 3-3 because at that time ischemic heart disease accounted for nearly half (46 percent) of all the cardiovascular listing-level allowances.

- For two other impairment codes, aortic aneurysm and congenital heart disease, the proportion of initial allowances made at Step 3 increased from 1994 to 1995 before resuming a steady decline. For example, the listing-level share of initial allowances for adults with congenital heart disease declined from 58 percent in 1990 to 48 percent in 1993, jumped to 68 percent by 1995, and then declined to 43 percent in 2008.

Summary of Adult Trends

This brief analysis of data on the disposition of adult cardiovascular claims over time shows that the general decrease in the use of the Listings as the basis for allowances is generally applicable to the cardiovascular body system listings.[6] This supports SSA's concern about the usefulness of the Listings as an administrative expedient to quickly identify allowances, which would save both the claimant's time and the agency's resources.

The analysis also indicates some variation at the listing level and at the impairment code level. This in turn indicates less need to revise certain cardiovascular listings, which are apparently functioning well (e.g., heart transplantation) and greater need to examine certain listings whose usefulness appears to be declining despite revisions in 1994 and 2006 (e.g., chronic ischemic heart disease). As mentioned above, the drop in the use of the Listings as a screen-in tool for allowances at the time of the 1994 revision, as well as the continued decline in their use as a screen-in tool since then, argues strongly for greater simplicity and clarity in the criteria and the tests required to establish diagnoses and determine clinical severity.

Disposition of Child Cardiovascular Disability Claims, 1999–2009

In recent years, SSA has decided about 7,000 initial claims annually by children for SSI benefits in which the primary impairment code was

[6] From 1989 to 2008, the share of all adult allowances that met or equaled the listings declined from 62.9 to 50.3 percent. During the same time period, the share of cardiovascular adult allowances that met or equaled the listings declined much more, from 63.1 to 25.6 percent (IOM staff analysis of unpublished data provided by SSA).

cardiovascular. The majority (about 60 percent) have been for congenital heart disease. The next three largest categories, at 6 to 7 percent each, have been for arrhythmias, aortic valve disorders, and valvular heart disease or other stenotic defects.[7]

The annual number of cardiovascular allowances to SSI children has been about 3,400 (3,600 in 2009). The annual allowance rate has been about 47 percent for the past decade. In recent years, approximately three-quarters of the allowances have been based on meeting or medically equaling the congenital heart disease listings (4.06 and 104.06), 6 percent were for meeting or medically equaling other cardiovascular listings, and 19 to 20 percent were for functionally equaling the listings.

REFERENCES

Leopold, R. 2003. *A year in the life of a million American workers*. New York: MetLife.

Lewin-VHI, Inc. 1995. *Labor market conditions, socioeconomic factors, and the growth of applications and awards for SSDI and SSI disability benefits: Final report*. Washington, D.C.: Department of Health and Human Services, Office of the Assistant Secretary for Planning and Evaluation and Social Security Administration. May 23.

Lloyd-Jones, D., R. J. Adams, T. M. Brown, M. Carnethon, S. Dai, G. De Simone, T. B. Ferguson, E. Ford, K. Furie, C. Gillespie, A. Go, K. Greenlund, N. Haase, S. Hailpern, P. M. Ho, V. Howard, B. Kissela, S. Kittner, D. Lackland, L. Lisabeth, A. Marelli, M. M. McDermott, J. Meigs, D. Mozaffarian, M. Mussolino, G. Nichol, V. Roger, W. Rosamond, R. Sacco, P. Sorlie, R. Stafford, T. Thom, S. Wasserthiel-Smoller, N. D. Wong, and J. Wylie-Rosett, on behalf of the American Heart Association Statistics Committee Stroke Statistics Subcommittee. 2010. Heart disease and stroke statistics—2010 update: A report from the American Heart Association. *Circulation* 121(7):e46–2e15.

NHLBI (National Heart, Lung, and Blood Institute). 2006. *Incidence and prevalence: 2006 chart book on cardiovascular and lung diseases*. Bethesda, MD: NHLBI. http://www.nhlbi.nih.gov/resources/docs/06a_ip_chtbk.pdf (accessed June 2, 2010).

NHLBI. 2009. *Morbidity & mortality: 2009 chart book on cardiovascular, lung, and blood diseases*. Bethesda, MD: NHLBI. http://www.nhlbi.nih.gov/resources/docs/2009_ChartBook.pdf (accessed June 2, 2010).

SSA (Social Security Administration). 2009a. *Annual statistical report on the Social Security Disability Insurance Program, 2008*. http://www.ssa.gov/policy/docs/statcomps/di_asr/2008/index.html (accessed June 2, 2010).

SSA. 2009b. *SSI annual statistical report, 2008*. http://www.ssa.gov/policy/statcomps/ssi_asr/index.html (accessed June 2, 2010).

[7] The numbers and percentages in this section on initial claims by child for cardiovascular impairments are based on IOM staff analyses of unpublished data provided by SSA.

4

Approaches to Revising the Cardiovascular Listings

ISSUES IN REVISING THE LISTINGS

This report primarily addresses the specific cardiovascular listings and several cardiovascular conditions for which listings might be useful (see Chapters 5 through 14). This chapter discusses issues common to all or most of the cardiovascular listings and the approach the committee took to addressing them. These include the criteria for evaluating listings, the trade-off between sensitivity and specificity inherent in designing a screening tool such as the listings, the limited predictive capacity of most clinical factors, the safety of exercise tests, and the impact of comorbidities (discussed in more detail in Chapter 15).

Attributes of Effective Listings

Ideally, listings have the following attributes:

- Up to date with advances in diagnosis and treatment and with changes in the nature of work;
- Consistent;
- Correct; and
- Useful (SSA, 2005).

Several of these attributes were emphasized in the Social Security Administration's (SSA's) presentation to this committee at its first meeting (SSA, 2009). The committee was urged to recommend revisions that would make the cardiovascular listings more inclusive; more up to date regarding the latest knowledge, science, and technology; and more user-friendly, that is, as objective as possible and requiring the minimum number of criteria to be fulfilled to meet a listing.

The committee kept these criteria in mind throughout its discussions, while recognizing the inherent trade-offs among them. The recommendations incorporate the latest knowledge and technology based on current clinical guidelines and scientific literature, but they would only require tests and other procedures that are widely available in medical settings throughout the country. If a claimant has had more sophisticated, cutting-edge diagnostic tests that are only available in leading medical centers, the results should be used, but are not required. In addition, some techniques required by clinical guidelines for a definitive diagnosis (e.g., right heart catheterization to establish pulmonary hypertension) are considered to be too risky for SSA to require claimants to have the procedure if they have not already had it.

Objective criteria may be easier to use and lead to more consistent decisions, but they do not necessarily lead to more correct decisions. The generally limited ability of objective clinical tests to predict functional capacity or work disability is discussed below.

The committee did not try to consider the changing nature of work, other than to be aware of the long-term trend away from physically demanding jobs to less strenuous, but more cognitively demanding, jobs. The committee also could not determine whether the current cardiovascular listings or proposed revisions are correct in terms of validity, that is, the extent to which they allow all claimants who are truly unable to engage in any gainful employment—and only those claimants. This would require further research.

The general approach taken by the committee to revising the cardiovascular listings is shown in an algorithm outlined in Box 4-1. The algorithm was designed to arrive at the listings-level criteria that were the most objective and easiest to administer while maintaining a reasonable degree of accuracy.

Diagnosis Alone

Few diagnoses are sufficient by themselves to meet the Listings. Examples in other body systems include amyotrophic lateral sclerosis and amputation of both hands. Most of the compassionate allowance conditions are based on diagnosis, such as aggressive, incurable cancers and certain rare diseases that are invariably fatal; none of them is a cardiovascular condition.

The committee is not recommending any diagnoses as sufficient to meet a cardiovascular listing, except the current listing for heart transplantation.

BOX 4-1
Committee's Approach to Revising the Listings

1. Determine if there is a diagnosis (e.g., International Classification of Diseases [ICD] code) that indicates either (A) a terminal illness of short duration or (B) a condition so severely incapacitating that it is nearly always work disabling and would be extremely likely to meet, if not exceed, the Social Security definition of disability. If so, make it a sufficient requirement for a listing-level allowance (also consider recommending it as a compassionate allowance if it is not already designated as such). If not, go to the next step.
2. Given a diagnosis that is not sufficient by itself to accurately differentiate disabled from nondisabled claimants, determine if an accepted measure of impairment severity exists that has been shown to have a high degree of association with incapacity to work or with serious functional limitations that would seem to preclude work. If so, make that degree of impairment severity a sufficient requirement (given that diagnosis) for a listing-level allowance. If not, go to the next step.
3. Given a diagnosis and impairment severity measure or measures that are not sufficient to accurately differentiate disabled from nondisabled claimants, require evidence of severe functional limitations.

It automatically allows benefits for a 12-month period after the procedure, which the committee would not recommend revising.

Diagnosis Plus *a Specific Degree of Medical Severity*

A number of listings require evidence of a certain degree of medical severity according to a specified test or examination, including one cardiovascular listing. For example, the current listing for peripheral artery disease (PAD) is met with a resting ankle-brachial index (ABI) of less than 0.50 or certain toe pressure values. Adjudicators find such listings to be objective and easy to apply, but the problem with most medical severity measures is their lack of sensitivity (i.e., their inability to identify many true positives), especially if they are set at a point of high specificity to prevent false positives. This stems from the limited capacity of most severity measures to predict degree of functional limitation or vocational capacity and is discussed more fully below.

The committee could have recommended clinical criteria so severe that anyone meeting them would almost certainly be unable to work. For example, the PAD listing could specify an ABI of less than 0.40, when critical leg ischemia requiring emergency intervention to avoid amputation becomes likely. The problem with this approach is that relatively few claimants who are truly unable to work would meet the criteria, which would undermine the purpose of the Listings. Their purpose is to allow claimants to meet the criteria quickly if they would be highly likely to do so after undergoing the usual in-depth, time-consuming evaluation.

The committee agreed that it would be appropriate for certain conditions to meet a listing based on diagnosis and severity alone. These include:

- Symptomatic severe aortic stenosis that meets certain anatomical impairment criteria determined by echocardiogram or heart catheterization because it is likely to be fatal in a short time unless treated successfully by surgery (see Recommendation 12-1).
- Symptomatic chronic venous insufficiency (CVI) with severe trophic skin changes or persistent venous ulcers (see Recommendation 9-1).

In several instances, the committee recommends that claimants should meet a listing on the basis of a certain degree of severity alone or, for a somewhat lower degree of severity, if they are severely functionally limited. Adding a second basis for meeting a listing that requires less impairment severity—if the claimant can demonstrate a marked limitation of capacity to function due to that impairment or impairments—increases the sensitivity of the Listings, that is, identifies more claimants who should be allowed. Examples include:

- Systolic heart failure with a left ventricular ejection fraction of 20 percent or less, because this severity would preclude gainful employment for nearly everyone, or with a left ventricular ejection fraction between 20 and 30 percent in conjunction with marked functional limitations (see Recommendations 5-3 and 5-1, respectively).
- Pulmonary hypertension with a mean pulmonary artery pressure of 40 mm Hg or higher, or with a mean pulmonary artery pressure between 25 and 40 mm Hg in conjunction with marked functional limitations (see Recommendations 11-1A and 11-1B, respectively).

Diagnosis Plus *a Specific Degree of Medical Severity* Plus *a Specific Degree of Whole-Person Functional Limitation*

In many conditions, even a substantial degree of impairment of an organ or body system does not always rule out capacity to work. In most cases, at a given degree of severity (e.g., ejection fraction less than 30 percent), most people will not be able to work, although some will have that capacity. Therefore, additional information is needed to establish whether a claimant is unable to work (i.e., has functional limitations considered to be tantamount to inability to work). Most of the current cardiovascular listings are structured this way. For example, given a diagnosis of systolic heart failure and an ejection factor of 30 percent or less, the current listing is not met unless the claimant is unable to perform 5 metabolic equivalents of task (METs) on an exercise test, or has had three or more episodes of acute heart failure, or has persistent symptoms "which very seriously limit the ability to independently initiate, sustain, or complete activities of daily living."

After reviewing evidence regarding the relationship of impairment measures (e.g., the ABI, ejection fraction, degree of left main artery stenosis, pulmonary artery pressure, valvular regurgitation volume to functional capacity), the committee concluded that such measures generally should be considered necessary, but not sufficient to meet a listing. Most of the recommendations for listing-level criteria therefore take the form of (1) an anatomical abnormality of a certain severity, and (2) a certain degree of functional limitation. This is the approach taken to the listing criteria for heart failure, ischemic heart disease (unless the ejection fraction is 20 percent or less), PAD, and CVI.

Diagnosis Plus *a Specific Degree of Functional Limitation*

In some cases, evidence of very serious functional limitations is all that is needed in addition to a diagnosis. Other than in many of the mental listings, this is not common in the adult Listings. It is always an option in the childhood Listings, where claimants may functionally equal the Listings. The committee concluded that this approach would not be suitable for any of the adult cardiovascular conditions.

Measurement Issues

The criteria in the cardiovascular listings are all measures obtained from using some kind of instrument or protocol. Examples of measures include left ventricular diameter, left ventricular ejection fraction, heart wall thickness, peak VO_2 and other cardiopulmonary exercise (CPX) test readings, New York Heart Association functional classification, Canadian Cardiovascular Society (CCS) angina classification, ST-segment depression and other electrocardiogram (ECG) readings, degree of artery stenosis, ABI, arterial O_2 saturation, mean pulmonary artery pressure, METs, amount of heart valve regurgitation, size and rate of growth of an aortic aneurysm, amount of reflux in a leg vein, and activities of daily living (ADLs). These measures are not perfect for a variety of reasons. The reading may not be representative if the process being measured is variable, such as blood pressure or heart rate. The image may be complex to read, such as an echocardiogram of a ventricle or the aorta. The measure may be an indirect estimate, such as METs from a treadmill test done without measuring respiratory gas exchange. The test may be of low quality because the equipment was not well maintained or the tester was not adequately trained and certified to conduct it.

Some of the measures are obtained objectively, for example, blood pressure readings. Others are subjective, based on patient self-report, such as CCS angina class or ADL score. The main issue, however, is the extent to which a given test or protocol measures the phenomenon of interest. The ABI, for example, is objective, based on the ratio of two blood pressure readings. It is a validated test of peripheral artery disease, because, on average, individuals with an ABI of 0.90 have been shown by simultaneous angiography to have a 50 percent blockage of a major leg artery. However, it is not a strong measure of walking or of stair climbing capacity (which are themselves proxy measures of the phenomenon of interest, namely, degree of disability). An ABI of 0.50 is positively but weakly associated with distance walked in 6 minutes. ADL scores, on the other hand, while based on patient self-report, are a significant predictor of entry into a nursing home (Gaugler et al., 2007), use of hospital services and physician services, and mortality (Dunlop et al., 1999).

In the context of measuring inability to engage in any gainful activity—the definition of someone who should be allowed at Step 3—the appropriate way to evaluate a listing is as a screening tool or diagnostic test. The purpose of the listing is to correctly identify individuals whose medical condition or conditions either meet or equal that listing or do not meet or equal that listing. The former are true positives who should be allowed. The latter are true negatives who should be sent on to Step 4 and, if necessary, Step 5 (they may still be allowed if they meet the inability to perform any *substantial* gainful activity, the standard at Step 5). Individuals not identified and allowed at Step 3 are false negatives and constitute a lost opportunity to save time and resources. Allowed individuals may be false positives, who obtain benefits they are not entitled to. The appropriate metrics in this situation are sensitivity, specificity, and related measures of test accuracy. These are discussed in the next section in the context of assessing the limitations of the listings.

Limitations of the Listings as a Screening Tool

The Listings are used to determine if a claimant can or cannot engage in any gainful activity, that is, perform any work for pay. In fact, the work capacity of a population of claimants with a given impairment will vary from no work to high-work capacity. There will always be claimants with conditions that are difficult to classify as totally incapacitating (therefore meeting or equaling the Listings) as opposed to almost totally incapacitating (therefore not meeting or equaling the Listings). This uncertainty results in classification errors, that is, false negatives (claimants who are denied, but should be allowed) and false positives (claimants who are allowed, but should have been denied). As with other diagnostic screening tools, restricting the criteria would reduce false positives (increase specificity) but also would increase false negatives (reduce sensitivity). Relaxing the criteria to reduce false negatives (thus allowing true positives to be allowed quickly) would also increase the number of false positives.

As the administrator of a government benefit program, SSA wants to keep the false-positive rate very low, but at the same time wants the Listings to be as sensitive as possible. Higher sensitivity would quickly allow a greater percentage of those who are truly unable to work to qualify for benefits, which is the purpose of having the Listings. Therefore, in formulating recommendations to improve them, the committee kept in mind the trade-off between sensitivity and specificity and SSA's preference for high specificity. Generally, given the variable relationship between medical impairment measures and functional capacity—and the desire to increase sensitivity without unduly lowering specificity—most of the recommendations require both (1) an anatomical abnormality of a certain severity and (2) a certain degree of functional limitation, as discussed in the previous section. The false negatives (i.e., claimants who are truly unable to work but are not allowed at Step 3) resulting from the relative lack of sensitivity are not denied. They proceed through the remaining steps of the decision process, which involve an in-depth medical and vocational evaluation, and if they are unable to work, they should be allowed at Step 5.

Limitations on the Predictive Ability of Clinical Factors

The limited ability of clinical factors to predict the degree of functional capacity of an individual with an impairment makes it more challenging to increase the sensitivity of the Listings and to maintain high specificity at the same time. For example, most people with a left ventricular ejection fraction of 30 percent or less will not be able to get to and from or function in the workplace, but some will have that capacity. Meanwhile, some individuals with an ejection fraction of 40 or even 50 percent will be totally incapacitated. The same is true of using an ABI of less than 0.50 to predict the work capacity of individuals with PAD—some will be able to work.

This variability in functional capacity among people with the same clinical test results increases the uncertainty and, therefore, creates the problem of false negatives and false positives discussed above. In these circumstances, lowering the ejection fraction to 20 percent or the ABI to 0.40 would ensure specificity, but it would also reduce sensitivity to the point that most true positives would not meet or equal the Listings and would have to go through the time- and resource-intensive Steps 4 and 5 of the disability decision process. Using an ejection fraction of 50 percent or an ABI of 0.70 would likely allow most of the true positives, but at the same time it would allow many individuals who could work.

In most of the recommendations, therefore, the committee tried to increase sensitivity by requiring objective clinical documentation of severe impairments consistent with incapacity to work *in most cases* (e.g., ejection fraction of less than 30 percent for heart failure) and evidence of very serious functional limitations, which would serve to screen out false positives.

Functional Assessment Tools

The mainstay of functional capacity testing in cardiovascular medicine is the exercise test conducted on a motorized treadmill or cycle ergometer with ECG and blood pressure monitoring. Exercise tests provide an objective measure of a person's maximal aerobic capacity and are commonly used to provide diagnostic and prognostic information. The information can also be compared with the aerobic demands of various jobs, usually expressed as METs (Ainsworth et al., 2000). The number of METs an individual can achieve can be estimated from a graded treadmill test with ECG findings or determined directly if the individual's intake of oxygen and output of carbon dioxide are measured. The latter test, called a CPX test, can also determine how fully the patient is exerting himself or herself by measuring a respiratory exchange ratio to determine a patient's level of effort (Balady et al., 2010).

Exercise testing is commonly performed for diagnostic and prognostic purposes on individuals with ischemic heart disease, heart failure, valvular heart disease (except for symptomatic aortic stenosis), peripheral artery disease, congenital heart disease, unexplained exertional dyspnea, and children with symptoms on exercise or "before certain athletic, recreational, or vocational activities" (Arena et al., 2007; Paridon et al., 2006). According to several reviews of recent studies, CPX testing is useful in determining functional capacity in patients with pulmonary arterial hypertension and heart failure (Arena et al., 2008, 2010).

Some individuals may not be suitable candidates for an exercise test but can undergo a pharmacologic stress test. A pharmacologic stress test is indicated for patients with severe debilitation or a noncardiovascular impairment that prevents them from achieving a maximal heart rate during an exercise stress test. In a pharmacologic stress test, cardiovascular stress is induced by a pharmacologic agent and the functional response assessed with echocardiography or other imaging modality, such as radionuclide imaging.

Individuals with leg impairments or other severe debilitation may be good candidates for a timed walk test, such as the distance walked in 6 minutes, although timed walk tests are not considered a substitute for treadmill or ergometry exercise testing in individuals for whom treadmill or ergometry testing are not contraindicated (Arena et al., 2007).

It is well established that a person's ability to perform specific everyday tasks is predictive of disability outcomes, such as nursing home entry and level of care needed in assisted living facilities. The best known measures are ADLs and instrumental activities of daily living (IADLs). ADLs are basic tasks of daily life, such as feeding oneself, dressing, bathing, using the toilet, and transferring (getting in and out of bed or a chair). IADLs are activities such as housework, preparing meals, shopping, managing money, and using the telephone (NRC, 2009). Tools for assessing capacity to perform ADLs and IADLs have been developed and validated for use in rehabilitation and long-term care settings (Katz, 1963; Katz and Apkom, 1976; Lawton and Brody, 1969; Mahoney et al., 1958).

Maximizing the Use of Exercise Testing

The introductory section of the cardiovascular system listings notes that exercise tolerance tests are widely used to determine functional capacity in patients with ischemic heart disease, heart failure, and peripheral artery disease. It is indicated that SSA might purchase an exercise test if it is needed to determine whether a claimant meets or equals a cardiovascular listing; however, the current cardiovascular listings are based on an overly strict assessment of the risk factors associated with the performance of these tests. In fact, an extensive body of research shows exercise testing to be safe in most cases and much safer than the criteria in the current listings assume (Arena et al., 2007; Balady et al., 2010; Gibbons et al., 2002).[1] The committee encourages SSA to revise section 4.00.C.8 to bring it in line with the current understanding of the safety of exercise tests.

Serious complications, such as myocardial infarction (MI), arrhythmia, and death, can occur as a result of exercise testing. The incidence is very low, however. Multiple studies indicate that the risks of a complication that requires hospitalization, MI, or sudden cardiac death during or immediately after an exercise test are less than or equal to 0.2 percent, 0.04 percent,

[1] The role of exercise testing in determining functional capacity is discussed in more detail in Chapters 5 (Heart Failure, Cardiomyopathy, and Right Heart Failure) and 7 (Ischemic Heart Disease).

and 0.01 percent, respectively (Myers et al., 2009, citing ACSM, 2006). Obviously, supervisory physicians should be well trained in the clinical indications for use of exercise testing and in signs and symptoms of serious adverse events to minimize risk to patients. According to American College of Cardiology/American Heart Association guidelines for exercise testing (Gibbons et al., 2002), absolute contraindications for exercise testing are an acute MI within the past 2 days, arrhythmias causing symptoms or hemodynamic compromise, symptomatic and severe aortic stenosis, uncontrolled symptomatic heart failure, acute pulmonary embolus or pulmonary infarction, acute myocarditis or pericarditis, and acute aortic dissection. Relative contraindications are left main coronary stenosis, moderate stenotic valve disease, electrolyte abnormalities, severe systolic hypertension (greater than 200 mm Hg), severe diastolic blood pressure (greater than 110 mm Hg), tachyarrhythmias or bradyarrhythmias, hypertrophic cardiomyopathy and other forms of outflow tract obstruction, mental or physical impairment leading to an inability to exercise adequately, and high-degree atrioventricular block.

Absolute indications for terminating an exercise test include a persistent drop in systolic blood pressure from baseline of more than 10 mm Hg despite an increase in workload (when accompanied by other evidence of ischemia); moderate to severe angina; central nervous system symptoms (e.g., ataxia, dizziness, or near syncope); signs of poor perfusion (e.g., cyanosis or pallor); technical difficulties monitoring the ECG or the systolic blood pressure; sustained ventricular tachycardia; ST elevation greater than or equal to 1 mm in leads without Q waves (other than V_1 or aVR); or the subject's request to stop. Relative indications for stopping include a drop in systolic blood pressure from baseline of more than 10 mm Hg despite an increase in workload (in the absence of other evidence of ischemia); ST or QRS changes such as excessive ST displacement (more than 2 mm of horizontal or down sloping) or marked axis deviation; arrhythmias other than sustained ventricular tachycardia; symptoms such as fatigue, shortness of breath, wheezing, leg cramps, or claudication; bundle-branch block or intraventricular conduction delay that cannot be distinguished from ventricular tachycardia; increasing chest pain; or hypertensive response (systolic blood pressure greater than 250 mm Hg or diastolic blood pressure greater than 115 mm Hg) (Fletcher et al., 2001; Gibbons et al., 2002).

Consideration of the Impact of Comorbidities

An extensive body of literature documents the presence and negative effects of comorbidities such as diabetes, obesity, chronic obstructive pulmonary disease, chronic kidney disease, malignancies, and major depression on the clinical outcomes and functional status of individuals with cardiovascular disease. The committee carefully considered whether to include factors such as the presence of severe chronic depression in the cardiovascular listings, but decided against it because of the variable effects of comorbidities on individuals. However, the committee assumes that SSA, in applying the cardiovascular listings, will implement its existing policies regarding comorbidities as fully as possible. These policies permit a claimant to equal a listing on a case-by-case basis (see further discussion of this issue in Chapter 15).

SUMMARY

This chapter has outlined the committee's approach to revising the cardiovascular listings. In summary, the committee kept in mind the administrative purpose of the Listings, which is to create a shortcut for the approval of claimants whose impairments are so severe that they would most likely be allowed after going through the more in-depth, but time-consuming, process of determining their residual vocational capacity.

The committee found that, for some conditions, an anatomical measure of severity is sufficient to meet the listing; however, for most conditions, impairment severity is a relatively insensitive measure of a person's capacity to function in the workplace or perform other usual life activities. Therefore, in revising most of the cardiovascular listings, the committee adopted the approach of recommending that claimants demonstrate both (1) severe impairment and (2) marked functional limitations. This approach was taken to increase the sensitivity of the Listings, and thus the share of deserving claimants allowed quickly, without increasing the false-positive rate appreciably.

We do not agree that this approach brings subjective functional considerations into purely objective medical decisions. Assessment of degree of anatomical impairment is certainly a medical function, performed as part of a regular medical evaluation of patients to determine treatment needs, but assessment of the person's functional capacity is also a medical function and can be performed in the medical setting and documented in the medical record.

The most objective way to determine functional capacity of cardiovascular patients is exercise testing, which can be performed by most cardiovascular patients. SSA's current criteria for deciding whether to pay for an exercise test are too restrictive given what is currently known about the safety of exercise testing, and the committee urges SSA to revise those criteria accordingly.

Evidence also shows that comorbidities prevalent among individuals with cardiovascular disease, such as depression and diabetes, not only worsen the cardiovascular disease, but also reduce functional capacity beyond the effects of the cardiovascular disease. The committee does not recommend revising SSA's current policies and procedures for considering comorbidities in the disability determination process, but urges SSA to provide adjudicators with up-to-date information about the impact of comorbidities and to support research on the effects of common cardiovascular comorbidities such as diabetes and major depression on functional capacity and disability (see Recommendation 16-1 in Chapter 16).

REFERENCES

ACSM (American College of Sports Medicine). 2006. *ACSM's guidelines for exercise testing and prescription*, 7th ed. Philadelphia, PA: Lippincott Williams & Wilkins.

Ainsworth, B. E., W. L. Haskell, M. C. Whitt, M. L. Irwin, A. M. Swartz, S. J. Strath, W. L. O'Brien, D. R. Bassett Jr., K. H. Schmitz, P. O. Emplaincourt, D. R. Jacobs Jr., and A. S. Leon. 2000. Compendium of physical activities: An update of activity codes and MET intensities. *Medicine and Science in Sports and Exercise* 32(Suppl):S498–S516.

Arena, R., J. Myers, M. A. Williams, M. Gulati, P. Kligfield, G. J. Balady, E. Collins, and G. Fletcher. 2007. Assessment of functional capacity in clinical and research settings: A scientific statement from the American Heart Association Committee on Exercise, Rehabilitation, and Prevention of the Council on Clinical Cardiology and the Council on Cardiovascular Nursing. *Circulation* 116:329–343.

Arena, R., J. Myers, and M. Guazzi. 2008. The clinical and research applications of aerobic capacity and ventilatory efficiency in heart failure: An evidence-based review. *Heart Failure Review* 13(2):245–269.

Arena, R., C. J. Lavie, R. V. Milani, J. Myers, and M. Guazzi. 2010. Cardiopulmonary exercise testing in patients with pulmonary hypertension: An evidence-based review. *Journal of Heart and Lung Transplantation* 29(2):159–173.

Balady, G. J., R. Arena, K. Sietsema, J. Myers, L. Coke, G. F. Fletcher, D. Forman, B. Franklin, M. Guazzi, M. Gulati, S. J. Keteyian, C. J. Lavie, R. Macko, D. Mancini, and R. V. Milani. 2010. Clinician's guide to cardiopulmonary exercise testing in adults. A scientific statement from the American Heart Association. *Circulation* 122:191–225.

Dunlop, D. D., S. L. Hughes, and L. M. Mannheim. 1999. Disability in activities of daily living: Patterns of change and a hierarchy of disability. *American Journal of Public Health* 87(3):378–383.

Fletcher, G. F., G. J. Balady, E. A. Amsterdam, B. Chaitman, R. Eckel, J. Fleg, V. F. Froelicher, A. S. Leon, I. L. Piña, R. Rodney, D. A. Simons-Morton, M. A. Williams, and T. Bazzarre. 2001. Exercise standards for testing and training: A statement for healthcare professionals from the American Heart Association. *Circulation* 104(14):1694–1740.

Gaugler, J. E., S. Duval, K. A. Anderson, and R. L. Kane. 2007. Predicting nursing home admission in the U.S.: A meta-analysis. *BMC Geriatrics* 7:13.

Gibbons, R. J., G. J. Balady, J. T. Bricker, B. R. Chaitman, G. F. Fletcher, V. F. Froelicher, D. B. Mark, B. D. McCallister, A. N. Mooss, M. G. O'Reilly, W. L. Winters Jr., R. J. Gibbons, E. M. Antman, J. S. Alpert, D. P. Faxon, V. Fuster, G. Gregoratos, L. F. Hiratzka, A. K. Jacobs, R. O. Russell, and S. C. Smith Jr. 2002. ACC/AHA 2002 guideline update for exercise testing: A report of the American College of Cardiology/American Heart Association Task Force on Practice Guidelines (Committee on Exercise Testing). *Journal of the American College of Cardiology* 40:1531–1540.

Katz, S., and C. Akpom. 1976. A measure of primary sociobiological function. *International Journal of Health Services* 6(3):493–508.

Katz, S., A. B. Ford, R. W. Moskowitz, B. A. Jackson, and M. W. Jaffee. 1963. Studies of illness in the aged: The index of ADL, a standardized measure of biological and psychosocial function. *Journal of the American Medical Association* 185:914–919.

Lawton, M. P., and E. Brody. 1969. Assessment of older people: Self-maintaining and instrumental activities of daily living. *Gerontologist* 9(3):179–186.

Mahoney, F. I., O. H. Wood, and D. W. Barthel. 1958. Rehabilitation of chronically ill patients: The influence of complications on the final goal. *Southern Medical Journal* 51(5):605–609.

Myers, J., R. Arena, B. Franklin, I. Pina, W. E. Kraus, K. McInnis, G. J. Balady; American Heart Association Committee on Exercise, Cardiac Rehabilitation, and Prevention of the Council on Clinical Cardiology, the Council on Nutrition, Physical Activity, and Metabolism, and the Council on Cardiovascular Nursing. 2009. Recommendations for clinical exercise laboratories: A scientific statement from the American Heart Association. *Circulation* 119(24):3144–3161.

NRC (National Research Council). 2009. *Improving the measurement of late-life disability in population surveys: Beyond ADLs and IADLs*. Washington, DC: The National Academies Press.

Paridon, S. M., B. S. Alpert, S. R. Boas, M. E. Cabrera, L. L. Caldarera, S. R. Daniels, T. R. Kimball, T. K. Knilans, P. A. Nixon, J. Rhodes, and A. T. Yetman. 2006. Clinical stress testing in the pediatric age group: A statement from the American Heart Association Council on Cardiovascular Disease in the Young, Committee on Atherosclerosis, Hypertension, and Obesity in Youth. *Circulation* 113(15):1905–1920.

SSA (Social Security Administration). 2005. Presentation on Listings issues by Barry Eigen, Executive Program Policy Officer, Office of Disability Programs, SSA, to Institute of Medicine Committee on Improving the Disability Decision Process, Washington, DC, August 4, 2005.

SSA. 2009. Presentation on the cardiovascular listings by Steven G. Steinberg, M.D., Cardiology Consultant, Office of Medical and Vocational Expertise, SSA, to Institute of Medicine Committee on Social Security Disability Criteria, Washington, DC, December 14, 2009.

5

Heart Failure, Cardiomyopathy, and Right Heart Failure

The approach to heart failure adopts the strategy of the current listings to require both a cardiac abnormality diagnostic of the condition and a functional limitation demonstrated by the patient, which recognizes the wide variability of the relationship between anatomic impairment and disability. The cardiac abnormality for heart failure is distinguished as either systolic failure with low ejection fraction or diastolic dysfunction with preserved ejection fraction. The recommendations are cognizant of the safety and utility of exercise testing, particularly if the exercise testing is combined with the determination of peak oxygen consumption. The recommendations would also allow the functional limitation requirement to be met by repeated hospitalizations. Although most cardiomyopathies will be evaluated as heart failure, unique considerations for hypertrophic cardiomyopathy led to the proposal of a separate indication. Although right heart failure is not a unique disease, it can occasionally dominate the clinical picture of left heart failure and other serious cardiac conditions. Therefore, right heart failure has been proposed as another route to meeting a listing.

DESCRIPTION

Heart failure is the inability of the heart to provide sufficient blood flow to meet the needs of the body for oxygenated blood during regular activity or to do so only with elevated pressures within the heart (Arena et al., 2007; Colucci and Braunwald, 1995). Heart failure is not one disease, but a chronic and progressive condition that can be the final common pathway from a number of structural or functional cardiac disorders that impair the ability of the heart to fill or empty (Arena et al., 2007). Heart failure can occur when the heart muscle is weak (systolic failure) or when it is stiff and unable to relax normally (diastolic failure). Cardiomyopathy, which means "disease of the heart muscle," is one of many causes of heart failure.

The syndrome of heart failure is often characterized by shortness of breath or fatigue, even during mild exertion. A common feature of heart failure decompensation is retention of excess fluid, which contributes to raise fluid pressures within the heart, lungs, and the rest of the body, which is termed *congestion*. When congestion occurs on the left side of the heart (left heart failure), it can lead to shortness of breath occurring during modest activity or at rest, particularly while lying down. Elevation of pressures can also occur in the veins draining into the right side of the heart, which can result in peripheral edema and abdominal swelling (ascites). These findings are often termed *right heart failure*. The type of heart muscle weakness is often described by the pumping strength of the heart, measured by the left ventricular ejection fraction (EF). This is the proportion of blood ejected from the ventricle with each beat, expressed either as a fraction (normally 0.55 to 0.70) or as a percentage of the total volume in the left ventricle (normally 55 to 70 percent).

The primary manifestations of heart failure are fatigue, dyspnea, and peripheral fluid retention, which alone or in combination may limit a patient's ability to perform activities (Gibbons et al., 2002) and potentially lead to impairment or disability. All three symptoms do not have to manifest for a patient to have heart failure. Although the full-blown chronic syndrome has sometimes been termed "congestive heart failure," clinical evidence of congestion (as described above) may or may not be present at the time of evaluation (Allen et al., 2008). For example, a patient may experience exercise intolerance from fatigue but have little fluid retention, or may be limited by peripheral swelling without reporting symptoms of fatigue or breathlessness.

EPIDEMIOLOGY

Heart failure is an ongoing public health challenge in the United States. In the adult population over age 20, the prevalence of heart failure is 2.6 percent. It is generally higher in men than in women but highest in black women. The lifetime risk of developing heart failure is one in five at age 40 for both men and women. The prevalence in patients between ages 20 and 39 is less than 0.5 percent of the population. In patients over age 45, the incidence of new cases is estimated at 670,000 annually. From ages 40 to 59, the prevalence is 1.9 per 100 men and 1.4 per 100 women (Lloyd-Jones et al., 2010). Overall, approximately 5.8 million people have heart failure in the United States, leading to more than 1 million hospitalizations each year and 12 to 15 million patient visits to treating physicians annually.

Heart failure with preserved ejection fraction (sometimes termed HFpEF, or diastolic heart failure) accounts for about half of all U.S. heart failure hospitalizations (Redfield et al., 2003). The majority of these patients are over age 70, and it is particularly common when patients have chronic hypertension, diabetes, and obesity. For the patients under age 65, diastolic heart failure is uncommon, except in association with longstanding severe hypertension, which is particularly prevalent in African-American men. Rare causes of this type of heart failure are amyloidosis and restrictive cardiomyopathy (Redfield et al., 2003). Although hypertrophic cardiomyopathy is present in about 1 in 500 persons, most people with this diagnosis remain highly functional and do not come under consideration for disability (Ho and Seidman, 2006).

Heart failure contributed to 282,754 U.S. deaths in 2006 (Lloyd-Jones et al., 2010). Median life expectancy for a person with heart failure has been described as less than 5 years (Allen et al., 2008), but many of these statistics are derived from the population older than those considered for disability. Some patients under age 65 who are in good general health other than cardiac disease may be considered for cardiac transplantation. Otherwise, mortality within 1 year can be expected for about half of patients in whom severe symptoms due to heart failure limit their daily life despite current medical therapies (Allen et al., 2008).

TYPES OF HEART FAILURE

Systolic Heart Failure

When the syndrome of heart failure occurs with an EF less than 40 percent, the dysfunction is often called "systolic heart failure," referring to weakened pumping strength. Heart failure with low EF is generally associated with enlargement of the heart (measured by left ventricular diameter on echocardiography, normally less than 5.4 cm in diameter). This is the most common type of heart failure in patients younger than age 65. The most common causes are cardiomyopathy, which means weakness of the heart muscle not resulting from another cardiac diagnosis, and coronary artery disease, which causes irreversible damage to the heart muscle and has usually been preceded by a myocardial infarction (heart attack), although these often occur silently.

Most cases of heart failure not otherwise specified are systolic heart failure. The major symptoms in heart failure, as described above, are the same whether the EF is low (less than 40 percent) or preserved (greater than

40 percent). These relate to fluid retention and congestion, leading to shortness of breath and swelling. However, the reduced pumping strength of the heart in systolic heart failure can also lead to decreased blood flow during periods of increased demand during activity, causing early fatigue and prolonged exhaustion after heavy activity, even without obvious breathlessness. When the disease becomes very advanced, the amount of blood flow to the body (cardiac output) may actually be lower than normal at rest, which is sometimes demonstrated during cardiac catheterization if specific measurements of cardiac output are made. When the reduction is so extreme that it is life threatening, it is called cardiogenic shock.

Diastolic Heart Failure

Heart failure can also occur with "preserved" EF, in which the heart muscle is stiff rather than weak, leading to impaired filling of the chambers of the heart. The strength of the heart muscle and amount of blood flow to the body are usually well maintained and EF is greater than 40 percent, although not always in the normal range of 55 to 70 percent. The major structural abnormality is increased stiffness of the heart muscle, usually with some increase in wall thickness. This stiffness leads to impaired filling of the heart, or diastolic dysfunction. Numerous measurements can be made on echocardiography to determine how well the heart can relax and fill (diastolic function); these vary by laboratory, but are usually summarized in echocardiographic reports as diastolic dysfunction that is "mild," "moderate," or "severe."

Most symptoms of diastolic heart failure relate to chronic shortness of breath during exertion, the same as for systolic heart failure. Symptoms of peripheral swelling may occur earlier in the course of diastolic heart failure than in systolic heart failure. However, the presentation and diagnosis are often dominated by repeated hospitalizations for episodes of sudden decompensation. These episodes are sometimes termed acute or "flash" pulmonary edema (fluid in the lungs with rapid development of severe shortness of breath).

Hypertrophic Cardiomyopathy

Hypertrophic cardiomyopathy is a condition in which the heart muscle is unusually thick, with left ventricular EF that can be above normal. This condition is usually diagnosed by echocardiography, which reveals both abnormal thickness of the heart muscle and abnormal diastolic function. Hypertrophic cardiomyopathy is sometimes considered a type of diastolic heart failure, but it is often considered a separate diagnosis due to unique aspects of therapy and prognosis. The symptoms of hypertrophic cardiomyopathy are most commonly exertional limitation due to shortness of breath or chest pain. Some patients may develop syncope or near syncope, particularly during or following exertion (Ho and Seidman, 2006).

Most cases are associated with a specific genetic abnormality of the heart muscle cell. Patients often have a family history of this disease, but some cases result from sporadic mutations, with no previously affected family members (Ho and Seidman, 2006).

Right Heart Failure

Right heart failure most commonly accompanies left heart failure, either because it is also affected by the primary cause of heart failure, or because the chronic effects of left heart failure have led to gradual deterioration of the right ventricular function. However, some patients may have a clinical picture dominated by right heart failure. Congenital heart disease with or without prior surgery may be associated with abnormal function of the right side of the heart. This may be due in some cases to congenital underdevelopment of the right side of the heart, but more commonly develops later from chronic excess load on the right ventricle. Other conditions that can lead to the syndrome of right heart failure include tricuspid valve disease, pulmonary hypertension, pericardial disease, and atypical right heart response to left ventricular dysfunction, with less severe abnormality of left ventricular EF or diastolic dysfunction than required to meet criteria for systolic or diastolic heart failure as described above.

DIAGNOSIS OF HEART FAILURE

Careful clinical evaluation is crucial to correctly diagnose and treat patients with symptoms that may be due to heart failure. The term *heart failure* can lead to confusion, because the heart is usually not truly "failing" to function, in which case death would result. Instead, the heart may provide an adequate blood flow for organs to function at rest but has limited capacity to increase output to meet the needs of the body during sustained activity and exertion. The most common criteria for diagnosing "systolic heart failure" include evidence that the pumping strength of the left ventricle is reduced (measured by the EF, normally 55 to 70 percent). In addition, the size of the heart is often enlarged. Both measurements are usually provided by echocardiography, but they can also be measured through other techniques that image the heart, such as nuclear imaging tests or magnetic resonance imaging (MRI).

Most patients with systolic heart failure do not detect any limitation until the EF is less than 40 percent. Some patients can live virtually normal lives with EFs as low as 20 percent, but most patients with disease this advanced have major activity limitations (Cohn et al., 1993; Levy et al., 2006; Stevenson et al., 1995). When the pressures in the heart are severely elevated at rest or the blood flow is severely reduced, heart failure is occasionally demonstrated by direct measurement of these pressures and flows during cardiac catheterization.

Diastolic heart failure remains challenging to diagnose from objective tests. Many criteria from echocardiographic assessment relate to how the heart relaxes; current debate remains about which are the most sensitive and specific. Different echocardiographic laboratories will concentrate on different measurements, yet most will describe diastolic dysfunction as mild, moderate, or severe.

Hypertrophic cardiomyopathy is also diagnosed by echocardiography. The unusual thickness of the ventricular muscle is a feature. In addition, about one in three patients may demonstrate some obstruction to flow through the left ventricle ("obstructive cardiomyopathy").

Currently, the most common and appropriate diagnosis and evaluation of a patient with heart failure or cardiomyopathy includes a comprehensive echocardiogram with Doppler flow studies, because it determines not only severity of disease as measured by ventricular EF, but also how the heart fills and relaxes, which chambers are involved, and whether abnormalities of heart muscle texture, heart valves, or pericardium are present. The comprehensive nature of this test is important because patients with heart failure often present with multiple cardiac impairments (Hunt et al., 2005). Other useful tests to determine the severity of impairment or cardiac abnormality include radionuclide ventriculography or MRI (Hunt et al., 2005). In addition, a blood test showing markedly elevated levels of natriuretic peptides (e.g., BNP, NT-proBNP) supports the diagnosis of heart failure, and these levels are often elevated in patients with symptomatic heart failure, whether it is with systolic heart failure (heart failure with low EF) or diastolic heart failure (heart failure with preserved EF). Normal values of these peptides vary in relation to age, gender, race, and body weight.

TREATMENT

The recommended treatment guidelines for heart failure are designated according to stages of symptoms and apply primarily to patients with systolic heart failure (Hunt et al., 2005). Medical therapy for patients with symptoms of systolic heart failure includes angiotensin-converting enzyme inhibitors or angiotensin II receptor antagonists, beta adrenergic blocking agents, and diuretics as needed to control fluid retention, which may entail multiple changes and use of more than one diuretic. Digoxin, hydralazine, and nitrate combinations or nitrates alone, and aldosterone may also be indicated in patients with symptoms that persist. Anticoagulation is indicated for some patients who are at particular risk for thromboembolic events. Implantable defibrillators may be indicated to decrease the risk of sudden death for some patients. Cardiac resynchronization therapy is a special form of pacing that may improve function in some patients with dysynchrony in the heart contraction pattern. Recurrent tachyarrhythmias may be treated with antiarrhythmic agents.

The recommended regimens for systolic heart failure may improve heart function as measured by increase in the EF and/or decrease in left ventricular enlargement. In general, the maximal impact of these therapies to improve objective cardiac function and exercise capacity may not be realized for 6 months or longer. Evaluation ideally would be deferred until after an adequate time for response to the appropriate medical regimen.

For diastolic heart failure, there are no specific treatment recommendations that are based on evidence from randomized trials. However, therapy should include vigorous efforts to control hypertension, usually with multiple drugs. Fluid retention should be treated aggressively with diuretics, which should be adjusted regularly to maintain fluid balance (Zile and Nappi, 2000).

For hypertrophic cardiomyopathy, therapy is guided primarily by control of the symptoms of exertional dyspnea and chest pain. Beta-blockers and calcium channel blockers are the mainstay of therapy, with occasional use of disopyramide in patients whose symptoms are not controlled with other agents. In patients who have specific risk factors for sudden death with hypertrophic cardiomyopathy, use of implantable defibrillators may be considered (Ho and Seidman, 2006).

The therapy of right heart failure usually includes high doses of diuretics to reduce signs of fluid retention. Therapy with diuretics does not treat the underlying cause of the heart failure, but is a key part of the medical regimen to minimize the impairment and discomfort caused by swelling of the legs or abdomen. The treatment regimen may also include therapies directed when feasible to treat the underlying cause of the right heart failure.

DISABILITY

Assessing Functional Capacity for Disability

Functional capacity is often described using the New York Heart Association Functional Classification System as a measure of symptom severity. Class I indicates no symptoms during vigorous activity. Class II includes symptoms with moderate activity that is greater than required for daily life (e.g., vigorous recreation). Class III symptoms are those occurring with less than the usual daily level of activity. Class IV symptoms occur at rest or with minimal exertion, such as dressing or walking from room to room. These four classes reflect subjective assessment by health care providers. The major information used for this classification is the description of symptoms by the care provider or patient. These are dynamic classifications, and patients can cross back and forth frequently between different levels of symptoms. When used to describe the severity of disease, the classifications are usually meant to describe the symptom level most of the time, rather than at the best or worst times.

Patients can have a diagnosis of heart failure without being disabled from working. As discussed above, the term *heart failure* is an unfortunate one because many patients included in this definition have mild or moderate symptoms that do not prevent gainful employment. It is widely recognized that symptoms and functional capacity in heart failure are not easily predicted or explained by the degree of impairment in cardiac function, such as reduction of left ventricular EF or increase in left ventricular size. Although these measurements are important for the diagnosis of cardiac impairment leading to heart failure, they rarely constitute sufficient basis to show disability. In extreme cases, very severe reduction of left ventricular EF, such as 20 percent or less, can be considered a surrogate for limited function and survival, and thus could warrant decision of disability without functional assessment (Cohn et al., 1993; Levy et al., 2006; Stevenson et al., 1995).

The most direct assessment of ability to work is the ability to perform physical exertion. A patient's ability to perform activities of daily living, work, and vigorous exertion requires the integration of cardiovascular, pulmonary, and circulatory systems (Arena et al., 2007; Fleg et al., 2000; Wilson et al., 1995). Exercise testing has been consistently demonstrated and widely accepted to be practical and safe for most patients with chronic heart failure (Balady et al., 2010). Either treadmill testing or bicycle exercise testing can be performed. The advantage of treadmill testing is that walking is a more familiar activity to many than bicycling; the advantage of bicycle testing is that workload can be controlled more strictly, and patients who have gait instability may feel more comfortable sitting on the bicycle. Treadmill testing is more common, and the protocol and listing criteria will be discussed as for a treadmill test. Bicycle testing may lead to slightly lower estimation of overall exercise capacity, but the difference is not believed to be sufficient to justify having different listing criteria for bicycle and treadmill exercise performance.

The evaluation of exercise capacity recognizes that "the subjective quality of symptoms can detract from objective, reproducible, and sensitive measurements. Personality, mood, culture, and idiosyncratic vacillations as well as cognition, literacy, and socioeconomics are among the factors that impact on these measures" (Balady et al., 2010:200). Measurements based on peak heart rate as a proportion of predicted maximal heart rate are now "confounded by beta-blockers and other heart-rate limiting medications," which include antiarrhythmic agents (Balady et al., 2010:200). Thus, "determination of peak VO_2 during a symptom-limited treadmill or bicycle cardiopulmonary exercise testing (CPX) is the most objective method to assess exercise capacity in heart failure patients. . . . It is a useful test to determine the severity of the disease and to help to determine whether heart failure is the cause of exercise limitation" (Balady et al., 2010:201).

The level of peak VO_2 less than 15 ml/kg is proposed as the listing criterion for exercise impairment, which is consistent with the level for pulmonary disability, also 15 ml/kg/min. Although there is some consideration of using a percentage of predicted peak oxygen consumption for age and gender, the level of exercise limitation at which no meaningful work can be performed is presumably an absolute rather than a relative number and should be independent of age and gender. It is also consistent with the general level of metabolic equivalents of task (METs), the factor by which resting energy demands are increased to do levels of work as required by most work with modest movement. Disability would be considered adequately documented if patients have objective evidence of limitation that prevent them from reaching oxygen consumption of 15 ml/kg/min by the end of exercise. An objective documentation of circulatory limitation is the respiratory exchange ratio (RER) of at least 1.1 or more, which indicates that anaerobic metabolism has been achieved, and that oxygen delivery has become inadequate to meet metabolic demands during exercise. An RER of 1.1 is the criterion for adequate exercise effort as recommended by the American Heart Association (AHA) 2010 guidelines on CPX in adults (Balady et al., 2010).

For patients performing symptom-limited exercise testing without gas exchange to measure peak VO_2, the level is defined by the estimated MET level of the exercise. The estimated MET level selected for patients without peak VO_2 measurement has generally been 5 or less. The specific experience with heart failure patients is that the actual peak oxygen consumption is usually significantly lower than that estimated from the MET level of the exercise stage. Thus a measured peak VO_2 of 15 ml/kg/min and the estimated MET level of 5 are not inconsistent.

Strengths and Limitations of Current Listing Criteria for Heart Failure

The Social Security Administration (SSA) currently reviews applicants' disability claims for heart failure based on specific diagnostic and clinical criteria. The current listing (see Box 5-1) incorporates measures of functioning into the evaluation, where the claimant is limited in activities of daily living and unable to perform an exercise test at the specified level. These criteria are required in combination.

BOX 5-1
Current Listing for Chronic Heart Failure

4.02 *Chronic heart failure* while on a regimen of prescribed treatment, with symptoms and signs described in 4.00D2. The required level of severity for this impairment is met when the requirements in *both A and B* are satisfied.

A. Medically documented presence of one of the following:

1. Systolic failure (see 4.00D1a(i)), with left ventricular end diastolic dimensions greater than 6.0 cm or ejection fraction of 30 percent or less during a period of stability (not during an episode of acute heart failure); or
2. Diastolic failure (see 4.00D1a(ii)), with left ventricular posterior wall plus septal thickness totaling 2.5 cm or greater on imaging, with an enlarged left atrium greater than or equal to 4.5 cm, with normal or elevated ejection fraction during a period of stability (not during an episode of acute heart failure);

AND

B. Resulting in one of the following:

1. Persistent symptoms of heart failure which very seriously limit the ability to independently initiate, sustain, or complete activities of daily living in an individual for whom an MC, preferably one experienced in the care of patients with cardiovascular disease, has concluded that the performance of an exercise test would present a significant risk to the individual; or
2. Three or more separate episodes of acute congestive heart failure within a consecutive 12-month period (see 4.00A3e), with evidence of fluid retention (see 4.00D2b(ii)) from clinical and imaging assessments at the time of the episodes, requiring acute extended physician intervention such as hospitalization or emergency room treatment for 12 hours or more, separated by periods of stabilization (see 4.00D4c); or
3. Inability to perform on an exercise tolerance test at a workload equivalent to 5 METs or less due to:

    a. Dyspnea, fatigue, palpitations, or chest discomfort; or
    b. Three or more consecutive premature ventricular contractions (ventricular tachycardia), or increasing frequency of ventricular ectopy with at least 6 premature ventricular contractions per minute; or
    c. Decrease of 10 mm Hg or more in systolic pressure below the baseline systolic blood pressure or the preceding systolic pressure measured during exercise (see 4.00D4d) due to left ventricular dysfunction, despite an increase in workload; or
    d. Signs attributable to inadequate cerebral perfusion, such as ataxic gait or mental confusion.

SOURCE: SSA, 2008.

The current listing criteria as described in Box 5-1 include and require evidence of each of two aspects of disease: (1) objective measurement of cardiac abnormality and (2) evidence of limited functional capacity. This construct has been useful and remains the basis of recommendations for a revised listing. However, review of the specific criteria for (1) and (2) suggested several areas for which newer definitions may be more applicable to contemporary populations and to current testing and therapies.

The current criteria of EF and left ventricular dimension for evaluation of systolic dysfunction remain highly relevant to assessment. However, diastolic dysfunction is a much more heterogeneous condition in terms of population, assessment, and clinical limitation. The requirement for increased wall thickness is neither sensitive nor specific for diastolic dysfunction. Newer measurements from echocardiography describe the ability of the heart to relax and fill.

Functional assessment in the current listing is severely limited by the previous position that exercise testing posed significant risk to patients with heart failure. The assessment of clinical limitation without exercise testing thus has been highly subjective. Newer experience, as reviewed in the American College of Cardiology (ACC)/AHA guidelines on cardiopulmonary exercise testing, suggests that exercise testing is safe in most patients with chronic heart failure in the absence of acute or recent clinical instability (Balady et al., 2010).

When available, exercise testing is the most helpful assessment. For patients in whom exercise tests can be performed, the current criterion of less than 5 METs is reasonable and can be estimated from the level of exercise performed. However, many reasons for *not* reaching that level of exercise are highly subjective, relying on patient descriptions of shortness of breath and fatigue. The complaint of palpitations can be replaced by the objective demonstration of arrhythmias, as all standard exercise tests are performed with electrocardiographic monitoring. However, frequent and consecutive premature ventricular contractions (PVCs), even brief runs of up to 10 beats of nonsustained ventricular tachycardia, are common in patients with heart failure and reduced EF; they are not generally considered criteria for exercise limitation except as discussed separately in the arrhythmia disability listing (see Chapter 13). The complaint of chest pain is subjective and should be substantiated by electrocardiographic evidence of myocardial ischemia. (The only population in which chest pain without demonstrable ischemia is generally acceptable as an indication of exercise limitation is hypertrophic cardiomyopathy, which as suggested above might be more conveniently considered separately.) The criterion of a fall in blood pressure is objective and a reasonable documentation of exercise limitation, but unusual in patients with heart failure. The previous listing criteria included exercise limited by signs of inadequate cerebral perfusion such as ataxic gait and mental confusion; these signs would raise concerns about other diagnoses, as they do not commonly occur during exercise testing, even in severely impaired patients with heart failure.

The current functional criterion of repeated hospitalizations is useful to characterize those patients whose heart failure is of a fluctuating and episodic nature. Although recurrent admissions can result from irregular compliance with medications and outpatient follow-up, they can occur even in patients with optimal management. Patients with severe disease and multiple hospitalizations are also likely to have objective impairment of exercise performance, but either would seem reasonable criteria for disability. Information regarding the frequency with which individual functional limitations are used as criteria is not currently accessible.

CONCLUSIONS AND RECOMMENDATIONS

After review of the current medical literature and related treatment and practice guidelines from ACC and AHA, the committee determined the chronic heart failure listing should be revised to include separate evaluation criteria for the following related conditions: chronic heart failure (both systolic and diastolic heart failure), hypertrophic cardiomyopathy, and right heart failure. The general diagnosis of cardiomyopathy (other than hypertrophic) would not have its own listing criteria, but would be evaluated according to one of these other three conditions.

The conceptual framework of the current listing criteria includes the determination of both (A) a measured anatomic or hemodynamic abnormality of cardiac function and (B) a demonstrated impairment of patient function, either chronically or intermittently. The requirement for both is consistent with the well-documented variability in the relationship between cardiac impairment and physical functioning in heart failure and cardiomyopathy.

RECOMMENDATION 5-1. Retain the current framework of listing 4.02 chronic heart failure, requiring both (A) an objective cardiac abnormality, and (B) a functional limitation. This framework would apply to each of the following: systolic heart failure, diastolic heart failure, hypertrophic cardiomyopathy, and right heart failure.

Systolic Heart Failure (Figure 5-1)

The criteria for systolic heart failure should include:

A. An objective cardiac abnormality demonstrated by a left ventricular ejection fraction of 30 percent or less (or an ejection

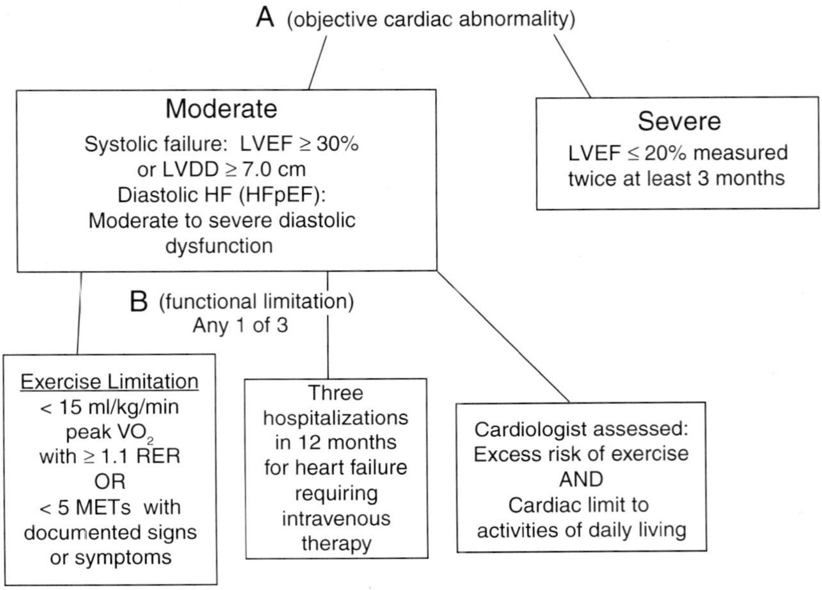

FIGURE 5-1 Recommended listing-level criteria for systolic and diastolic heart failure.
NOTES: HF = heart failure; LVDD = left ventricular diastolic dysfunction; LVEF = left ventricular ejection fraction; METs = metabolic equivalents of task; RER = respiratory exchange ratio.

fraction of a systemic ventricle in congenital heart disease without an anatomic, systemic left ventricle), or a left ventricular diameter of 7 cm or greater,

AND

B. A functional abnormality demonstrated by one of three criteria:

1. **Exercise testing (see Recommendation 5-2); or**
2. **Cardiologist-assessed excessive risk of exercise testing and cardiac limit to activities of daily living; or**
3. **Three hospitalization-equivalent events in the past 12 months.**

Diastolic Heart Failure (Figure 5-1)

The criteria for diastolic heart failure should include:

A. An objective cardiac abnormality demonstrated by moderate or severe diastolic dysfunction, usually indicated by echocardiography,

AND

B. A functional abnormality can be demonstrated by one of three criteria:

1. **Exercise testing (see Recommendation 5-2); or**
2. **Cardiologist-assessed excessive risk of exercise testing and cardiac limit to activities of daily living; or**
3. **Three hospitalization-equivalent events in the past 12 months.**

The criterion of three hospitalizations is anticipated to be met more frequently for diastolic heart failure than it is for the more common systolic heart failure, for which the exercise limitation may be more commonly met.

Hypertrophic Cardiomyopathy (Figure 5-2)

The criteria for hypertrophic cardiomyopathy should include:

A. An objective cardiac abnormality demonstrated by a left ventricular or septal wall thickness greater than 15 mm in the absence of another known cause for left ventricular hypertrophy (e.g., hypertension, aortic valve disease),

AND

B. A functional abnormality demonstrated by one of three criteria:

1. **Exercise testing (see Recommendation 5-2); or**
2. **Cardiologist-assessed excessive risk of exercise testing and cardiac limit to activities of daily living; or**
3. **Three hospitalization-equivalent events in the past 12 months.**

Due to the characteristics of their cardiac function or symptoms, some patients with hypertrophic cardiomyopathy may be considered too high

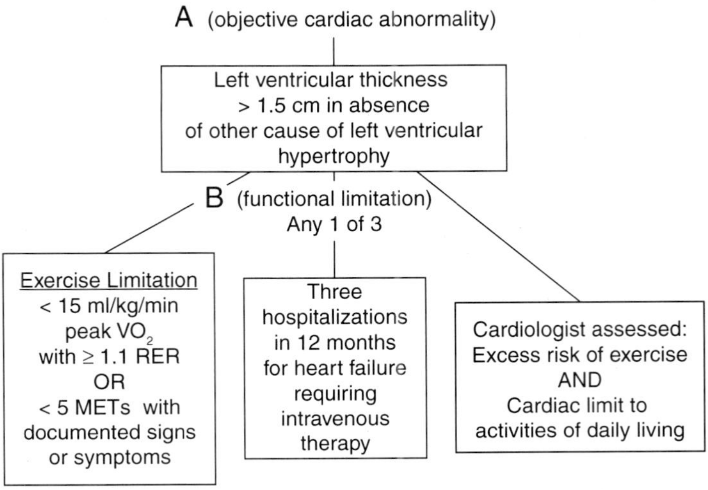

FIGURE 5-2 Recommended listing-level criteria for hyptertrophic cardiomyopathy. NOTE: METs = metabolic equivalents of task; RER = respiratory exchange ratio.

risk for exercise testing, particularly those with very thick ventricular thicknesses or demonstration of a large pressure gradient ("obstruction") inside the left ventricle. If these patients are identified by their physicians as having severe symptoms and being at excessive risk for exercise testing, they will meet the functional limitation criteria.

- Hypertrophic cardiomyopathy excluded from exercise testing with cardiologist documentation of the following:
    - o Major risk associated with exercise testing (see Recommendation 5-2), and
    - o Symptoms from hypertrophic cardiomyopathy resulting in limitation of ability to independently perform activities of daily living.

Right Heart Failure (Figure 5-3)

The criteria for right heart failure should require both an objective cardiac diagnosis implicated as a cause of right heart failure and clinical evidence of functional limitation manifest as severe systemic venous congestion:

A. An objective cardiac abnormality demonstrated by one of the following:

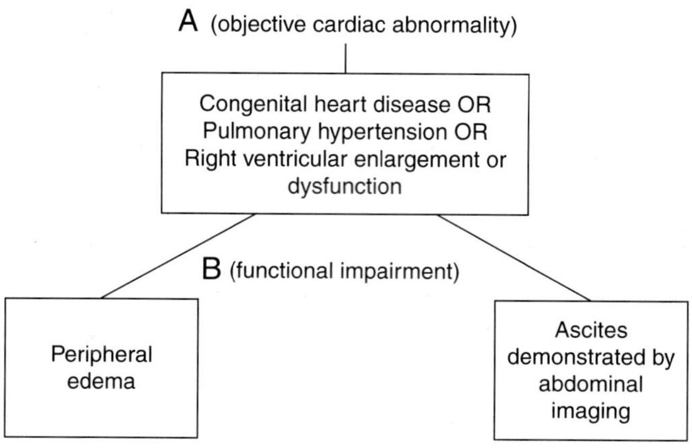

FIGURE 5-3 Recommended listing-level criteria for right heart failure.

1. Congenital heart disease; or
2. Pulmonary hypertension; or
3. Right ventricular enlargement or dysfunction.

AND

B. Functional abnormalities meeting criteria for right heart failure:

1. Systemic venous congestion despite chronic diuretic therapy, assessed twice with at least 3 months in between, causing either

- **Peripheral edema to the knee or above; or**
- **Severe ascites documented by abdominal imaging study.**

Some patients may have primary peripheral edema that can become severe, particularly in the presence of obesity, without an underlying cause of heart failure. They are *not* to be included here. Intra-abdominal fluid accumulation (ascites) sufficient for listing would have to be documented by abdominal imaging, because it cannot reliably be distinguished from abdominal adiposity.

Exercise Testing

Based on its review of the 2010 ACC/AHA exercise guidelines, the committee concludes that the listing criteria to evaluate claimants for disability should include objective measures performed during exercise tests. These measures are considered safe and reasonable for most patients with heart failure. The listing criteria accordingly should reflect the updated guidelines for exercise testing.

> **RECOMMENDATION 5-2. Revise the exercise criteria to reflect the current acceptability of exercise testing as safe in heart failure and the objective measurements that can now be performed during exercise testing. Limitation is defined as a standard treadmill test (or bicycle test) performed at a workload equivalent to one of the following criteria:**
>
> - **Less than 15 ml/kg/min peak VO_2/(oxygen consumption) on cardiopulmonary exercise test; or**
> - **Less than 5 metabolic equivalents of task if using standard treadmill test without gas exchange.**

The applicant may satisfy the exercise test criteria for disability listing by failing to reach one of these limits due to documented evidence of cardiac limitation. This is easiest with the CPX test, which requires less subjective interpretation.

On cardiopulmonary exercise testing, if the RER is greater than or equal to 1.1, the presence of anaerobic metabolism and inadequate oxygen delivery to the exercising muscles can be considered present, which can indicate a cardiovascular limitation. The reason for including the cardiopulmonary exercise testing is that the simultaneous measurement of gas exchange enables determination of the degree of effort and cardiac limitation. This makes it easier and more objective to exclude intentional underperformance on standardized exercise testing.

If standard exercise testing without gas exchange is the test information provided, objective evidence of true cardiac limitation can be as follows:

- Signs may include fall in blood pressure, evidence of myocardial ischemia from ST-segment depression or elevation, or ventricular tachycardia. These will rarely be present. Otherwise, termination of a standard treadmill test would need to be validated by subjective evidence from the evaluator that exercise was limited by cardiac causes.
- Severe symptoms may include angina, dyspnea, and claudication.

Signs and symptoms should be documented as related to heart failure, and not an unrelated condition.

The occurrence of frequent or consecutive PVCs are common at rest and during exercise in patients with heart failure and should not be considered adequate reason to terminate the exercise test unless accompanied by other evidence of exercise limitation. Prolonged runs of ventricular tachycardia as the basis of termination of exercise testing would be evaluated under the arrhythmia disability criteria in most cases. The occurrence of one such episode, even if specific therapy were required for termination, should trigger specific therapy of the arrhythmia and subsequent repeat exercise testing if a person is seeking disability under the heart failure criteria.

Severe Reduction of Ejection Fraction

An EF of 20 percent or less represents a decrease to less than one-third of normal heart pumping function. This severe level of impairment is generally associated with marked functional limitation and limitation in survival. However, this impairment occasionally can be seen in conjunction with another severe condition that is reversible, such as a severe viral infection or bacterial sepsis. The committee proposed that the EF of 20 percent or less be documented twice with at least 3 months intervening to allow time for improvement of any reversible process. Although little systematic evidence documents patients' functional status with very low EF, the committee's expert judgment is that patients with an EF of 20 percent or less would most likely be severely impaired and therefore should be considered for listing-level disability.

The committee recognizes that some individuals, particularly those in their teens or twenties, will be able to work and may even be asymptomatic. This means that a listing requiring only an EF of 20 percent or less will not be 100 percent specific. As an administrative expedient, however, this recommended listing would be specific enough and the number of worthy claimants who would be quickly and easily allowed outweighs the probability that a few individuals who could work would be allowed. Asymptomatic individuals are most likely to be young. They are likely to continue working, even if they are aware they have a very low EF, because the level of benefits they could anticipate receiving would be very low relative to what they could earn by continuing to work. The listing could include a criterion that a claimant must be symptomatic as well as have an EF of 20 percent or less, but this would require adjudicators to determine from the medical records whether the claimant is symptomatic. Adding a second criterion of functional limitation, which is more subjective to document, would complicate the application of what could be a simple listing.

RECOMMENDATION 5-3. Add an additional listing route in which the objective cardiac abnormality of a left ventricular ejection fraction of 20 percent or less, documented twice with at least 3 months intervening, is sufficiently severe that demonstration of functional limitation is not needed to meet the listing.

REFERENCES

Allen, L. A., J. E. Yager, M. J. Funk, W. C. Levy, J. A. Tulsky, M. T. Bowers, G. C. Dodson, C. M. O'Connor, and G. M. Felker. 2008. Discordance between patient-predicted and model-predicted life expectancy among ambulatory patients with heart failure. *Journal of the American Medical Association* 299(21):2533–2542.

Arena, R., J. Myers, M. A. Williams, M. Gulati, P. Kligfield, G. J. Balady, E. Collins, and G. Fletcher. 2007. Assessment of functional capacity in clinical and research settings: A scientific statement from the American Heart Association Committee on Exercise, Rehabilitation, and Prevention of the Council on Clinical Cardiology and the Council on Cardiovascular Nursing. *Circulation* 116:329–343.

Balady, G. J., R. Arena, K. Sietsema, J. Myers, L. Coke, G. F. Fletcher, D. Forman, B. Franklin, M. Guazzi, M. Gulati, S. J. Keteyian, C. J. Lavie, R. Macko, D. Mancini, and R. V. Milani, on behalf of the American Heart Association Exercise, Cardiac Rehabilitation, Prevention Committee of the Council on Clinical Cardiology, Council on Epidemiology Prevention, Council on Peripheral Vascular Disease, and Interdisciplinary Council on Quality of Care Outcomes Research. 2010. Clinician's guide to cardiopulmonary exercise testing in adults. A scientific statement from the American Heart Association. *Circulation* 122:191–225.

Cohn, J. N., G. R. Johnson, R. Shabetai, H. Loeb, F. Tristani, T. Rector, R. Smith, and R. Fletcher. 1993. Ejection fraction, peak exercise oxygen consumption, cardiothoracic ratio, ventricular arrhythmias, and plasma norepinephrine as determinants of prognosis in heart failure. The V-HeFT VA Cooperative Studies Group. *Circulation* 87(6 Suppl): V15–V16.

Colucci, W. S., and E. Braunwald. 1995. Heart failure: Cardiac function and dysfunction. In *Atlas of heart diseases,* 4th ed., edited by W. S. Colucci. Philadelphia, PA: Blackwell Science. Pp. 128–142.

Fleg, J. L., I. L. Piña, G. J. Balady, B. R. Chaitman, B. Fletcher, C. Lavie, M. C. Limacher, R. A. Stein, M. Williams, and T. Bazzarre. 2000. Assessment of functional capacity in clinical and research applications: An advisory from the Committee on Exercise, Rehabilitation, and Prevention, Council on Clinical Cardiology, American Heart Association. *Circulation* 102:1591–1597.

Gibbons, R. J., G. J. Balady, J. T. Bricker, B. R. Chaitman, G. F. Fletcher, V. F. Froelicher, D. B. Mark, B. D. McCallister, A. N. Mooss, M. G. O'Reilly, W. L. Winters Jr., E. M. Antman, J. S. Alpert, D. P. Faxon, V. Fuster, G. Gregoratos, L. F. Hiratzka, A. K. Jacobs, R. O. Russell, and S. C. Smith Jr. 2002. ACC/AHA 2002 guideline update for exercise testing. *Journal of the American College of Cardiology* 40:1531–1540.

Ho, C. Y., and C. E. Seidman. 2006. A contemporary approach to hypertrophic cardiomyopathy. *Circulation* 113(24):e858–e862.

Hunt, S. A., W. T. Abraham, M. H. Chin, A. M. Feldman, G. S. Francis, T. G. Ganiats, M. Jessup, M. A. Konstam, D. M. Mancini, K. Michl, J. A. Oates, P. S. Rahko, M. A. Silver, L. W. Stevenson, and C. W. Yancy. 2005. Guideline update for the diagnosis and management of chronic heart failure in the adult. *Circulation* 112:e154–235.

Levy, W. C., D. Mozaffarian, D. T. Linker, S. C. Sutradhar, S. D. Anker A. B. Cropp, I. Anand, A. Maggioni, P. Burton, M. D. Sullivan, B. Pitt, P. A. Poole-Wilson, D. L. Mann, and M. Packer. 2006. The Seattle heart failure model: Prediction of survival in heart failure. *Circulation* 113(11):1424–1433.

Lloyd-Jones, D., R. J. Adams, T. M. Brown, M. Carnethon, S. Dai, G. De Simone, T. B. Ferguson, E. Ford, K. Furie, C. Gillespie, A. Go, K. Greenlund, N. Haase, S. Hailpern, P. M. Ho, V. Howard, B. Kissela, S. Kittner, D. Lackland, L. Lisabeth, A. Marelli, M. M. McDermott, J. Meigs, D. Mozaffarian, M. Mussolino, G. Nichol, V. L. Roger, W. Rosamond, R. Sacco, P. Sorlie, R. Stafford, T. Thom, S. Wasserthiel-Smoller, N. D. Wong, J. Wylie-Rosett, and on behalf of the American Heart Association Statistics Committee Stroke Statistics Subcommittee. 2010. Heart disease and stroke statistics—2010 update: A report from the American Heart Association. *Circulation* 121(7):e46–e215.

Redfield, M. M., S. J. Jacobsen, J. C. Burnett Jr., D. W. Mahoney, K. R. Bailey, and R. J. Rodeheffer. 2003. Burden of systolic and diastolic ventricular dysfunction in the community: Appreciating the scope of the heart failure epidemic. *Journal of the American Medical Association* 289(2):194–202.

SSA (Social Security Administration). 2008. *Listing of impairments—Adult listings (Part A). Disability evaluation under Social Security (Blue Book).* http://www.socialsecurity.gov/disability/professionals/bluebook/AdultListings.htm (accessed July 22, 2010).

Stevenson, L. W., G. Couper, B. Natterson, G. Fonarow, M. A. Hamilton, M. Woo, and J. W. Creaser. 1995. Target heart failure populations for newer therapies. *Circulation* 92(9 Suppl):II 174–181.

Wilson, J. R., G. Rayos, T. K. Yeoh, and P. Gothard. 1995. Dissociation between peak exercise oxygen consumption and hemodynamic dysfunction in potential heart transplant candidates. *Journal of the American College of Cardiology* 26(2):429–435.

Zile, M. R., and J. Nappi. 2000. Diastolic heart failure. *Current Treatment Options in Cardiovascular Medicine* 2(5):439–450.

6

Heart Transplantation

The current listing for heart transplantation does not need to be revised, but the Social Security Administration should reevaluate heart transplant recipients 9 months after surgery to avoid a potential gap in benefits should the claimant continue to be disabled due to residual impairment or due to noncardiac causes.

DESCRIPTION

A heart transplant may be an option for some individuals if standard medical and pacing device therapy cannot successfully treat the symptoms associated with heart failure. Patients who have undergone heart transplantation may experience some physical limitations regarding activities of daily living. Return to work is possible with increased functional status, but may not be the case with every individual who has undergone heart transplantation. Treatment adherence and psychological support after transplant are important indicators for successful functional recovery. In current clinical practice, patients who have undergone cardiac transplantation often take a 6-month period to adequately recover. Cardiac rehabilitation for transplant recipients includes exercise retraining. Medical therapy initially includes high doses of immunosuppression to decrease the chance of rejection. This increases the risk of infection, which diminishes as immunosuppression doses are decreased during the first 6 months after transplantation. The risks of both infection and rejection decrease to a relatively low level by the end of the first year.

EPIDEMIOLOGY

In 2008, 2,163 cardiac transplants were performed in the United States (Lloyd-Jones et al., 2010). Because heart failure affects nearly 6 million Americans, many more heart transplants could be possible if more donor hearts were available for transplantation. In the United States, more than 72 percent of heart transplant recipients are male; 65.5 percent are white; 19.4 percent are between ages 35 and 49, and 54.2 percent are age 50 or older (Lloyd-Jones et al., 2010). Individuals who undergo heart transplantation have a high survival rate (see Table 6-1).

The Social Security Administration currently grants disability to individuals who have undergone a heart transplant for 1 year after transplantation (see Box 6-1) with instruction to evaluate individuals with residual impairment after 1 year under the appropriate cardiac listing. As indicated above, cardiac transplants are shown to be highly successful in improving the functional capacity of recipients past an approximate 6-month recovery period.

CONCLUSIONS AND RECOMMENDATIONS

The committee concludes the current listing evaluation criterion for heart transplant recipients is appropriate. During the first year after the procedure, patients who receive a cardiac transplant should meet the listing and receive disability. If heart transplant recipients continue to experi-

TABLE 6-1 Survival Rates After Heart Transplantation, by Sex

Survival Rates	Men	Women
1-year	88.0%	77.2%
3-year	79.3%	77.2%
5-year	73.1%	67.4%

SOURCE: Lloyd-Jones et al., 2010.

BOX 6-1
Current Listing for Heart Transplant

4.09 Heart Transplant. Consider under a disability for 1 year following surgery; thereafter, evaluate residual impairment under the appropriate listing.

SOURCE: SSA, 2008.

ence functional impairment after rehabilitation, residual impairment will likely manifest as a specific cardiac condition that may then be evaluated under another, appropriate listing, such as heart failure or ischemic heart disease.

RECOMMENDATION 6-1. Maintain the current listing criterion for heart transplant recipients, meaning the claimant meets the listing (4.09) for 1 year after transplantation surgery.

The committee recommends individuals allowed under the heart transplant listing who continue to experience impairment should begin the evaluation process at 9 months after being granted disability due to their heart transplants. Beginning the evaluation process 3 months prior to the end of the benefit period will allow those who may qualify under another appropriate listing to avoid a gap in benefits.

RECOMMENDATION 6-2. Reevaluate heart transplant recipients for disability 9 months after surgery to avoid a potential gap in benefits should the claimant continue to be disabled because of residual impairment from transplantation or other cardiac or noncardiac causes.

Physical functional limitations are generally low in the heart transplant population. However, individuals require a period of time to prevent the likelihood of infection, rejection of the donor heart, or other possible complications that may occur due to the transplant in the period directly following transplantation. Although most patients may be fully functional after a 6-month rehabilitation period, the committee concludes that extending the period of disability benefits to 1 year is reasonable, allowing individuals enough time to adequately recover and potentially resume employment or other useful activities.

REFERENCES

Lloyd-Jones, D., R. J. Adams, T. M. Brown, M. Carnethon, S. Dai, G. De Simone, T. B. Ferguson, E. Ford, K. Furie, C. Gillespie, A. Go, K. Greenlund, N. Haase, S. Hailpern, P. M. Ho, V. Howard, B. Kissela, S. Kittner, D. Lackland, L. Lisabeth, A. Marelli, M. M. McDermott, J. Meigs, D. Mozaffarian, M. Mussolino, G. Nichol, V. L. Roger, W. Rosamond, R. Sacco, P. Sorlie, R. Stafford, T. Thom, S. Wasserthiel-Smoller, N. D. Wong, and J. Wylie-Rosett, on behalf of the American Heart Association Statistics Committee Stroke Statistics Subcommittee. 2010. Heart disease and stroke statistics—2010 update: A report from the American Heart Association. *Circulation* 121(7):e46–e215.

SSA (Social Security Administration). 2008. *Listing of impairments—Adult listings (Part A). Disability evaluation under Social Security (Blue Book).* http://www.ssa.gov/disability/professionals.bluebook/AdultListings.htm (accessed May 3, 2010).

7

Ischemic Heart Disease

This chapter describes the evaluation and management of ischemic heart disease, which has evolved significantly over the past decade. In particular, several clinical trials have documented the benefits of revascularization in patients with acute ischemic syndromes as well as the efficacy of medical therapy, including lifestyle modification in patients with stable coronary disease. A fundamental premise in establishing new listing criteria for ischemic heart disease disability is the linking of anatomic or structural evidence of coronary heart disease (CHD) with both functional impairment and severe anginal symptoms. A flow diagram has been introduced that depicts five pathways to meet listings, including clinical, standard exercise testing, stress imaging, and angiographic anatomic criteria, with one pathway specific for patients with prior coronary artery bypass graft and severe CHD. Because many patients with ischemic heart disease are unable to exercise, standard stress electrocardiographic criteria for ischemia (the sole determinant of objective ischemia assessment in prior cardiovascular disability listings) have been expanded significantly to encompass nonexercise modalities (including nuclear imaging and echocardiography provoked by pharmacologic vasodilator stress) to assess the presence of severe inducible ischemia that, when combined with severe angina (Canadian Cardiovascular Society Class III or IV) would meet a cardiovascular disability listing. Additionally, the criteria by which angiographic CHD meet a listing have been specified, and severe CHD is defined by greater than or equal to 50 percent left main stenosis and/or greater than or equal to 70 percent proximal/mid stenoses in greater than or equal to two native arteries or bypass grafts. These updated criteria now provide a significantly enhanced and evidence-based approach for making disability determinations based on anatomic and functional criteria in patients with severe angina.

DESCRIPTION

Ischemia is defined as inadequate blood supply (circulation) to a local area due to blockage of the blood vessels supplying the area. Ischemic means that an organ (e.g., the heart) is not getting enough blood and oxygen. Ischemic heart disease, also called coronary heart disease (CHD) or coronary artery disease, is the term given to heart problems caused by narrowed heart (coronary) arteries that supply blood to the heart muscle. Although the narrowing can be caused by a blood clot or by constriction of the blood vessel, most often it is caused by buildup of plaque, called atherosclerosis. When the blood flow to the heart muscle is completely blocked, the heart muscle cells die, which is termed a heart attack or myocardial infarction (MI). Most people with early (less than 50 percent narrowing) CHD do not experience symptoms or limitation of blood flow. However, as the atherosclerosis progresses, especially if left untreated, symptoms may occur. They are most likely to occur during exercise or emotional stress, when the demand for the oxygen carried by the blood increases.

The discomfort experienced when the heart muscle is deprived of adequate oxygen is called angina pectoris. This is a clinical syndrome characterized by discomfort in the chest, jaw, shoulder, back, or arms that is typically aggravated by exertion or emotional stress and relieved promptly with rest or by taking nitroglycerin. Angina usually occurs in patients with CHD, but also can occur in individuals with valvular disease, hypertrophic cardiomyopathy, and uncontrolled hypertension. Infrequently, patients with normal coronary arteries may experience angina related to coronary spasm or endothelial dysfunction (Gibbons et al., 2002a).

Angina is classified using the Canadian Cardiovascular Society (CCS) scheme, which grades angina or an anginal equivalent (e.g., exertional dyspnea) based on a description of the level of activity that causes symptoms (Table 7-1). Class I is defined by angina that occurs with strenuous or rapid or prolonged exertion at work or recreation, but not with ordinary physical activity. Class I activities include chopping wood, climbing hills, cycling, aerobic ballet, ballroom (fast) or square dancing, jogging a 10-minute mile, rope skipping, skating, skiing, playing tennis or squash, and walking 5 miles per hour. Class II is defined by angina that slightly limits ordinary activity, such that angina is precipitated by walking or climbing stairs rapidly, walk-

TABLE 7-1 Canadian Cardiovascular Society Functional Classification of Angina

Class	Definition	Limitations
I	No limitation of ordinary activity. Angina occurs with strenuous, rapid, or prolonged exertion at work or recreation.	Angina may occur with chopping wood, climbing hills, cycling, aerobic ballet, ballroom (fast) or square dancing, jogging a 10-minute mile, rope skipping, skating, skiing, playing tennis or squash, and walking 5 miles per hour.
II	Slight limitation of ordinary activity.	Angina may occur with walking or climbing stairs rapidly, walking uphill, walking or climbing stairs after meals; in cold or in wind; under emotional stress; only during the first few hours after awakening; or with walking more than two blocks on level ground and climbing more than one flight of ordinary stairs at a normal pace and in normal conditions.
III	Marked limitation of ordinary physical activity.	Angina may occur with walking one or two blocks on level ground, and climbing one flight of stairs in normal conditions and at normal pace, playing a musical instrument, performing household chores, gardening, vacuuming, walking a dog, or taking out the trash.
IV	Inability to perform any physical activity without discomfort.	Angina may occur at rest.

SOURCE: Adapted from Goldman et al., 1981.

ing uphill, walking or climbing stairs after meals; in cold or in wind; under emotional stress; only during the first few hours after awakening; or with walking more than two blocks on level ground and climbing more than one flight of ordinary stairs at a normal pace and in normal conditions. Class III is defined by marked limitation of ordinary physical activity such that angina is precipitated by walking one or two blocks on level ground, climbing one flight of stairs in normal conditions and at normal pace, playing a musical instrument, performing household chores, gardening, vacuuming, walking a dog, or taking out the trash. Class IV is defined by inability to carry on any physical activity without discomfort; anginal syndrome may be present at rest (Campeau, 1976, 2002; Goldman et al., 1981). As many as 3 to 4 million Americans may have silent ischemia, or ischemia without pain, or a heart attack without prior warning. People with angina may also have undiagnosed episodes of silent ischemia. Furthermore, those who have had heart attacks or individuals with diabetes are at risk for developing silent ischemia.

EPIDEMIOLOGY

On the basis of data from the National Health and Nutrition Examination Survey (NHANES) for the period 2003 to 2006, an estimated 17.6 million Americans age 20 or older have CHD, with an overall prevalence of 7.9 percent (9.1 percent in men and 7 percent in women). The overall prevalence of MI is 3.6 percent (4.7 percent in men and 2.6 percent in women). The estimated annual incidence of MI is 935,000, which includes 610,000 new and 325,000 recurrent infarctions. The overall prevalence of angina pectoris is 4.6 percent, with age-adjusted prevalence higher in women than men. CHD accounts for more than half of all cardiovascular events in men and women under age 75. The lifetime risk of developing CHD after age 40 is 49 percent for men and 32 percent for women (Lloyd-Jones et al., 2010).

CHD is the leading cause of death in both men and women. It caused one of every six U.S. deaths in 2006; CHD mortality was 425,425, and MI mortality was 141,462. Approximately every 25 seconds, an American will experience a coronary event, and approximately every minute a death will be attributed to a coronary event. Approximately every 34 seconds, an American will have an MI and 15 percent will die of it (Lloyd-Jones et al., 2010).

In addition, in 2006, 1,115,000 inpatient diagnostic cardiac catheterizations were performed as well as 661,000 inpatient percutaneous coronary interventions (PCIs) and 253,000 coronary artery bypass surgery (CABG) procedures. The estimated direct and indirect cost of coronary heart disease for 2010 is $177.1 billion (Lloyd-Jones et al., 2010).

DIAGNOSTIC CRITERIA AND METHODS

CHD can be diagnosed in several ways. Patients with documented (prior) MI or coronary artery revascularization (either with PCI or CABG) have CHD. Moreover, the presence of typical angina suggests a clinical diagnosis of CHD, but most often requires confirmation by additional diagnostic tests, such as coronary angiography. However, this test is an invasive and relatively costly procedure associated with a low, yet definite, risk of an adverse event. Coronary angiography is most often performed following an abnormal stress test or in the setting of an acute coronary syndrome (unstable angina or heart attack) in individuals who are candidates for revascularization (either by PCI or CABG).

Exercise Stress Tests

Stress testing is usually performed using an exercise tolerance test (ETT) with a treadmill or, occasionally, with bicycle ergometry. The most commonly applied treadmill protocol is the Bruce protocol, with the modified Bruce, Naughton, Balke (Balke-Ware), Wilson, Taylor, or "ramp" protocols used in some patients. Noting the specific protocol is important because protocols differ by the rate at which the workload increases. The workload achieved during a test for any given protocol can be estimated in units of metabolic equivalents of task (METs) from published nomograms (Fletcher et al., 2001; Thompson et al., 2010). Completion of the first stage of the Bruce protocol is equivalent to 5 METs.

Exercise testing can be performed with electrocardiogram (ECG) monitoring alone or combined with a cardiac imaging test: single photon emission computed tomography (SPECT), positron emission tomography (PET), or with echocardiography imaging. Each modality has specific criteria for an abnormal test. An abnormal exercise ECG is defined by ST-segment displacement, usually an ST-segment depression greater than or equal to 1 mm, measured 0.08 seconds after the J-point, that is horizontal or downsloping (Gibbons et al., 2002b). ST-segment elevation greater than or equal to 1 mm in leads without Q waves occurs infrequently, but this is also considered an abnormal response. An abnormal SPECT or PET study is defined by a perfusion defect (Klocke et al., 2003), with a defect that is the same with rest or exercise (a fixed defect) suggesting infarction. An abnormal exercise echocardiogram is a wall motion abnormality (Pellikka et al., 2007). Usually, such an abnormality that develops or worsens during exercise represents ischemia, whereas a wall motion abnormality that is present at rest and unchanged (fixed) with exercise indicates infarction. The presence of either ischemia or infarction on a stress-imaging study is consistent with the diagnosis of CHD in a patient with angina symptoms.

Stress test results are commonly reported in a dichotomous manner: normal or abnormal, positive or negative for ischemia, and so on. However, for a positive test, the degree of severity of abnormality provides additional information. All stress-testing modalities are limited by their false-positive results (abnormal stress test result, but CHD is not present) and false-negative results (normal stress test result, but CHD is present). Due to variability in image interpretation and imaging artifacts, isolated small mild abnormalities on stress SPECT or stress echocardiogram may be false-positive results, but the more severely abnormal results are more likely to represent a true-positive test (i.e., CHD is present). Additionally, a more severely abnormal test result is associated with an increased likelihood of multivessel CHD and a worse prognosis.

An abnormal test result at a low workload is one of the most reliable indications of a high likelihood of multivessel CHD (McNeer et al., 1978). Other variables associated with multivessel CHD or worse prognosis are shown in Table 7-2 (Dubach, 1988; Gibbons et al., 2002a,b; Klocke et al., 2003; McNeer, 1978; Pellikka et al., 2007). Earlier versions of the CHD

TABLE 7-2 Other Variables Associated with Multivessel CHD or Worse Prognosis

ETT	SPECT	Echocardiogram
Magnitude ST-segment depression	Number of perfusion defects	High WMI score
Number of leads ST-segment depression	High SSS	Decrease in LVEF
Duration ST-segment depression in recovery period	High SRS	Number of segments with WMA
Angina (especially if limiting symptom)	TID	n/a
Decrease in systolic BP below baseline	n/a	WMA involving multiple coronary artery territories
Chronotropic incompetence	Defects involving multiple coronary artery territories	Rest LVEF < 35 percent
Abnormal heart rate recovery	Rest LVEF at < 35 percent	Increase in ESV
High-risk Duke treadmill score[a]	Tℓ 201 lung uptake	n/a

[a] The Duke treadmill score can be calculated as follows: Duration (minutes Bruce protocol) – 5 X magnitude ST-segment deflection (mm) – angina index.

NOTE: BP = blood pressure; CHD = coronary heart disease; ESV = end systolic volume; ETT = exercise tolerance test; LVEF = left ventricular ejection fraction; SPECT = single-photon emission computerized tomography; SRS = summed reversibility score; SSS = summed stress score; TID = transient ischemic dilatation; WMA = wall motion abnormality; WMI = wall motion index.

SOURCES: Dubach et al., 1988; Gibbons et al., 2002a,b; Klocke et al., 2003; McNeer, 1978; Pellikka et al., 2007.

listings included detailed descriptions of interpretation of the exercise ECG. However, most reports in patient records do not provide these descriptors, but rather they simply categorize the exercise ECG as being normal or abnormal, positive or negative. Exercise duration is included in most reports. Similarly, for the stress-imaging procedures, the results can be characterized most accurately by applying the 17-segment model advocated by the American Heart Association (AHA) (Cerqueira et al., 2002). This model can be used to develop a summed stress score or summed reversibility score for SPECT imaging and a wall motion index score for echocardiography. These scoring systems have been validated as accurate tools for prognostic purposes. However, this information is not usually included in reports. Instead, the anatomical location of the defects (reflecting coronary artery distribution) and exercise duration are most often included in exercise imaging reports.

Nuclear and echocardiographic imaging can localize the site of ischemia, although the correlation with angiographic CHD is not perfect. The assignment of coronary artery territories by imaging to anatomical CHD at angiography is as follows: anterior/anteroseptal—left anterior descending artery; inferior/inferoseptal—right coronary artery; lateral—circumflex artery (Cerqueira et al., 2002). Involvement of the lateral territory may be further specified as anterolateral or inferolateral. The artery supplying the apex is variable. For this reason, defects involving the apex alone are not assigned to a coronary artery territory. In addition to multiple coronary artery territories, other markers shown by imaging usually represent extensive ischemia. For nuclear imaging this marker is transient ischemic dilatation, or poststress dilatation of the left ventricle. For echocardiography these markers include a decrease in left ventricular ejection fraction (LVEF) or an increase in end systolic volume between rest and exercise.

In contrast to the imaging modalities, the exercise ECG cannot localize the site of ischemia. Thus, for application of the exercise ECG, there cannot be a requirement for involvement of greater than or equal to two coronary artery territories (for further discussion, refer to the following paragraph, as well as to item 3 in the section on concluding concepts and Recommendation 7-3). Nonetheless, studies have shown that the development of ischemic ECG changes at a low workload is associated with a high likelihood of multivessel CHD (McNeer, 1978). Another variable that can be measured during exercise testing and that occurs less commonly than ECG changes, but also reflects multivessel CHD and a poor prognosis, is a decrease in systolic blood pressure at peak exercise greater than or equal to 10 mm Hg below the baseline blood pressure (Dubach et al., 1988).

To facilitate application of the listings in a uniform manner across the stress-testing modalities, a claimant will meet a listing if exercise capacity is limited (less than or equal to 5 METs), combined with objective evidence of CHD. Given the poor specificity of single mild abnormalities on SPECT or echocardiographic imaging, the presence of defects involving less than or equal to two coronary artery territories is required to increase the likelihood that the claimant has CHD before being granted disability. This requirement for involvement of less than or equal to two-vessel CHD is analogous to the coronary angiogram criteria.

The criteria to meet a listing through the use of an exercise stress test (standard treadmill test, nuclear SPECT or PET, echocardiography) include exercise duration less than or equal to 5 METs and objective evidence for significant ischemia defined in Table 7-3.

Pharmacologic (Nuclear and Echocardiography) Stress Tests

Pharmacologic stress testing using SPECT, PET, or echocardiographic imaging is reserved for patients who are either unable to perform dynamic

TABLE 7-3 Criteria to Meet a Listing Through the Use of an Exercise Stress Test

Exercise Workload Less Than or Equal to 5 METs Plus at Least One of the Following Criteria:	
Criterion	Modality
Ischemic ECG	Standard treadmill
Decrease in systolic BP ≥ 10 mm Hg below baseline	Standard treadmill
Fixed/reversible perfusion defects ≥ 2 coronary territories	Nuclear imaging (SPECT or PET)
Transient ischemic dilation	Nuclear imaging (SPECT or PET)
Fixed/reversible regional wall motion abnormality ≥ 2 coronary territories	Echocardiography
Decrease in LVEF between rest and exercise	Echocardiography
Increase in ESV between rest and exercise	

NOTE: BP = blood pressure; ECG = electrocardiogram; ESV = end systolic volume; LVEF = left ventricular ejection fraction; METs = metabolic equivalents of task; PET = positron emission tomography; SPECT = single-photon emission computerized tomography.

exercise or unable to achieve at least 85 percent of the age-predicted maximal heart rate with exercise, which is the effort level required to achieve adequate sensitivity to detect coronary artery stenosis capable of causing angina (Klocke et al., 2003; Pellikka et al., 2007). Pharmacologic stress does not consistently cause angina or ECG changes of ischemia, so only the imaging results are diagnostic. Pharmacologic agents are administered intravenously in place of dynamic exercise stress, and the resulting perfusion or wall motion response is compared with the resting state and is interpreted using the same criteria for perfusion defects and wall motion abnormalities listed above for dynamic exercise.

The most frequently used pharmacologic stress agents for SPECT and PET are the vasodilators dipyridamole, adenosine, and regadenoson, which increase blood flow through the coronary arteries, but only modestly increase heart rate in most patients. Many patients experience chest discomfort during the administration of these agents, which should not be interpreted as angina. The agents create differences in blood flow between coronary arteries that have high-grade blockages and normal arteries, which result in perfusion defects that can be detected using radioactive imaging.

The most frequently used pharmacologic agent in stress echocardiography is dobutamine, a positive inotropic agent that increases the force or energy of muscular contractions and increases heart rate and blood pressure. Dobutamine is administered intravenously in increasing doses until the patient reaches 85 percent of the maximal age-predicted heart rate. Atropine may also be required in some patients. If the patient does not achieve 85 percent of the heart rate response, the resulting images may underestimate the presence of CHD. The positive inotropic effect and increases in heart rate and blood pressure may cause angina and result in abnormal wall motion at peak stress in portions of the heart muscle supplied by coronary arteries with high-grade blockages. Dobutamine may also be used for SPECT imaging.

Coronary CT Angiography

Coronary computed tomography (CT) angiography is an imaging technique during which an iodinated contrast dye is injected through a peripheral vein and images of the coronary arteries are taken using a CT system. It provides images of the coronary arteries similar to those obtained using coronary angiography, during which the dye is injected directly into the coronary arteries using an arterial catheter. It is most useful in patients with an intermediate risk of coronary heart disease. In patients with extensive calcium deposits or prior coronary artery stents, detection of stenosis is difficult (Budoff et al., 2006). Tremendous progress has been made in changing this technique, but lack of standardization and unresolved technical issues do not allow it to be used in place of coronary angiography as a basis for determining disability (Mark et al., 2010; Miller et al., 2008).

TREATMENT

Comprehensive management of angina and stable CHD entails multiple therapeutic approaches, including the following:

- Identification and treatment of associated diseases that can precipitate or worsen angina and ischemia;
- Cardiac risk factor identification and intervention;
- Application of pharmacological and nonpharmacological interventions for secondary prevention;
- Pharmacological and symptomatic management of angina and ischemia; and
- Myocardial revascularization with PCI or CABG surgery, when indicated.

A multidimensional management approach integrates all of these considerations, often simultaneously, in each patient. Among pharmacotherapies, three drug classes have been demonstrated to reduce mortality and morbidity in patients with stable CHD and preserved left ventricular (LV) function: aspirin, angiotensin-converting enzyme (ACE) inhibition, and effective lipid lowering. Beta-blockers have been shown to reduce mortality in patients with prior MI (CAPRICORN Investigators, 2001). Other therapies such as nitrates, beta-blockers, calcium channel blockers, and ranolazine have been shown to improve angina and exercise performance and to reduce ischemia, but have not been proven to reduce mortality in patients with stable CHD.

Clinical practice guidelines for the diagnosis and treatment of chronic stable angina (Fraker et al., 2007; Gibbons et al., 2002a), unstable angina/non-ST-segment elevation myocardial infarction (Anderson et al., 2007), and ST-segment elevation myocardial infarction (Antman et al., 2004; Kushner et al., 2009), have been jointly published by AHA and the American College of Cardiology (ACC). These guidelines detail the indications and timing of medical therapy (including lifestyle modification) and revascularization with PCI and/or CABG (Eagle et al., 2004) and provide guidance for secondary prevention that includes risk factor reduction (Smith et al., 2006). Although revascularization has specific indications, treatment with medical therapy, lifestyle modification, and risk factor reduction is recommended across the spectrum of CHD in both stable and unstable patients and following a coronary event or revascularization.

Recent Advances

The most recent advance in medical therapy consists of the introduction of ranolazine (Chaitman, 2006; Chaitman et al., 2004; Morrow et al., 2007). Nonpharmacologic treatments include spinal cord stimulation (Taylor et al., 2009) and enhanced external counterpulsation (EECP) (Akhtar et al., 2006; Michaels et al., 2004; Soran et al., 2006) for the treatment of angina and ischemia. Advances in revascularization include development of drug-eluting stents (Novack et al., 2009), the introduction of percutaneous support devices in patients undergoing PCI (Goldstein et al., 1998), and increased use of off-pump techniques, as well as minimal access and robotic procedures in patients undergoing CABG (Poston et al., 2008; Sabik et al., 2002). Interest and experience also have been growing in the performance of hybrid revascularization procedures (Stahl et al., 2002) using a collaborative approach between interventional cardiologists and cardiothoracic surgeons.

Ranolazine is the newest antianginal agent approved by the Food and Drug Administration and the first new drug class for angina since calcium channel blockers (CCBs) were introduced 30 years ago. Ranolazine acts by reducing intracellular calcium overload in ischemic myocytes by inhibiting late inward sodium current entry. The net effect of reduced late inward sodium current is a reduction in LV wall tension and myocardial oxygen demand, thereby reducing angina and ischemia. Ranolazine increases exercise tolerance in patients with stable angina, reduces episodes of recurrent ischemia, and provides additional antianginal benefit in patients who are already on intensive antianginal therapy with beta-blockers and CCBs. While multiple nonspecific side effects of ranolazine have been reported, the drug is well tolerated in clinical practice. The most common side effects are dizziness (6.2 percent), headache (5.5 percent), constipation (4.5 percent), and nausea (4.4 percent), which are more commonly observed at the 1,000 mg twice a day dose. Mean QT prolongation noted in clinical trials ranges from 6 to 8 milliseconds; the clinical relevance of the modest QT prolongation that occurs in a dose-related manner is unclear, but there has been no increased risk of a serious proarrhythmic effect (torsades de pointes) or sudden cardiac death reported in a large, placebo-controlled trial of more than 6,500 patients (MERLIN Trial) (Morrow et al., 2007).

EECP is an alternative treatment for patients with refractory angina. It is generally administered as 35 sequential treatments (1 hour daily; 5 days per week) over 7 weeks. EECP was shown to increase the time to ST-segment depression during exercise testing, reduce angina, and improve health-related quality of life for at least 1 year in a randomized, double-blind study of patients with chronic stable angina (Soran et al., 2006). EECP does not reduce ischemia on myocardial perfusion imaging, and the mechanisms underlying its effects are poorly understood.

Side Effects of Treatments

Nitroglycerin and nitrates can cause vasodilation-induced headache, a decrease in blood pressure, and, more rarely, severe hypotension with bradycardia. The vasodilation by nitroglycerin may be markedly exaggerated and prolonged in the presence of the phosphodiesterase inhibitors sildenafil (Viagra), vardenafil (Levitra), and tadalafil (Cialis), so these agents should not be used concurrently with nitrates.

Most of the adverse effects of beta-blockers occur as a consequence of the known properties of these drugs and include cardiac effects (e.g., severe sinus bradycardia, sinus arrest, reduced LV contractility), bronchoconstriction, fatigue, mental depression, nightmares, gastrointestinal upset, sexual dysfunction, intensification of insulin-induced hypoglycemia, and cutaneous reactions. Lethargy, weakness, and fatigue may be caused by reduced cardiac output or may arise from a direct effect on the central nervous system. Bronchoconstriction results from blockade of $beta_2$ receptors in the tracheobronchial tree. As a consequence, reversible obstructive lung disease (e.g., asthma) may be considered as relative contraindications to beta-blockers, even to $beta_1$-selective agents (Egred et al., 2005).

Calcium channel blockers are potent vasodilators, which may lead to dizziness, hypotension, and reflex tachycardia—particularly with some dihydropyridines. Peripheral edema can occur, usually with the dihydropyridines. Both verapamil and diltiazem can cause bradycardia or conduction disturbances, particularly if coadministered with beta-blockers. Diltiazem and verapamil may exacerbate or precipitate heart failure in patients with reduced LV ejection fraction.

Trends in Morbidity and Mortality

Data from the Framingham Heart Study showed the overall death rates from CHD decreased by 64 percent from 1950 to 1999. From 1996 to 2006, the annual death rate due to CHD declined by 36.4 percent, and the actual number of deaths declined by 21.9 percent (Lloyd-Jones et al., 2010). An analysis of NHANES CHD mortality data between 1980 and 2000 revealed that approximately 47 percent of the decline in mortality could be explained by the use of medical and surgical treatment (including secondary prevention therapies after myocardial infarction or revascularization, initial treatment of MI or unstable angina, treatment of heart failure, revascularization for chronic angina, and other therapies, including antihypertensive and lipid-lowering primary prevention strategies), whereas approximately 44 percent of the mortality decline was attributed to changes in risk factors (including lower total cholesterol, systolic blood pressure, and smoking prevalence, and decreased physical inactivity) (Lloyd-Jones et al., 2010).

According to data from the National Registry of Myocardial Infarction, in-hospital mortality following acute MI declined from 11.2 percent in 1940 to 9.4 percent in 1999 (Lloyd-Jones et al., 2010). Moreover, a recent analysis of the Medicare fee-for-service population revealed that the adjusted hospitalization rate for acute MI declined by 5.8 percent per year from 2002 through 2007, although there was a slower rate of decline in African American patients compared with white patients (Chen et al., 2010).

DISABILITY

Many patients with CHD and chronic stable angina have a reduced functional capacity, particularly those with CCS Class III or IV angina. Revascularization has been shown to be more effective in reducing angina than maximal medical therapy, at least initially (Boden, 2007b), and patients who are not candidates for revascularization may experience disabling symptoms. About 30 percent of patients never return to work after coronary revascularization, and 15 to 20 percent rate their own health as fair or poor despite revascularization (Writing Group for the BARI Investigators, 1997). In addition, health expenditures from lost productivity from morbidity and mortality from CHD in 2010 are estimated to be at $11.3 billion and $69.8 billion, respectively (Lloyd-Jones et al., 2010).

Disability and Work

Only a modest relationship exists between the extent of anatomic CHD or myocardial ischemia and the severity of cardiac symptoms and functional impairment. In patients with a recent MI, the size or location of the MI, a history of previous MI, and poor ventricular function predict functional impairment and return to work after the event (Herlitz et al., 1994; Maeland and Havik, 1986; Rost and Smith, 1992; Smith and O'Rourke, 1988), but these medical factors account for only part of observed disability in these patients. Measures of cardiac functional capacity, such as exercise treadmill performance, correlate well with the ability to participate in strenuous activities, but they correlate only weakly with the ability to perform more routine tasks of daily living and less strenuous work-related activities (Neill et al., 1985).

Angina and fatigue are the most common symptoms limiting sustained work activities (Mital et al., 2004). Both can be significantly improved in most patients using standard medical and surgical treatments. However, a recent review of the literature found that 90 percent of patients experience improvement in symptoms following CABG, but only about 50 percent return to work (Mital et al., 2004). Although treatments are usually successful in decreasing symptoms and improving exercise tolerance, they do not necessarily result in a return to premorbid activities such as work. In short, disability is only partly explained by the severity of CHD and its symptoms.

Higher socioeconomic status (Abbott and Berry, 1991; Maeland and Havik, 1986; Rannevik, 1988), more education (Herlitz et al., 1994; Hlatky et al., 1986; Maeland and Havik, 1986, 1987; Mark et al., 1992; Speziale et al., 1996), younger age (Boudrez et al., 1994; Speziale et al., 1996), and looking forward to returning to work (Boll et al., 1987; Mittag et al., 2001) predict return to work after an acute coronary event. Alternatively, having a job that is physically strenuous or unsatisfying predicts a lower likelihood of returning to work (Boudrez and De Backer, 2000; Drory et al., 2005; Froom et al., 1999; Myrtek et al., 1997; Sellier et al., 2003; Shanfield, 1990; Wenger et al., 1985).

Psychological and social factors also both predict return to work and eventual disability (Cay and Walker, 1988; Maeland and Havik, 1987; Soderman et al., 2003), sometimes even better than the severity of cardiac disease (de Jonge et al., 2006; Sullivan et al., 1997). Depression is one of the most important noncardiac predictors of functional impairment and disability in patients with heart disease (Papakostas, 2009). In 2004, the World Health Organization found that depression was the leading cause of years lost due to disability for both men and women worldwide (WHO, 2008). When both depression and heart disease are present, their effects on functional status are at least additive. Thus, a claimant who does not quite meet the cardiovascular listings yet is depressed may nevertheless be disabled (Carney and Freeland, 2008).

Work Disability and Patients with CHD

Age, gender, education level, physical work capacity, and type of occupation, as well as psychosocial factors, play a critical role in whether a person returns to work after CHD events (Mital et al., 2004). The determinants of return to work are complex and are not necessarily determined by cardiac findings alone. Persons who have been unemployed for an extended period of time have a more difficult time integrating into the workforce. Cardiac rehabilitation programs can address the physical and psychosocial matters necessary to return to work (Wenger et al., 1995). However, these findings have been challenged, suggesting that this depends on the services that such programs offer with respect to occupational and psychological services.

It has been reported that following CABG, only 30 to 40 percent of patients reported that "heart problems" were the reason for not returning to work (Mital et al., 2004). The factors identified as determining return to work are as follows:

- Demographic (age, education, predictability of income);
- Sociological (reaction or attitude to disability, attitude of significant others toward disability);
- Vocational (predictability of employment status, attitude toward work);
- Medical (degree of severity of disability, presence of secondary disease); and
- Psychosocial (motivation to work, adaptability to change, intelligence) (Safilious-Rothchild, 1970).

It has also been documented that return to work depended on educational level attained: 78 percent of those with a college degree, 65 percent of those who completed technical school, 62 percent with a high school diploma, and 40 percent with elementary school education returned to work (Wenger et al., 1985).

One study reported that 85 to 90 percent of patients returned to work within 3 months after an MI (Froelicher et al., 1994). Women who had previously worked, older workers, blue-collar workers with physically strenuous jobs, and people with psychiatric problems had lower rates of returning to work (Shanfield, 1990). Social factors, in addition to medical problems, have been found to be major determinants of return to work.

Occupational work evaluation programs that use simulated work conditions to identify physical and psychological workplace stresses may have a role for disability evaluations, but others suggest that standard clinical testing is sufficient to identify ability to work (Dennis, 1990; Mital et al., 2004). The work simulation consisted mostly of upper arm dynamic work simulations, yet most production and service jobs involve physical movement, postural changes, carrying, and exertion over prolonged periods of time and would therefore require different simulation activities for complete work assessment (Mital et al., 2004).

The most important and decisive factors that influence return to work after a cardiac event are psychological in nature, and availability of disability benefits cannot be ignored (Mital et al., 2004). It has been reported that when patients in the coronary care unit were asked after their MI if they thought they would return to work by 6 months, their responses were highly predictive of actual return, whereas those patients who stated that they did not think they would return to work actually did not (Sivarajan and Newton, 1984). Others have found similar results in patients who were asked prior to CABG about their desire to return to work (Boll et al., 1987).

One approach used in research is the Sickness Impact Profile (SIP), which assesses a number of different domains of how sickness impacts activities *today* (Bergner et al., 1981). SIP is a 136-item self- or interviewer-administered, behaviorally based, health status questionnaire. Everyday activities in 12 categories are measured. The 12 categories are as follows:

1. Sleep and rest;
2. Emotional behavior;
3. Body care and movement;
4. Home management;
5. Mobility;
6. Social interaction;
7. Ambulation;
8. Alertness behavior;
9. Communication;
10. Work;
11. Recreation and pastimes; and
12. Eating.

Respondents endorse items that describe themselves and are related to their health. The SIP is scored and weighted according to the number and type of items endorsed. Scoring can be done at the level of categories and dimensions as well as at the total SIP level. Both physical and psychosocial domains as well as a total score are provided. This may be worth considering in research studies of disability to determine how such SIP scores correlate with standard exercise testing to establish capacity and provide a functional measure below which a person would be considered disabled.

In summary, there appears to be no single measure or combination of measures to determine fitness for any work. Given the combination of physical and psychological demands of work, the decision to return to work is likely dependent to a large extent on alternatives available to the patients. The extent to which individuals seek disability insurance after one or more cardiac events is a complex question in need of careful study.

Disability and Functional Limitation

Function with respect to cardiac disease is optimally assessed when the cardiovascular system is subjected to either physical or emotional stress testing; hence, numerous well-known stress-testing methods (both physical and emotional) have been developed, such as the step, bicycle ergometer, and exercise tolerance tests. More recently, the 6-minute walk test has evolved, either because the patient population was considered too frail to embark on a treadmill test or because of the unavailability of appropriate equipment. It is used most frequently in patients with heart failure (ATS, 2002).

Whether a graded exercise test correlates with the patient's everyday activities such as walking and housework has been evaluated. Patients' exercise performance was evaluated using a Naughton protocol, which provides a wide range of exercise durations to avoid submaximal exercise in patients with very low exercise tolerance. Exercise was stopped when the symptomatic endpoints—either angina or inability to continue to exercise because of extreme fatigue—were reached. Ventricular tachycardia and hypotension were other endpoints, and each patient achieved maximal effort according to his or her own symptoms (Neill et al., 1985).

Although this study aimed to identify limitations in self-care activities of daily living, it did not address limitations in performance of a minimal amount of work. It was concluded that low-exercise capacity due to angina does not necessarily prevent patients from carrying out their routine avocational activities. Further advancement in the medical management of CHD since 1985 is likely to better control symptoms of ischemia. It was also concluded that interventions to restore exercise capacity to normal might have little or no impact on behavior because there are many nonmedical determinants of adequate function for work (Neill et al., 1985).

Ischemic Heart Disease in Children

Ischemic heart disease in children is often due to structural anomalies of the proximal coronary arteries, coronary fistulae, Kawasaki disease, or injury to the coronary arteries during cardiac surgery. Ischemia may be evaluated using stress or resting echocardiography, radionuclide perfusion studies, or cardiac magnetic resonance imaging, but two abnormalities in two territories are not necessary for diagnosis of ischemia in children. Treatment of ischemia may involve surgical or cardiac interventional approaches.

CURRENT LISTING

The current listing for ischemic heart disease was updated in 2006 (72 FR 2312) when the cardiovascular Final Rule for Revised Medical Criteria for Evaluating Cardiovascular Impairments went into effect, replacing the previous 1994 listing (59 FR 55874). See Boxes 7-1 and 7-2 for the current adult and children ischemic heart disease listings.

CONCLUDING CONCEPTS

1. Treatment of CHD can dramatically improve a claimant's functional status. For instance, a claimant may have undergone medical testing with results that would meet the listing, but then may undergo coronary revascularization with complete resolution of ischemia and no functional limitations. Therefore, any claimant who has undergone revascularization should be reassessed 3 months or more following the revascularization procedure to determine his or her functional limitations. Similar improvements could also occur with optimal medical therapy, but less frequently than following revascularization.
2. Certain tests more accurately identify the presence of CHD than others. Functional limitation can be more accurately assessed by objective testing than by subjective symptoms. Consequently, there is a hierarchy of preferred tests. Specifically, a claimant may have results from both stress testing and cardiac catheterization (and coronary angiography) that could be discrepant. For instance, an exercise test may show severe ischemia, which alone might meet the listing criteria, but at catheterization minimal disease may be evident. The findings from catheterization should override the findings from a stress test. The same issue applies to the results of stress imaging as opposed to the stress electrocardiogram. In terms of determining functional limitation, objective testing performed on the

BOX 7-1
Current Adult Listing for Ischemic Heart Disease

4.04 Ischemic heart disease, with symptoms due to myocardial ischemia, as described in 4.00E3–4.00E7, while on a regimen of prescribed treatment (see 4.00B3 if there is no regimen of prescribed treatment), with one of the following:

A. Sign- or symptom-limited exercise tolerance test demonstrating at least one of the following manifestations at a workload equivalent to 5 METs or less:

1. Horizontal or downsloping depression, in the absence of digitalis glycoside treatment or hypokalemia, of the ST segment of at least –0.10 millivolts (–1.0 mm) in at least 3 consecutive complexes that are on a level baseline in any lead other than a VR, and depression of at least –0.10 millivolts lasting for at least 1 minute of recovery; or
2. At least 0.1 millivolt (1 mm) ST elevation above resting baseline in non-infarct leads during both exercise and 1 or more minutes of recovery; or
3. Decrease of 10 mm Hg or more in systolic pressure below the baseline blood pressure or the preceding systolic pressure measured during exercise (see 4.00E9e) due to left ventricular dysfunction, despite an increase in workload; or
4. Documented ischemia at an exercise level equivalent to 5 METs or less on appropriate medically acceptable imaging, such as radionuclide perfusion scans or stress echocardiography.

OR

B. Three separate ischemic episodes, each requiring revascularization or not amenable to revascularization (see 4.00E9f), within a consecutive 12-month period (see 4.00A3e).

OR

C. Coronary artery disease, demonstrated by angiography (obtained independent of Social Security disability evaluation) or other appropriate medically acceptable imaging, and in the absence of a timely exercise tolerance test or a timely normal drug-induced stress test, an MC, preferably one experienced in the care of patients with cardiovascular disease, has concluded that performance of exercise tolerance testing would present a significant risk to the individual, with both 1 and 2:

1. Angiographic evidence showing:
   a. 50 percent or more narrowing of a nonbypassed left main coronary artery; or
   b. 70 percent or more narrowing of another nonbypassed coronary artery; or
   c. 50 percent or more narrowing involving a long (greater than 1 cm) segment of a nonbypassed coronary artery; or
   d. 50 percent or more narrowing of at least two nonbypassed coronary arteries; or
   e. 70 percent or more narrowing of a bypass graft vessel; and
2. Resulting in very serious limitations in the ability to independently initiate, sustain, or complete activities of daily living.

SOURCE: SSA, 2008a.

BOX 7-2
Current Childhood Listing for Ischemic Heart Disease

What is ischemic heart disease (IHD) and how will we evaluate it in children? IHD results when one or more of your coronary arteries is narrowed or obstructed or, in rare situations, constricted due to vasospasm, interfering with the normal flow of blood to your heart muscle (ischemia). The obstruction may be the result of an embolus, a thrombus, or plaque. When heart muscle tissue dies as a result of the reduced blood supply, it is called a myocardial infarction (heart attack). Ischemia is rare in children, but when it occurs, its effects on children are the same as on adults. If you have IHD, we will evaluate it under 4.00E and 4.04 in part A.

SOURCE: SSA, 2008b.

treadmill should override symptom criteria (CCS III) whenever the stress-testing information and symptom criteria are discrepant. For instance, if the records indicate that a claimant has functional Class IV symptoms, but he or she then performs a stress test and exercises for 10 minutes, the results of the stress test should apply.

3. Although there is not a perfect correlation between functional limitation and symptoms and the extent of CAD, the claimant with three-vessel CAD will be much more likely to be limited by his or her CHD than a claimant who may have a 70 percent stenosis in a single branch vessel. Thus, the committee has recommended requiring that a claimant have at least two-vessel CAD by angiography. Recognizing that not all claimants will have undergone coronary angiography, the requirement for two coronary territories by stress imaging makes the application of the noninvasive criteria somewhat analogous to the invasive criteria.
4. Medical therapy is the cornerstone of treatment for patients with CHD no matter whether revascularization with PCI or CABG is performed. Effective lifestyle interventions for CHD include smoking cessation (Critchley and Capewell, 2003), dietary intervention (de Lorgeril et al., 1999; Leren, 1970), and exercise (O'Connor et al., 1989; Oldridge et al., 1988). Effective pharmacologic interventions include aspirin (Antithrombotic Trialists' Collaboration, 2002), beta-blockers (Lau et al., 1992; Yusuf et al., 1985), ACE inhibitors (Al-Mallah et al., 2006; Khalil et al., 2001), and statins (Baigent et al., 2005), which may reduce mortality among patients with CHD. Calcium channel blockers, long-acting nitrates, and ranolazine decrease angina symptoms and myocardial ischemia, but have not been shown to decrease mortality or MI in CHD patients.

ACC, AHA, and CCS recommend comprehensive lifestyle and pharmacologic interventions with specific risk factor targets (Antman et al., 2008; Gibbons et al., 2002a; Smith et al., 2006), although most cardiovascular clinical trials have tested a single intervention. The multiple simultaneous lifestyle and pharmacologic interventions (referred to as "optimal medical therapy") tested in the Clinical Outcomes Utilizing Revascularization and Aggressive Drug Evaluation (COURAGE) Trial (Boden et al., 2007b) exemplify the therapeutic model for routine clinical practice (Table 7-4).

FINAL CONCLUSIONS AND RECOMMENDATIONS

We have concluded that the extent of coronary artery disease alone, as assessed by coronary angiography, in the absence of symptoms does not render an applicant disabled at the listings level, and that evidence of functional limitations should also be required to meet the listings (see Figures 7-1 and 7-2).

RECOMMENDATION 7-1. The committee recommends that the definitive diagnosis of coronary heart disease (diagnosed by documented prior myocardial infarction OR prior coronary revascularization OR specific criteria on exercise or stress-imaging tests OR coronary angiography) in patients with Canadian Cardiovascular Society Class III or IV angina or anginal-equivalent symptoms be coupled with a functional limitation to meet a listing.

RECOMMENDATION 7-2. The committee recommends that one of four functional limitations be present to meet a listing:

1. **Clinical: Documentation of three separate ischemic episodes requiring unplanned hospitalization (inpatient or observation status), each requiring revascularization (three separate percutaneous coronary intervention [PCI] procedures or two PCI and one coronary artery bypass graft [CABG] procedure) if amenable to revascularization, within a consecutive 12-month period;**

OR

2. **Exercise stress test (with or without imaging): Ischemic response defined by ST-segment depression of greater than or equal to 1 mm measured 0.08 seconds after the J-point that is horizontal or downsloping in configuration or ST-segment elevation greater than or equal to 1 mm in leads without Q**

TABLE 7-4 Optimal Pharmacologic Therapy Based on the COURAGE Trial[a]

Medication Class	Indications
Aspirin	All subjects
Thienopyridine	In subjects with contraindication to aspirin; all PCI subjects (duration depends on BMS versus DES); post-MI/ACS for up to 1 year
ACE inhibitor	Hypertension, diabetes, LV systolic dysfunction, chronic kidney disease
Angiotensin-receptor blocker	Individuals with hypertension, diabetes, LV systolic dysfunction, or chronic kidney disease who are intolerant of ACE inhibitors
Beta-blocker	All post-MI patients unless contraindicated;[b] all others[c]
Thiazide diuretic	Hypertension, as indicated
Calcium antagonist	Hypertension; angina/ischemia
Long-acting nitrate	Angina/ischemia
Late inward Na^+ current inhibitor: ranolazine	Angina/ischemia
Other antianginal agents: ivabradine, trimetazadine, nicorandil	Angina/ischemia
Statin	All subjects
Niacin: extended-release niacin	LDL > 70 mg/dL (1.8 mmol/L), non-HDL > 100 mg/dL (2.6 mmol/L) if TG > 150 mg/dL (1.7 mmol/L) on statin, HDL < 40 mg/dL (1.0 mmol/L) in men, HDL < 50 mg/dL (1.3 mmol/L) in women
Cholesterol absorption inhibitor: ezetimibe	LDL > 70 mg/dL (1.8 mmol/L) on maximally tolerated dose of statin
Bile acid sequestrant	LDL > 70 mg/dL (1.8 mmol/L) on maximally tolerated dose of statin
Fibrate	TG > 150 mg/dL (1.7 mmol/L) on statin (not recommended for low HDL when TG < 150 mg/dL [1.69 mmol/L])
Omega-3 fatty acids	All subjects receive 1 gm/d; 2-4 gm/d to lower non-HDL < 100 mg/dL (2.6 mmol/L)

NOTE: ACE = angiotensin-converting enzyme; BMS = bare metal stents; DES = drug-eluting stent; HDL = high-density lipoprotein cholesterol; LDL = low-density lipoprotein cholesterol; LV = left ventricle; MI/ACS = myocardial infarction/acute coronary syndrome; PCI = percutaneous coronary intervention; TG = triglycerides.

[a] Subject to modification, pending finalization and subsequent changes to American College of Cardiology/American Heart Association (ACC/AHA) and European Society of Cardiology clinical practice guidelines for stable ischemic heart disease.

[b] Class I, Level of Evidence A, recommendation according to ACC/AHA guidelines.

[c] Class IIa, Level of Evidence C, recommendation according to ACC/AHA guidelines.

SOURCES: Boden et al., 2006, 2007a; Maron et al., 2010; O'Gara, 2010.

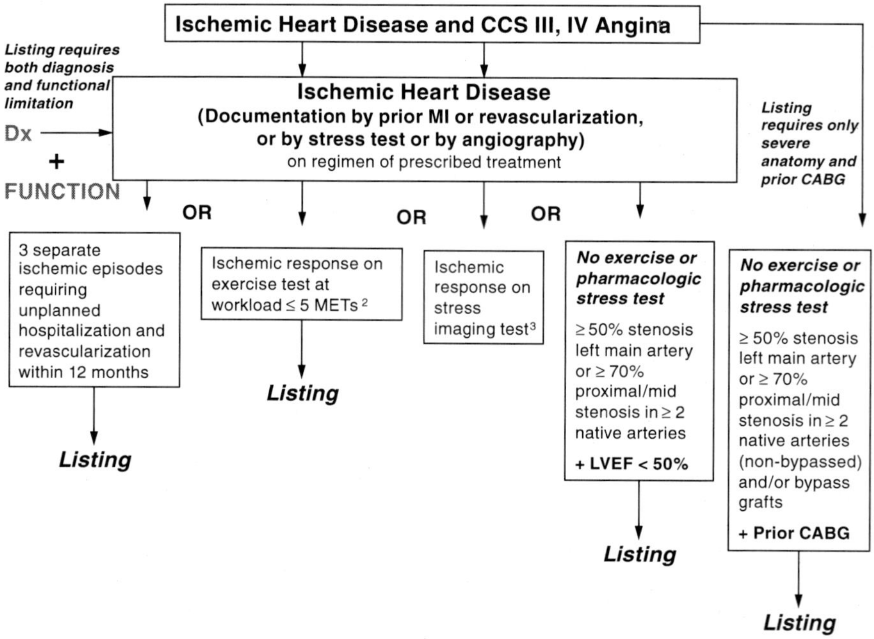

FIGURE 7-1 Coronary heart disease listings.
NOTE: CABG = coronary artery bypass graft; CCS = Canadian Cardiovascular Society; Dx = diagnosis; LVEF = left ventricular ejection fraction; METs = metabolic equivalents of task; MI = myocardial infarction.
[1] Defined in report: Canadian Cardiovascular Society Class III or IV.
[2] Defined in report: See Recommendation 7-2.
[3] Defined in report: See Recommendation 7-2.

waves or fall in systolic blood pressure greater than or equal to 10 mm Hg below resting systolic blood pressure at a workload of less than or equal to 5 metabolic equivalents of task;

OR

3. **Stress-imaging test: Ischemic response with either exercise or pharmacologic vasodilator stress indicated by greater than or equal to two reversible and/or fixed regional myocardial perfusion defects during nuclear testing and transient ischemic dilation *or* resting left ventricular ejection fraction (LVEF) less than 50 percent, OR greater than or equal to two reversible and/or fixed regional wall motion abnormalities and either a fall in LVEF OR resting LVEF less than 50 percent;**

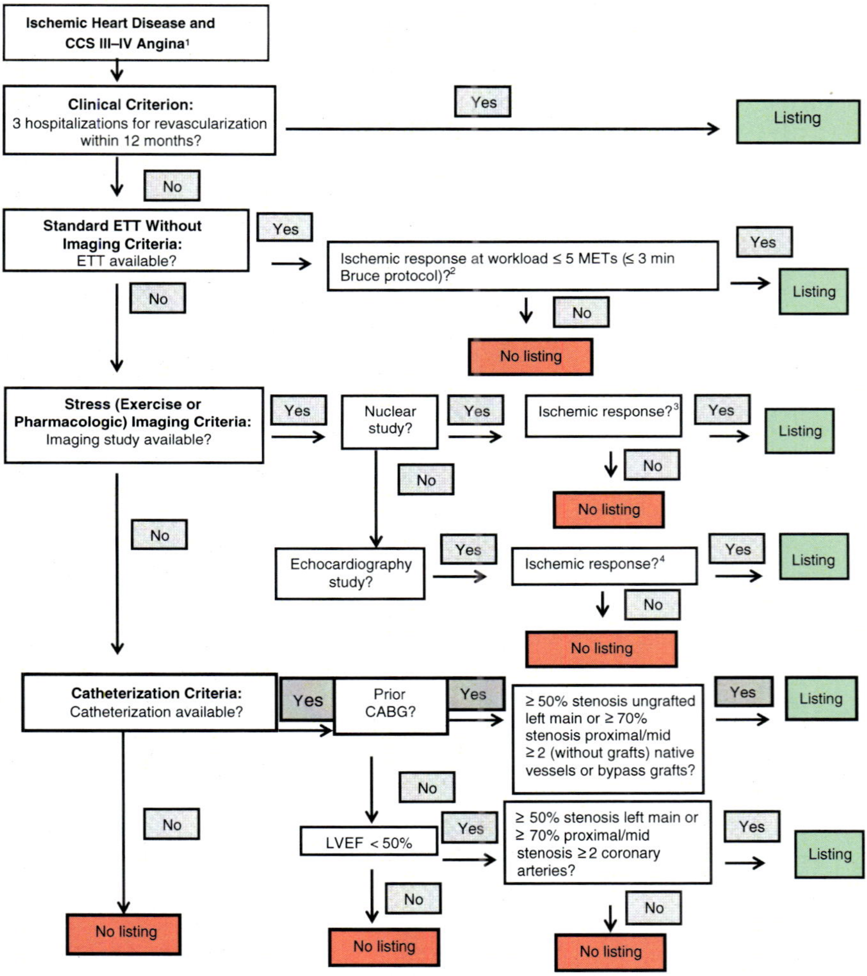

FIGURE 7-2 Coronary heart disease listings: Ischemic heart disease ladder flow diagram.

NOTE: CABG = coronary artery bypass graft; CCS = Canadian Cardiovascular Society; ETT = exercise tolerance test; LVEF = left ventricular ejection fraction; METs = metabolic equivalents of task.

[1] Defined: Canadian Cardiovascular Society Class III or IV.

[2] Defined in report: See Recommendation 7-2.

[3] Defined in report: See Recommendation 7-2.

[4] Defined in report: See Recommendation 7-2.

OR

4. **Among patients who have not had prior CABG, severe coronary heart disease with either 50 percent stenosis in the left main artery or greater than or equal to 70 percent stenosis in the proximal or midportion of greater than or equal to two major coronary arteries and a LVEF less than 50 percent.**

RECOMMENDATION 7-3. The committee recommends that patients with prior coronary artery bypass graft and either severe disease in native coronary arteries that have not been bypassed (greater than or equal to 50 percent stenosis in the left main artery or greater than or equal to 70 percent stenosis in the proximal or midportion of greater than or equal to two major native coronary arteries) and/or greater than or equal to 70 percent stenosis in greater than or equal to two bypass grafts and with Canadian Cardiovascular Society Class III or IV angina (or angina-equivalent symptoms) meet a listing.

RECOMMENDATION 7-4. The committee recommends that children who are disabled prior to interventions are considered as disabled until 6 months following surgery and then reevaluated. The table of pharmacologic interventions for ischemia in adults cannot be applied to children as necessarily appropriate therapies.

REFERENCES

Abbott, J., and N. Berry. 1991. Return to work during the year following first myocardial infarction. *British Journal of Clinical Psychology* 30(Pt 3):268–270.

Akhtar, M., G. F. Wu, Z. M. Du, Z. S. Zheng, and A. D. Michaels. 2006. Effect of external counterpulsation on plasma nitric oxide and endothelin-1 levels. *American Journal of Cardiology* 98(1):28–30.

Al-Mallah, M. H., I. M. Tleyjeh, A. A. Abdel-Latif, and W. D. Weaver. 2006. Angiotensin-converting enzyme inhibitors in coronary artery disease and preserved left ventricular systolic function: A systematic review and meta-analysis of randomized controlled trials. *Journal of the American College of Cardiology* 47(8):1576–1583.

Anderson, J. L., C. D. Adams, E. M. Antman, C. R. Bridges, R. M. Califf, D. E. Casey Jr., W. E. Chavey II, F. M. Fesmire, J. S. Hochman, T. N. Levin, A. M. Lincoff, E. D. Peterson, P. Theroux, N. K. Wenger, R. S. Wright, S. C. Smith Jr., A. K. Jacobs, J. L. Halperin, S. A. Hunt, H. M. Krumholz, F. G. Kushner, B. W. Lytle, R. Nishimura, J. P. Ornato, R. L. Page, and B. Riegel. 2007. ACC/AHA 2007 guidelines for the management of patients with unstable angina/non-ST-elevation myocardial infarction: A report of the American College of Cardiology/American Heart Association Task Force on Practice Guidelines (Writing Committee to Revise the 2002 Guidelines for the Management of Patients with Unstable Angina/Non-ST-Elevation Myocardial Infarction) developed in collaboration with the American College of Emergency Physicians, the Society for Cardiovascular Angiography and Interventions, and the Society of Thoracic Surgeons endorsed by the American Association of Cardiovascular and Pulmonary Rehabilitation and the Society for Academic Emergency Medicine. *Journal of the American College of Cardiology* 50(7):e1–e157.

Antithrombotic Trialists' Collaboration. 2002. Collaborative meta-analysis of randomised trials of antiplatelet therapy for prevention of death, myocardial infarction, and stroke in high risk patients. *British Medical Journal* 324(7329):71–86.

Antman, E. M., D. T. Anbe, P. W. Armstrong, E. R. Bates, L. A. Green, M. Hand, J. S. Hochman, H. M. Krumholz, F. G. Kushner, G. A. Lamas, C. J. Mullany, J. P. Ornato, D. L. Pearle, M. A. Sloan, S. C. Smith Jr., J. S. Alpert, J. L. Anderson, D. P. Faxon, V. Fuster, R. J. Gibbons, G. Gregoratos, J. L. Halperin, L. F. Hiratzka, S. A. Hunt, and A. K. Jacobs. 2004. ACC/AHA guidelines for the management of patients with ST-elevation myocardial infarction: A report of the American College of Cardiology/American Heart Association Task Force on Practice Guidelines (Committee to Revise the 1999 Guidelines for the Management of Patients with Acute Myocardial Infarction). *Circulation* 110(9): e82–e293.

Antman, E. M., M. H. Hand, P. W. Armstrong, E. R. Bates, L. A. Green, L. K. Halasyamani, J. S. Hochman, H. M. Krumholz, G. A. Lamas, C. J. Mullany, D. L. Pearle, M. A. Sloan, S. C. Smith Jr.; 2004 Writing Committee Members: E. M. Antman, D. T. Anbe, P. W. Armstrong, E. R. Bates, L. A. Green, M. Hand, J. S. Hochman, H. M. Krumholz, F. G. Kushner, G. A. Lamas, C. J. Mullany, J. P. Ornato, D. L. Pearle, M. A. Sloan, S. C. Smith Jr.; and Task Force Members: S. C. Smith Jr., A. K. Jacobs, C. D. Adams, J. L. Anderson, C. E. Buller, M. A. Creager, S. M. Ettinger, J. L. Halperin, S. A. Hunt, H. M. Krumholz, F. G. Kushner, B. W. Lytle, R. Nishimura, R. L. Page, B. Riegel, L. G. Tarkington, and C. W. Yancy. 2008. 2007 focused update of the ACC/AHA 2004 guidelines for the management of patients with ST-elevation myocardial infarction: A report of the American College of Cardiology/American Heart Association Task Force on Practice Guidelines: Developed in collaboration with the Canadian Cardiovascular Society endorsed by the American Academy of Family Physicians: 2007 Writing Group to Review New Evidence and Update the ACC/AHA 2004 Guidelines for the Management of Patients with ST-Elevation Myocardial Infarction, writing on behalf of the 2004 writing committee. *Circulation* 117(2):296–329.

ATS (American Thoracic Society). 2002. ATS statement: Guidelines for the six-minute walk test. *American Journal of Respiratory & Critical Care Medicine* 166(1):111–117.

Baigent, C., A. Keech, P. M. Kearney, L. Blackwell, G. Buck, C. Pollicino, A. Kirby, T. Sourjina, R. Peto, R. Collins, R. Simes, and Cholesterol Treatment Trialists' (CTT) Collaborators. 2005. Efficacy and safety of cholesterol-lowering treatment: Prospective meta-analysis of data from 90,056 participants in 14 randomised trials of statins. *Lancet* 366(9493):1267–1278.

Bergner, M., R. A. Bobbitt, W. B. Carter, and B. S. Gilson. 1981. The sickness impact profile: Development and final revision of a health status measure. *Medical Care* 19(8):787–805.

Boden, W. E., R. A. O'Rourke, K. K. Teo, P. M. Hartigan, D. J. Maron, W. Kostuk, M. Knudtson, M. Dada, P. Casperson, C. L. Harris, J. A. Spertus, L. Shaw, B. R. Chaitman, G. B. J. Mancini, D. S. Berman, and W. S. Weintraub. 2006. Design and rationale of the Clinical Outcomes Utilizing Revascularization and Aggressive DruG Evaluation (COURAGE) trial: Veterans Affairs cooperative studies program no. 424. *American Heart Journal* 151:1173–1179.

Boden, W. E., R. A. O'Rourke, K. K. Teo, P. M. Hartigan, D. J. Maron, W. Kostuk, M. Knudtson, M. Dada, P. Casperson, C. L. Harris, J. A. Spertus, L. Shaw, B. R. Chaitman, G. B. J. Mancini, D. S. Berman, G. Gau, and W. S. Weintraub. 2007a. The evolving pattern of symptomatic coronary artery disease in the United States and Canada: Baseline characteristics of the Clinical Outcomes Utilizing Revascularization and Aggressive DruG Evaluation (COURAGE) trial. *American Journal of Cardiology* 99:208–212.

Boden, W. E., R. A. O'Rourke, K. K. Teo, P. M. Hartigan, D. J. Maron, W. J. Kostuk, M. Knudtson, M. Dada, P. Casperson, C. L. Harris, B. R. Chaitman, L. Shaw, G. Gosselin, S. Nawaz, L. M. Title, G. Gau, A. S. Blaustein, D. C. Booth, E. R. Bates, J. A. Spertus, D. S. Berman, G. B. J. Mancini, and W. S. Weintraub, for the COURAGE Trial Research Group. 2007b. Optimal medical therapy with or without PCI for stable coronary disease. *The New England Journal of Medicine* 356:1503–1516.

Boll, A., L. Klatt, J. Koch, and A. F. Langbehn. 1987. Psychosocial factors influencing return to work after coronary artery bypass surgery (CABS). *International Journal of Rehabilitation Research* 10:145–154.

Boudrez, H., and G. De Backer. 2000. Recent findings on return to work after an acute myocardial infarction or coronary artery bypass grafting. *Acta Cardiologica* 55(6):341–349.

Boudrez, H., G. De Backer, and B. Comhaire. 1994. Return to work after myocardial infarction: Results of a longitudinal population based study. *European Heart Journal* 15(1):32–36.

Budoff, M. J., S. Achenbach, R. S. Blumenthal, J. J. Carr, J. G. Goldin, P. Greenland, A. D. Guerci, J. A. C. Lima, D. J. Rader, G. D. Rubin, L. J. Shaw, and S. E. Wiegers. 2006. Assessment of coronary artery disease by cardiac computed tomography: A scientific statement from the American Heart Association Committee on Cardiovascular Imaging and Intervention, Council on Cardiovascular Radiology and Intervention, and Committee on Cardiac Imaging, Council on Clinical Cardiology. *Circulation* 114(16):1761–1791.

Campeau, L. 1976. Grading of angina pectoris. *Circulation* 54:5223.

Campeau, L. 2002. The Canadian Cardiovascular Society grading of angina pectoris revisited 30 years later. *Canadian Journal of Cardiology* 18(4):371–379.

CAPRICORN Investigators. 2001. Capricorn Trial abstract. *Lancet* 357:1385–1390.

Carney, R. M., and K. E. Freedland. 2008. Depression in patients with coronary heart disease. *American Journal of Medicine* 121:S20–S27.

Cay, E. L., and D. D. Walker. 1988. Psychological factors and return to work. *European Heart Journal* 9(Suppl L):74–81.

Cerqueira, M. D., N. J. Weissman, V. Dilsizian, A. K. Jacobs, S. Kaul, W. K. Laskey, D. J. Pennell, J. A. Rumberger, T. Ryan, and M. S. Verani. 2002. Standardized myocardial segmentation and nomenclature for tomographic imaging of the heart: A statement for healthcare professionals from the Cardiac Imaging Committee of the Council on Clinical Cardiology of the American Heart Association. *Circulation* 105(4):539–542.

Chaitman, B. R. 2006. Ranolazine for the treatment of chronic angina and potential use in other cardiovascular conditions. *Circulation* 113(20):2462–2472.

Chaitman, B. R., C. J. Pepine, J. O. Parker, J. Skopal, G. Chumakova, J. Kuch, W. Wang, S. L. Skettino, and A. A. Wolff. 2004. Effects of ranolazine with atenolol, amlodipine, or diltiazem on exercise tolerance and angina frequency in patients with severe chronic angina: A randomized controlled trial. *Journal of the American Medical Association* 291(3):309–316.

Chen, J., S.-L. T. Normand, Y. Wang, E. E. Drye, G. C. Schreiner, and H. M. Krumholz. 2010. Recent declines in hospitalizations for acute myocardial infarction for Medicare fee-for-service beneficiaries: Progress and continuing challenges. *Circulation* 121(11): 1322–1328.

Critchley, J. A., and S. Capewell. 2003. Mortality risk reduction associated with smoking cessation in patients with coronary heart disease: A systematic review. *Journal of the American Medical Association* 290(1):86–97.

de Jonge, P., T. A. Spijkerman, R. H. S. van den Brink, and J. Ormel. 2006. Depression after myocardial infarction is a risk factor for declining health related quality of life and increased disability and cardiac complaints at 12 months. *Heart* 92(1):32–39.

de Lorgeril, M., P. Salen, J.-L. Martin, I. Monjaud, J. Delaye, and N. Mamelle. 1999. Mediterranean diet, traditional risk factors, and the rate of cardiovascular complications after myocardial infarction: Final report of the Lyon diet heart study. *Circulation* 99(6):779–785.

Dennis, C. 1990. Vocational capacity with cardiac impairment. In *Medical perspectives in vocational assessment of impaired workers*, edited by S. J. Scheer. Rockville, MD: Aspen Publishers. Pp. 301–334.

Drory, Y., S. Kravetz, N. Koren-Morag, U. Goldbourt, and Israel Study Group on First Acute Myocardial Infarction. 2005. Resumption and maintenance of employment after a first acute myocardial infarction: Sociodemographic, vocational and medical predictors. *Cardiology* 103(1):37–43.

Dubach, P., V. F. Froelicher, J. Klein, D. Oakes, M. Grover-McKay, and R. Friis. 1988. Exercise-induced hypotension in a male population. Criteria, causes, and prognosis. *Circulation* 78(6):1380–1387.

Eagle, K. A., R. A. Guyton, R. Davidoff, F. H. Edwards, G. A. Ewy, T. J. Gardner, J. C. Hart, H. C. Herrmann, L. D. Hillis, A. M. Hutter Jr., B. W. Lytle, R. A. Marlow, W. C. Nugent, T. A. Orszulak, E. M. Antman, S. C. Smith Jr., J. S. Alpert, J. L. Anderson, D. P. Faxon, V. Fuster, R. J. Gibbons, G. Gregoratos, J. L. Halperin, L. F. Hiratzka, S. A. Hunt, A. K. Jacobs, and J. P. Ornato. 2004. ACC/AHA 2004 guideline update for coronary artery bypass graft surgery: Summary article: A report of the American College of Cardiology/American Heart Association Task Force on Practice Guidelines (Committee to Update the 1999 Guidelines for Coronary Artery Bypass Graft Surgery). *Circulation* 110(9):1168–1176.

Egred, M., S. Shaw, B. Mohammad, P. Waitt, and E. Rodrigues. 2005. Under-use of beta-blockers in patients with ischaemic heart disease and concomitant chronic obstructive pulmonary disease. *QJM: An International Journal of Medicine* 98(7):493–497.

Fletcher, G. F., G. J. Balady, E. A. Amsterdam, B. Chaitman, R. Eckel, J. Fleg, V. F. Froelicher, A. S. Leon, I. L. Pina, R. Rodney, D. A. Simons-Morton, M. A. Williams, and T. Bazzarre. 2001. Exercise standards for testing and training: A statement for healthcare professionals from the American Heart Association. *Circulation* 104(14):1694–1740.

Fraker, T., and S. D. Fihn, writing on behalf of the 2002 Chronic Stable Angina Writing Committee. 2007. 2007 chronic angina focused update of the ACC/AHA 2002 guidelines for the management of patients with chronic stable angina: A report of the American College of Cardiology/American Heart Association Task Force on Practice Guidelines Writing Group to Develop the Focused Update of the 2002 Guidelines for the Management of Patients with Chronic Stable Angina. *Journal of the American College of Cardiology* 50:2264–2274.

Froelicher, E. S., L. L. Kee, K. M. Newton, B. Lindskog, and M. Livingston. 1994. Return to work, sexual activity, and other activities after acute myocardial infarction. *Heart & Lung* 23(5):423–435.

Froom, P., C. Cohen, J. Rashcupkin, E. Kristal-Boneh, S. Melamed, J. Benbassat, and J. Ribak. 1999. Referral to occupational medicine clinics and resumption of employment after myocardial infarction. *Journal of Occupational & Environmental Medicine* 41(11):943–947.

Gibbons, R. J., J. Abrams, K. Chatterjee, J. Daley, P. C. Deedwania, J. S. Douglas, T. B. Ferguson Jr., S. D. Fihn, T. D. Fraker Jr., J. M. Gardin, R. A. O'Rourke, R. C. Pasternak, and S. V. Williams (members of the Committee to Update the 1999 Guidelines for the Management of Patients with Chronic Stable Angina), and R. J. Gibbons, E. M. Antman, J. S. Alpert, D. P. Faxon, V. Fuster, G. Gregoratos, L. F. Hiratzka, A. K. Jacobs, and S. C. Smith Jr. (members of the Task Force on Practice Guidelines). 2002a. *ACC/AHA 2002 guideline update for the management of patients with chronic stable angina: A report of the American College of Cardiology/American Heart Association Task Force on Practice Guidelines (Committee on the Management of Patients with*

Chronic Stable Angina). http://www.acc.org/clinical/guidelines/stable/stable.pdf (accessed July 8, 2010).

Gibbons, R. J., G. J. Balady, J. T. Bricker, B. R. Chaitman, G. F. Fletcher, V. F. Froelicher, D. B. Mark, B. D. McCallister, A. N. Mooss, M. G. O'Reilly, W. L. Winters Jr., and Task Force members, E. M. Antman, J. S. Alpert, D. P. Faxon, V. Fuster, G. Gregoratos, L. F. Hiratzka, A. K. Jacobs, R. O. Russell, and S. C. Smith Jr. 2002b. ACC/AHA 2002 guideline update for exercise testing: A report of the American College of Cardiology/American Heart Association Task Force on Practice Guidelines (Committee to Update the 1997 Exercise Testing Guidelines). *Circulation* 106:1883–1892.

Goldman, L., B. Hashimoto, E. F. Cook, and A. Loscalzo. 1981. Comparative reproducibility and validity of systems for assessing cardiovascular functional class: Advantages of a new specific activity scale. *Circulation* 64(6):1227–1234.

Goldstein, D. J., M. C. Oz, and E. A. Rose. 1998. Implantable left ventricular assist devices. *New England Journal of Medicine* 339(21):1522–1533.

Herlitz, J., B. W. Karlson, M. Sjölin, H. E. Ekvall, and A. Hjalmarson. 1994. Prognosis during one year of follow-up after acute myocardial infarction with emphasis on morbidity. *Clinical Cardiology* 17(1):15–20.

Hlatky, M. A., T. Haney, J. C. Barefoot, R. M. Califf, D. B. Mark, D. B. Pryor, and R. B. Williams. 1986. Medical, psychological and social correlates of work disability among men with coronary artery disease. *American Journal of Cardiology* 58(10):911–915.

Khalil, M. E., A. W. Basher, E. J. Brown Jr., and I. A. Alhaddad. 2001. A remarkable medical story: Benefits of angiotensin-converting enzyme inhibitors in cardiac patients. *Journal of the American College of Cardiology* 37(7):1757–1764.

Klocke, F. J., M. G. Baird, B. H. Lorell, T. M. Bateman, J. V. Messer, D. S. Berman, P. T. O'Gara, B. A. Carabello, R. O. Russell Jr., M. D. Cerqueira, M. G. St. John Sutton, A. N. DeMaria, J. E. Udelson, J. W. Kennedy, M. S. Verani, K. A. Williams, E. M. Antman, S. C. Smith Jr., J. S. Alpert, G. Gregoratos, J. L. Anderson, L. F. Hiratzka, D. P. Faxon, S. A. Hunt, V. Fuster, A. K. Jacobs, R. J. Gibbons, and R. O. Russell. 2003. ACC/AHA/ASNC guidelines for the clinical use of cardiac radionuclide imaging—Executive summary: A report of the American College of Cardiology/American Heart Association Task Force on Practice Guidelines (ACC/AHA/ASNC Committee to Revise the 1995 Guidelines for the Clinical Use of Cardiac Radionuclide Imaging). *Circulation* 108:1404–1418.

Kushner, F. G., M. Hand, S. C. Smith Jr., S. B. King III, J. L. Anderson, E. M. Antman, S. R. Bailey, E. R. Bates, J. C. Blankenship, D. E. Casey Jr., L. A. Green, J. S. Hochman, A. K. Jacobs, H. M. Krumholz, D. A. Morrison, J. P. Ornato, D. L. Pearle, E. D. Peterson, M. A. Sloan, P. L. Whitlow, and D. O. Williams. 2009. 2009 focused updates: ACC/AHA guidelines for the management of patients with ST-elevation myocardial infarction (updating the 2004 guideline and 2007 focused update) and ACC/AHA/SCAI guidelines on percutaneous coronary intervention (updating the 2005 guideline and 2007 focused update): A report of the American College of Cardiology Foundation/American Heart Association Task Force on Practice Guidelines. *Journal of the American College of Cardiology* 54(23):2205–2241.

Lau, J., E. Antman, J. Jimenez-Silva, B. Kupelnick, F. Mosteller, and T. Chalmers. 1992. Cumulative meta-analysis of therapeutic trials for myocardial infarction. *New England Journal of Medicine* 327(4):248–254.

Leren, P. 1970. The Oslo diet-heart study: Eleven-year report. *Circulation* 42(5):935–942.

Lloyd-Jones, D., R. J. Adams, T. M. Brown, M. Carnethon, S. Dai, G. De Simone, T. B. Ferguson, E. Ford, K. Furie, C. Gillespie, A. Go, K. Greenlund, N. Haase, S. Hailpern, P. M. Ho, V. Howard, B. Kissela, S. Kittner, D. Lackland, L. Lisabeth, A. Marelli, M. M. McDermott, J. Meigs, D. Mozaffarian, M. Mussolino, G. Nichol, V. Roger, W. Rosamond, R. Sacco, P. Sorlie, R. Stafford, T. Thom, S. Wasserthiel-Smoller, N. D. Wong, and J. Wylie-Rosett, on behalf of the American Heart Association Statistics Committee

Stroke Statistics Subcommittee. 2010. Heart disease and stroke statistics—2010 update: A report from the American Heart Association. *Circulation* 121(7):e46–e215.

Maeland, J. G., and O. E. Havik. 1986. Return to work after a myocardial infarction: The influence of background factors, work characteristics and illness severity. *Scandinavian Journal of Social Medicine* 14(4):183–195.

Maeland, J. G., and O. E. Havik. 1987. Psychological predictors for return to work after a myocardial infarction. *Journal of Psychosomatic Research* 31(4):471–481.

Mark, D. B., L. C. Lam, K. L. Lee, N. E. Clapp-Channing, R. B. Williams, D. B. Pryor, R. M. Califf, and M. A. Hlatky. 1992. Identification of patients with coronary disease at high risk for loss of employment. A prospective validation study. *Circulation* 86(5):1485–1494.

Mark, D. B., D. S. Berman, M. J. Budoff, J. J. Carr, T. C. Gerber, H. S. Hecht, M. A. Hlatky, J. M. Hodgson, M. S. Lauer, J. M. Miller, R. L. Morin, D. Mukherjee, M. Poon, G. D. Rubin, and R. S. Schwartz. 2010. ACCF/ACR/AHA/NASCI/SAIP/SCAI/SCCT 2010 expert consensus document on coronary computed tomographic angiography: A report of the American College of Cardiology Foundation Task Force on Expert Consensus Documents. *Journal of the American College of Cardiology* 55(23):2663–2699.

Maron, D. J., W. E. Boden, R. A. O'Rourke, P. M. Hartigan, K. J. Calfas, G. B. J. Mancini, J. A. Spertus, M. Dada, W. J. Kostuk, M. Knudtson, C. L. Harris, S. P. Sedlis, R. G. Zoble, L. M. Title, G. Gosselin, S. Nawaz, G. T. Gau, A. S. Blaustein, E. R. Bates, L. J. Shaw, D. S. Berman, B. R. Chaitman, W. S. Weintraub, and K. K. Teo, for the COURAGE Trial Research Group. 2010. Intensive multifactorial intervention for stable coronary artery disease: Optimal medical therapy in the COURAGE (Clinical Outcomes Utilizing Revascularization and Aggressive Drug Evaluation) trial. *Journal of the American College of Cardiology* 55(13):1348–1358.

McNeer, J. F., J. R. Margolis, K. L. Lee, J. A. Kisslo, R. H. Peter, Y. Kong, V. S. Behar, A. G. Wallace, C. B. McCants, and R. A. Rosati. 1978. The role of the exercise test in the evaluation of patients for ischemic heart disease. *Circulation* 57(1):64–70.

Michaels, A. D., G. Linnemeier, O. Soran, S. F. Kelsey, and E. D. Kennard. 2004. Two-year outcomes after enhanced external counterpulsation for stable angina pectoris (from the International EECP Patient Registry [IEPR]). *American Journal of Cardiology* 93:461–464.

Miller, J. M., C. E. Rochitte, M. Dewey, A. Arbab-Zadeh, H. Niinuma, I. Gottlieb, N. Paul, M. E. Clouse, E. P. Shapiro, J. Hoe, A. C. Lardo, D. E. Bush, A. deRoos, C. Cox, J. Brinker, and J. A. C. Lima. 2008. Diagnostic performance of coronary angiography by 64-row CT. *New England Journal of Medicine* 359:2324–2336.

Mital, A., A. Desai, and A. Mital. 2004. Return to work after a coronary event. *Journal of Cardiopulmonary Rehabilitation* 24(6):365–373.

Mittag, O., K. D. Kolenda, K. J. Nordman, J. Bernien, and C. Maurischat. 2001. Return to work after myocardial infarction/coronary artery bypass grafting: Patients' and physicians' initial viewpoints and outcome 12 months later. *Social Science & Medicine* 52(9):1441–1450.

Morrow, D. A., B. M. Scirica, E. Karwatowska-Prokopczuk, S. A. Murphy, A. Budaj, S. Varshavsky, A. A. Wolff, A. Skene, C. H. McCabe, and E. Braunwald, for the MERLIN-TIMI 36 Trial Investigators. 2007. Effects of ranolazine on recurrent cardiovascular events in patients with non-ST-elevation acute coronary syndromes: The MERLIN-TIMI 36 randomized trial. *Journal of the American Medical Association* 297(16):1775–1783.

Myrtek, M., A. Kaiser, B. Rauch, and G. Jansen. 1997. Factors associated with work resumption: A 5 year follow-up with cardiac patients. *International Journal of Cardiology* 59(3):291–297.

Neill, W. A., L. G. Branch, G. De Jong, N. E. Smith, C. A. Hogan, P. J. Corcoran, A. M. Jette, E. M. Balasco, and S. Osberg. 1985. Cardiac disability. The impact of coronary heart disease on patients' daily activities. *Archives of Internal Medicine* 145(9):1642–1647.

Novack, V., D. Cutlip, N. Kleiman, M. Pencina, L. Mauri, C.-H. Yen, P. Berger, S. Goldberg, M. Kellett, R. Waksman, M. Hong, A. E. Raizner, and D. J. Cohen. 2009. In-hospital and 1-year outcomes among unselected percutaneous coronary intervention patients treated with either sirolimus- or paclitaxel-eluting stents: Results from the EVENT (Evaluation of Drug Eluting Stents and Ischemic Events) Registry. *Journal of the American College of Cardiology: Cardiovascular Interventions* 2(8):767–775.

O'Connor, G., J. Buring, S. Yusuf, S. Goldhaber, E. Olmstead, R. Paffenbarger Jr., and C. Hennekens. 1989. An overview of randomized trials of rehabilitation with exercise after myocardial infarction. *Circulation* 80(2):234–244.

O'Gara, P. T. 2010. The COURAGE (Clinical Outcomes Utilizing Revascularization and Aggressive Drug Evaluation) trial: Can we deliver on its promise? *Journal of the American College of Cardiology* 55:1359–1361.

Oldridge, N. B., G. H. Guyatt, M. E. Fischer, and A. A. Rimm. 1988. Cardiac rehabilitation after myocardial infarction: Combined experience of randomized clinical trials. *Journal of the American Medical Association* 260(7):945–950.

Papakostas, G. I. 2009. Major depressive disorder: Psychosocial impairment and key considerations in functional improvement. *American Journal of Managed Care* 15:S316–S321.

Pellikka, P. A., S. F. Nagueh, A. A. Elhendy, C. A. Kuehl, S. G. Sawada, and the American Society of Echocardiography. 2007. American Society of Echocardiography recommendations for performance, interpretation, and application of stress echocardiography. *Journal of the American Society of Echocardiography* 20(9):1021–1241.

Poston, R. S., R. Tran, M. Collins, M. Reynolds, I. Connerney, B. Reicher, D. Zimrin, B. P. Griffith, and S. T. Bartlett. 2008. Comparison of economic and patient outcomes with minimally invasive versus traditional off-pump coronary artery bypass grafting techniques. *Annals of Surgery* 248(4):638–646.

Rannevik, P. K. 1988. Predicting return to work after acute myocardial infarction: Significance of clinical data, exercise test variables and beta-blocker therapy. *Cardiology* 75:230–236.

Rost, K., and G. R. Smith. 1992. Return to work after an initial myocardial infarction and subsequent emotional distress. *Archives of Internal Medicine* 152(2):381–385.

Sabik, J. F., A. M. Gillinov, E. H. Blackstone, C. Vacha, P. L. Houghtaling, J. Navia, N. G. Smedira, P. M. McCarthy, D. M. Cosgrove, and B. W. Lytle. 2002. Does off-pump coronary surgery reduce morbidity and mortality? *Journal of Thoracic and Cardiovascular Surgery* 124(4):698–707.

Safilious-Rothchild, C. 1970. The successful rehabilitant. In *The sociology and social psychology of disability and rehabilitation*, edited by C. Safilious-Rothchild. New York: Random House. Pp. 216–249.

Sellier, P., P. Varaillac, G. Chatellier, M. C. D'Agrosa-Boiteux, H. Douard, C. Dubois, P. C. Goepfert, C. Monpère, and A. S. Pierre, on behalf of the investigators of the PERISCOP study. 2003. Factors influencing return to work at one year after coronary bypass graft surgery: Results of the PERISCOP study. *European Journal of Cardiovascular Prevention & Rehabilitation* 10(6):469–475.

Shanfield, S. B. 1990. Return to work after an acute myocardial infarction: A review. *Heart & Lung* 19(2):109–117.

Sivarajan, E. S., and K. M. Newton. 1984. Exercise, education, and counseling for patients with coronary artery disease. *Clinics in Sports Medicine* 3(2):349–369.

Smith, G. R., Jr., and D. F. O'Rourke. 1988. Return to work after a first myocardial infarction. A test of multiple hypotheses. *Journal of the American Medical Association* 259(11):1673–1677.

Smith, S. C., Jr., J. Allen, S. N. Blair, R. O. Bonow, L. M. Brass, G. C. Fonarow, S. M. Grundy, L. Hiratzka, D. Jones, H. M. Krumholz, L. Mosca, R. C. Pasternak, T. Pearson, M. A. Pfeffer, and K. A. Taubert. 2006. AHA/ACC guidelines for secondary prevention for patients with coronary and other atherosclerotic vascular disease: 2006 update: Endorsed by the National Heart, Lung, and Blood Institute. *Circulation* 113(19):2363–2372.

Soderman, E., J. Lisspers, and O. Sundin. 2003. Depression as a predictor of return to work in patients with coronary artery disease. *Social Science & Medicine* 56(1):193–202.

Soran, O., E. D. Kennard, A. G. Kfoury, and S. F. Kelsey. 2006. Two-year clinical outcomes after enhanced external counterpulsation (EECP) therapy in patients with refractory angina pectoris and left ventricular dysfunction (report from the International EECP Patient Registry). *American Journal of Cardiology* 97(1):17–20.

Speziale, G., F. Bilotta, G. Ruvolo, K. Fattouch, and B. Marino. 1996. Return to work and quality of life measurement in coronary artery bypass grafting. *European Journal of Cardio-Thoracic Surgery* 10(10):852–858.

SSA (Social Security Administration). 2008a. *Listing of impairments—Adult listings (Part A). Disability evaluation under Social Security (Blue Book).* http://www.socialsecurity.gov/disability/professionals/bluebook/AdultListings.htm (accessed July 22, 2010).

SSA. 2008b. *Listing of impairments—Childhood listings (Part B). Disability evaluation under Social Security (Blue Book).* http://www.socialsecurity.gov/disability/professionals/bluebook/ChildhoodListings.htm (accessed July 22, 2010).

Stahl, K. D., W. D. Boyd, T. A. Vassiliades, and H. L. Karamanoukian. 2002. Hybrid robotic coronary artery surgery and angioplasty in multivessel coronary artery disease. *Annals of Thoracic Surgery* 74(4):S1358–S1362.

Sullivan, M. D., A. Z. LaCroix, C. Baum, L. C. Grothaus, and W. J. Katon. 1997. Functional status in coronary artery disease: A one-year prospective study of the role of anxiety and depression. *American Journal of Medicine* 103(5):348–356.

Taylor, R., J. De Vries, E. Buchser, and M. DeJongste. 2009. Spinal cord stimulation in the treatment of refractory angina: Systematic review and meta-analysis of randomised controlled trials. *BMC Cardiovascular Disorders* 9(1):13.

Thompson, W. R., N. F. Gordon, and L. S. Pescatello. 2010. Clinical exercise testing. In *ACSM's guidelines for exercise testing and prescription*, 8th ed., edited by W. R. Thompson, N. F. Gordon, and L. S. Pescatello. Philadelphia, PA: Wolters Kluwer/Lippincott Williams & Wilkins. Pp. 105–115.

Wenger, N. K., D. Almeida, J. M. Bradford, and S. B. King. 1985. Return to work after coronary artery bypass surgery: Problems and prospects. In *Return to work after coronary artery bypass surgery: Psychosocial and economic aspects*, edited by P. J. Walter. New York: Springer-Verlag. Pp. 323–331.

Wenger, N. K., E. S. Froelicher, P. A. Ades, K. Berra, J. A. Blumenthal, C. M. E. Certo, A. M. Dattilo, D. Davis, R. F. DeBusk, J. J. P. Drozda, B. J. Fletcher, B. A. Franklin, H. Gaston, P. Greenland, P. E. McBride, C. G. A. McGregor, N. B. Oldridge, J. C. Piscatella, and F. J. Rogers. 1995. *Clinical practice guidelines on cardiac rehabilitation.* Washington, DC: Agency for Health Care Policy and Research and the National Heart, Lung, and Blood Institute.

WHO (World Health Organization). 2008. *The global burden of disease: 2004 update.* Geneva, Switzerland: WHO Press.

Writing Group for the BARI (Bypass Angioplasty Revascularization Investigation) Investigators. 1997. Five-year clinical and functional outcome comparing bypass surgery and angioplasty in patients with multivessel coronary disease: A multicenter randomized trial. *Journal of the American Medical Association* 277(9):715–721.

Yusuf, S., R. Peto, J. Lewis, R. Collins, and P. Sleight. 1985. Beta blockage during and after myocardial infarction: An overview of the randomized trials. *Progress in Cardiovascular Diseases* 27(5):335–371.

8

Peripheral Artery Disease

The recommendations in this chapter arose from issues concerning the symptomatic expression of peripheral artery disease (PAD), assessment of PAD's severity, and consistency with other listings. Not all symptomatic patients with PAD present with intermittent claudication. Some symptoms are atypical, and the most severe cases present not with claudication, but with rest pain. In terms of assessing impairment severity, the ankle-brachial index (ABI) is a good test, but in some instances it needs to be augmented or replaced by other testing techniques. In addition, because hemodynamic severity as measured by ABI and other techniques is not strongly associated with degree of symptoms or functional limitation, evidence of functional limitation consistent with severe PAD should also be required. Logically, and for consistency with other cardiovascular listings, three hospitalizations within 1 year for PAD should be a way to meet the functional criterion. Also, for consistency with other listings, the functional limitation for PAD should be the same as that defined for the musculoskeletal system, that is, inability to ambulate effectively.

DESCRIPTION

Peripheral artery disease[1] (PAD) is a condition that occurs when arteries outside the heart and brain become narrowed or obstructed. The

[1] The Atherosclerotic Peripheral Vascular Disease Interdisciplinary Working Group, commissioned by the American Heart Association, recommended updated nomenclature for vascular

most common cause of PAD is a buildup of plaque inside the arteries, called atherosclerosis, which reduces the flow of blood to the extremities. Most people with early PAD do not experience symptoms. However, if left untreated, PAD may progress to the point that the muscles are starved for oxygen when a person uses them to walk or climb stairs. The resulting pain, called claudication, is usually intermittent, that is, it goes away when the person stops exercising. In more severe cases of PAD, the person may experience pain even when resting, and leg or foot wounds may not heal normally. In a small percentage of cases, the circulation of blood may become so reduced that severe ischemic muscle damage results, and amputation may be required.

Medically, PAD is of grave concern because it is a strong sign of systemic atherosclerosis and thus a high risk of a heart attack, ischemic stroke, and vascular death. The risk of heart attack is 20 to 60 percent higher, the risk of stroke is 40 percent higher, and the risk of death from coronary heart disease is two to six times higher than in people without PAD (Hirsch et al., 2006). Several studies have shown that the more severe the symptoms of PAD, the higher the mortality rate due to heart attack or stroke (Belch et al., 2003).

PAD itself rarely causes death (unless an ischemic limb is untreated for too long), but it can cause substantial morbidity and disability. Individuals with PAD have a reduced peak exercise capacity that limits their range of physical functioning. For example, they have less capacity to walk than otherwise similar individuals without PAD. If they have progressed to intermittent claudication, they have substantial limitations on their capacity to walk. In severe cases, claudication, muscle weakness or numbness, ischemic leg pain at rest, or ulceration will interfere with a person's ability to work.

EPIDEMIOLOGY

According to the National Health and Nutrition Examination Survey (NHANES), approximately 5 percent of U.S. adults ages 40 or older (more than 5 million individuals) had PAD (defined as an ankle-brachial index [ABI] of less than 0.90 in either leg) for the period 1999 to 2002 (Paulose-Ram et al., 2005). Of these, approximately one-fourth had moderate to severe PAD, defined as an ABI less than 0.70 in either leg. These rates went up sharply with age and were higher among men than women, among non-Hispanic blacks than among non-Hispanic whites or Mexican Americans, and in individuals with diabetes than nondiabetic individuals. A more recent systematic review of U.S. prevalence, that included NHANES findings

---

diseases in 2008, including the use of the term *peripheral artery disease* in place of *peripheral arterial disease* or *peripheral vascular disease* (Hiatt et al., 2008a).

and was corrected for biases—such as not including persons with previous revascularization or a high ABI (i.e., an ABI greater than 1.4), found a PAD prevalence of 8.5 million in 2000 (Allison et al., 2007).

The majority of individuals with PAD are asymptomatic. According to several large population studies, the prevalence of symptomatic PAD (i.e., claudication) by age group is about 0.6 percent for those ages 30 to 39, 1.2 percent for those ages 40 to 49, 2.3 percent for those ages 50 to 59, and 3.2 percent for those ages 60 to 64. Prevalence increases sharply among older individuals—to 6 percent among those ages 64 to 69 and 7 percent among those ages 70 to 74 (Norgren et al., 2007).

Intermittent claudication is approximately twice as common among PAD patients with diabetes. PAD in nondiabetic patients also progresses more quickly and is more likely to involve distal vessels, and the need for amputation because of critical leg ischemia is 5 to 10 times higher (Norgren et al., 2007).

DIAGNOSTIC CRITERIA AND METHODS

The physical examination of patients presenting with pain during exercise includes checking for abnormal leg pulses, for bruits, and for cool or ulcerated skin. However, physical examination findings are not sufficient for a diagnosis of PAD, even combined with a history of risk factors, such as smoking, high blood pressure, or high cholesterol (Criqui et al., 1985; Khan et al., 2006).

The definitive method or "gold standard" for diagnosing PAD is contrast angiography because of its ability to provide detailed information about arterial anatomy. However, contrast angiography is invasive and carries some risk. Therefore, the American College of Cardiology/American Heart Association (ACC/AHA) guidelines for the management of patients with PAD recommend that contrast angiography be used only when revascularization is contemplated (Class I Recommendation, Level of Evidence: B) (Hirsch et al., 2006).

Short of situations in which revascularization is being considered, the ACC/AHA guidelines indicate that "Patients with vascular disorders can usually be assured that an accurate anatomic diagnosis will be made with modern noninvasive vascular diagnostic techniques (e.g., ankle- and toe-brachial indices, segmental pressure measurements, pulse volume recordings, duplex ultrasound imaging, Doppler waveform analysis, and exercise testing)" and that "these tests will usually provide adequate information for creation of a therapeutic plan." When required, these physiological and anatomic data can be supplemented by use of magnetic resonance angiography (MRA), computed tomography angiography (CTA), and selective use of invasive aortic and lower extremity angiographic techniques (Hirsch et al., 2006:e490).

Ankle-Brachial and Toe-Brachial Indexes

Ankle-Brachial Index

The most common method to establish or rule out a diagnosis of lower extremity PAD is the ABI because it is reasonably accurate, has good sensitivity and excellent specificity, and is easy to perform, inexpensive, and noninvasive. The ABI is the ratio of systolic blood pressure at the ankle to the systolic blood pressure in the brachial artery of the upper arm. Normal ABI values are between 1.00 and 1.40.[2] Abnormal ABI values are 0.90 or less (values of 0.91 through 0.99 are considered to be borderline) (Hirsch et al., 2006). An ABI of 0.90 usually indicates vessel blockage in a major vessel of at least 50 percent (Dormandy et al., 1999).

ABI values of 0.41 to 0.90 are considered to represent mild to moderate PAD. Values of 0.40 or less indicate severe PAD and a high risk of amputation due to critical limb ischemia (Hirsch et al., 2006). A 20 percent or greater decrease in the ABI after exercise is also diagnostic for PAD, and the more severe the disease, the longer it takes for the ankle pressure to return to normal after exercise (Gerhard-Herman et al., 2006).

Studies of the sensitivity, specificity, and accuracy of the ABI as a tool to diagnose peripheral artery blockage of 50 percent or more, using contrast angiography as the standard, have found that the ABI has a sensitivity of 72 to 95 percent, specificity of 96 to 100 percent, positive predictive value of 90 to 100 percent, negative predictive value of 96 to 99 percent, and overall accuracy of 98 percent (Hirsch et al., 2006). In unselected populations, sensitivity is about 80 percent and specificity is about 96 percent (higher values are from studies that compare extremes: patients scheduled for intervention with young healthy controls) (Criqui and Ninomiya, 2006).

The highest brachial and ankle blood pressure readings are used in clinical practice and are required by the current listing for PAD. However, two recent studies have found that the ABI based on the average pressure in each ankle has the strongest statistical association with leg function (Allison et al., 2010; McDermott et al., 2000). One of the studies, the Multi-Ethnic Study of Atherosclerosis (MESA), compared three ways to measure ankle pressure in a given leg to compute the ABI: (1) the higher of the dorsalis pedis artery and posterior tibial artery pressures, (2) the lower of the dorsalis pedis artery and posterior tibial artery pressures, and (3) the mean of these two ankle pressures (Allison et al., 2010). The prevalence of PAD in the study population was three times higher using the lower pressure than

[2] Although the ACC/AHA guidelines specify the upper end of the normal ABI range to be 1.3 (Hirsch et al., 2006), recent data from the Ankle Brachial Index Collaboration strongly suggest it should be 1.4 (Ankle Brachial Index Collaboration, 2008).

using the higher pressure. The MESA study also calculated the sensitivity and specificity of the alternative ABIs in predicting several subclinical measures of atherosclerosis (e.g., coronary artery calcium, thickness of carotid artery plaque) and several risk factors (e.g., smoking, dyslipidemia). The finding was that using the ABI based on the lower pressure reading is more sensitive, but less specific than the ABI based on the higher pressure (the average of the two pressures was intermediate). In other words, using the higher pressure reading results in a specificity of 98 to 99 percent, which results in few false positives. However, the lower sensitivity leads to more false negatives. On the other hand, while using the lower pressure value is more sensitive, it is less specific and results in more false positives.

Toe-Brachial Index

The major limitation of the ABI as a diagnostic test is its inability to obtain accurate results with incompressible arteries due to medial calcification, which can occur in patients with conditions such as diabetes or chronic kidney disease. When the ABI is greater than or equal to 1.40, the toe-brachial index (TBI) should be used because arteries in the toes are much less likely to be calcified. The TBI procedure is similar to the ABI procedure except that it is performed with a photoplethysmograph infrared light sensor and a very small blood pressure cuff placed around the toe. A TBI less than 0.70 is sufficient to diagnose PAD (Hirsch et al., 2006). Ischemic rest pain is common when toe pressures are less than 30 mm Hg (Rutherford et al., 1997). A case-control study of 56 men with stable claudication and toe pressures less than 40 mm Hg found that 34 percent progressed to rest pain, ulceration, or gangrene over 31 months, compared with 9 percent of age-, sex-, and race-matched controls, and that those with diabetes had the highest incidence of deterioration (Bowers et al., 1993).

Test Availability

The ABI has been in use in clinical practice for some time, but it remains more likely to be found in a specialized vascular laboratory than in primary care settings (Mohler et al., 2004). This test is relatively inexpensive and can be done in 15 minutes or less by a trained nurse (Criqui et al., 2008; Pearson et al., 2009). Nevertheless, two-thirds of the participants in a recent program to implement the ABI measurement in primary care outpatient clinics had not measured the ABI of patients prior to participation. They reported that moderate to major barriers to administering the ABI included time constraints (56 percent), lack of reimbursement (45 percent), and limited staff availability (45 percent) (Mohler et al., 2004).

The TBI is rarely measured in primary care because measurement of toe pressure is more time consuming and technically difficult and requires additional equipment (Brooks et al., 2001).

Other Diagnostic Methods

Other noninvasive, inexpensive, and relatively safe diagnostic methods that provide diagnostic discrimination include segmental pressure measurements, pulse volume recordings, duplex ultrasonography, Doppler waveform analysis, and ABI after exercise testing (Hirsch et al., 2006). Segmental pressure measurements help to identify the location of arterial blockages. Pulse volume recording is another useful technique for diagnosing PAD, especially in people with incompressible arteries. Continuous-wave Doppler ultrasound measurements of blood flow with duplex imaging are useful in assessing PAD severity and location. Pulse volume recording and Doppler ultrasound are often used to assess the results of revascularization.

Exercise treadmill tests are used to diagnose PAD, provide objective evidence of the degree of the functional limitations of PAD, identify any non-PAD exercise limitations, and determine the safety of prescribing an exercise program, as well as to measure the response to therapy. According to the ACC/AHA guidelines, a standardized exercise protocol should be used with a motorized treadmill to measure pain-free walking distance and maximal walking distance. Generally, the treadmill should be programmed to provide a progressive workload beginning at a less intense level than used for healthy individuals and patients with coronary heart disease, such as the Gardner-Skinner, Hiatt, or Naughton protocols. ABI values should be determined before and after the test to ensure that the claudication symptoms are due to PAD and not to other causes (Hirsch et al., 2006). A decrease in ABI of 15 to 20 percent is diagnostic of PAD (Norgren et al., 2007).

Treadmill testing is not suitable for patients who, due to age or other reasons, are not able to exert themselves enough to allow reliable results. In such cases, a 6-minute walk test may be used to obtain an objective assessment of functional limitation and response to therapy (Hirsch et al., 2006). Another useful exercise test is the "heel rise test," where the patient repeatedly raises up on his or her toes with hands outstretched against a wall for balance. The drop in ankle pressure with this test correlates quite highly with that seen during a standard treadmill test (Amirhamzeh et al., 1997; McPhail et al., 2001).

MRA and CTA, as with contrast angiography, could be used to diagnose PAD, but they are expensive; are usually done with intravenous contrast, which is invasive; and are considered to be most useful for identifying patients who are suitable candidates for endovascular or surgical revascularization (Hirsch et al., 2006).[3]

TREATMENT

Clinical guidelines for diagnosis and management of PAD in the United States were first issued by ACC and AHA in 2005 (Hirsch et al., 2006), although clinicians previously accepted the idea that they should aggressively treat PAD symptoms to reduce functional loss, increase quality of life, and decrease rates of amputation. Also well recognized was the idea that aggressive risk factor modification was needed to lower the incidence of cardiovascular events, especially heart attack and stroke, stemming from the systemic atherosclerosis that a diagnosis of PAD strongly signals (Belch et al., 2003).

The 2005 ACC/AHA guidelines emphasize the reduction of atherosclerotic risk factors, such as smoking, diabetes, high cholesterol, hypertension, lack of exercise, and poor diet (Hirsch et al., 2006). These steps are prescribed primarily to reduce the likelihood of a heart attack or stroke, but they may also slow atherosclerosis of the lower limbs, and thus slow, halt, or reverse the progressive loss of functional capacity and the development of critical limb ischemia and limb loss.

Ideally, patients with PAD should be treated aggressively for their underlying atherosclerosis. Treatment includes smoking cessation, taking antihypertensive and lipid-lowering medications, controlling diabetes when present, and taking blood-thinning medications such as aspirin or clopidogrel.[4] Therapies known to improve the effects of claudication specifically on functional capacity (e.g., exercise tolerance or walking distance) include smoking cessation, supervised walking exercise, medication, and if indicated, revascularization through angioplasty or surgery. Specific findings include the following:

- Patients with intermittent claudication who stop smoking are much less likely to progress to rest pain (Jonason and Bergström, 1987) or critical leg ischemia (Hobbs and Bradbury, 2003). However, a meta-analysis did not find that smoking cessation improved maximal treadmill walking distance (Girolami et al., 1999).

---

[3] MRA is also contraindicated for patients with pacemakers.

[4] A recent study found that only 33 percent of PAD patients were receiving beta-blockers, 29 percent angiotensin-converting enzyme, or ACE, inhibitors, and 31 percent cholesterol-lowering medications, and that only 46 percent had a hemoglobin A1c of less than 7 percent (Rehring et al., 2005).

The ACC/AHA guidelines recommend that individuals with PAD who smoke should be advised to stop smoking and be offered comprehensive smoking cessation interventions, including behavior modification therapy, nicotine replacement therapy, or bupropion (Class I Recommendation, Level of Evidence: B) (Hirsch et al., 2006).

- Many studies have shown that supervised exercise training doubles pain-free walking distance and maximal walking time on average (Hirsch et al., 2007; Watson et al., 2008). The ACC/AHA guidelines recommend a program of supervised exercise training as an initial treatment modality for patients with intermittent claudication. The supervised exercise training should be performed for a minimum of 30 to 45 minutes, at least 3 times per week, for 12 or more weeks (Class I Recommendation, Level of Evidence: A) (Hirsch et al., 2006). However, few such programs exist because of lack of reimbursement by health insurers.
- Cilostazol, a phosphodiesterase inhibitor, was approved by the Food and Drug Administration (FDA) in 1999 for the treatment of claudication after it was shown in six controlled clinical trials to increase pain-free and maximal constant-load treadmill walking distances by 65 to 98 percent and 40 to 76 percent, respectively (Regensteiner et al., 2002). The same meta-analysis found that patients on cilostazol reported significantly greater gains in community walking distances and speeds according to the Walking Impairment Questionnaire than did patients on placebo.

  The ACC/AHA guidelines agree that cilostazol (100 mg orally two times per day) is an effective therapy to improve symptoms and increase walking distance in patients with lower extremity PAD and intermittent claudication. Therefore, the guidelines recommend that a therapeutic trial of cilostazol should be considered in all patients with lifestyle-limiting claudication (Class I Recommendation, Level of Evidence: A). Cilostazol cannot be used in patients with heart failure, however, because of possible adverse side effects (Hirsch et al., 2006).

  Pentoxifylline (400 mg three times per day) may be considered as second-line alternative therapy to cilostazol to improve walking distance in patients with intermittent claudication, although improvement has been shown to be better with cilostazol (Class IIb Recommendation, Level of Evidence: A) (Hirsch et al., 2006). No other medications are recommended at this time, or have been approved by FDA, although a number are being developed and tested.

  The most common side effects of cilostazol are gastrointestinal complaints, including nausea or change in stool characteristics (approximately 15 percent for each), headache (approximately 30 percent), and palpitations (9 percent). Side effects usually lessen with continued use (Carman and Fernandez, 2006). A study of long-term effects of cilostazol did not find increased mortality or serious bleeding events (Hiatt et al., 2008b). The most common side effects of pentoxifylline are also gastrointestinal (Carman and Fernandez, 2006).

The absolute gains in distance from medication are modest. For example, patients taking cilostazol were able to walk an average of 100 additional meters on a graded treadmill test before they were forced to stop by symptoms (350 instead of 250 meters) (Regensteiner et al., 2002).

- Revascularization should be considered for patients with severe, lifestyle-limiting symptoms, such as severe claudication or rest pain despite medical therapy for 3 months. Endovascular procedures (e.g., percutaneous angioplasty and stents) are usually effective, but open surgical procedures (e.g., bypass or endarterectomy) are indicated in certain patients (Hirsch et al., 2007).

  According to the ACC/AHA guidelines for PAD, endovascular procedures are indicated for individuals with a vocational or lifestyle-limiting disability because of intermittent claudication when clinical features suggest a reasonable likelihood of symptomatic improvement with endovascular intervention and (1) there has been an inadequate response to exercise or pharmacological therapy or (2) there is a very favorable risk–benefit ratio (e.g., focal aortoiliac occlusive disease) (Class I Recommendation, Level of Evidence: A) (Hirsch et al., 2006).

  Surgical revascularization for claudication is rarely indicated. Patients are initially treated with an endovascular intervention, and bypass surgery is an option only if that fails. According to the guidelines, surgical interventions are indicated for individuals with claudication symptoms who have a significant functional disability that is vocational or lifestyle limiting, who are unresponsive to exercise or pharmacotherapy, and who have a reasonable likelihood of symptomatic improvement (Class I Recommendation, Level of Evidence: B) (Hirsch et al., 2006).

DISABILITY

Blood carries oxygen and nutrients needed for the body to live and function. PAD results in reduced blood flow to the muscles and nerves of the lower extremities. In advanced cases, the reduced flow of blood can cause muscle pain, weakness, and numbness when an individual walks or even, in more severe cases, when an individual is at rest. A person with advanced PAD may also develop leg ulcers that will not heal. In the most severe instances, the muscles may die and the lower leg or foot must be amputated. The resulting limitations on mobility may become severe enough to prevent an individual with PAD from engaging in substantial gainful activity.

PAD and Work

An intensive literature search found neither research on the participation of persons with PAD in the workforce generally, nor more detailed analyses of workforce participation by ABI score or by any other objective laboratory test result or medical finding. This lack of research on the employment effects of PAD may be explained by its relatively low prevalence in the working-age population. Furthermore, most people who have PAD are asymptomatic, and many people with ischemic symptoms think these are due to aging or other medical conditions and do not report them.

An article on the impact of surgery for PAD on returning to work examined a retrospective follow-up study in Finland of 67 middle-aged patients (mean equals 53 years). Of those, 63 had a positive outcome based on vascular criteria. Of the 50 patients not yet retired at the time of the surgery, 41 returned to work. After 10 years, only 9 of the 41 who had returned to work were still working. Of the rest, 13 had retired (most due to the progression of PAD), and 19 had died. A preoperative ABI less than or equal to 0.50 or less was associated with increased risk of death but not with the rate of return to work (Peräkylä et al., 1994).

PAD and Functional Limitation

In the absence of research on the predictors of employment of those with PAD, its impact on functions that are plausibly related to work, such as exercise tolerance or ability to walk a certain distance or speed, must serve as proxies for work disability. A number of studies have examined the association between ABI and various measures of functional ability (Eberhardt et al., 2005; McDermott et al., 1998, 2002, 2007, 2009; Selvin and Hirsch, 2008). A few studies have looked at the association of PAD with measures of peak exercise capacity on a treadmill (Hiatt et al., 1990).

These studies consistently found that patients with PAD are functionally impaired and that the degree of functional limitation increased as clinical measures of impairment worsened. The studies found, for example, that:

- Less than 40 percent of the participants with an ABI lower than 0.40 could walk continuously for 6 minutes compared with more

than 95 percent of those with an ABI between 1.00 and 1.50 (McDermott et al., 2002);
- Patients with abnormal (less than 0.90) ABIs walked significantly shorter distances than those with normal ABIs (McDermott et al., 1998);
- The hazard ratios for losing the ability to walk one-quarter mile or walk up and down one flight of stairs without assistance more than 5 years from diagnosis were 4.16 for severe PAD (ABI less than 0.50), 3.82 for moderate PAD (ABI between 0.50 and 0.69), and 3.22 for mild PAD (ABI between 0.70 and 0.89) (McDermott et al., 2009); and
- The NHANES 1999–2004 survey found that 51 percent of individuals ages 60 and older with an ABI less than 0.90 reported difficulty walking for a quarter mile, walking up 10 steps without resting, or walking from one room to another on the same level, compared with 33 percent of those in the same age group overall (Selvin and Hirsch, 2008).

Studies have also found that the impact of PAD on health-related quality of life is substantial. In one study, the impact was comparable to that of other cardiovascular conditions, although PAD patients were most affected by calf pain while other cardiovascular patients were most affected by chest pain, shortness of breath, and palpitations (Regensteiner et al., 2008).

Although ABI and other measures of hemodynamic severity are clearly associated with functional capacity, especially at the very low and high ends of the scale, they are not strong predictors of functional limitations. For example, the correlation of ABI at rest with walking ability on a treadmill of a given individual is low (Hiatt et al., 1988). This is probably due to a number of factors, including individual differences in comorbidities, muscle pathology, leg blood flow, and conditioning (Brass et al., 2004: McDermott et al., 2001). As a result, some patients with a low ABI will have little walking impairment, while others with a higher ABI will have marked walking impairment (Hirsch et al., 2006). In this situation, ABI or other blood pressure measure is not sufficient to sharply differentiate claimants who are unable to work from those who are able to work without additional evidence of functional limitations consistent with incapacity to work.

CURRENT LISTING

The listing for PAD requires the existence of intermittent claudication plus specified test results based on ankle or toe blood pressure readings (Box 8-1). This results in four sublistings for PAD. The first, 4.12A, requires intermittent claudication and a resting ABI less than 0.50. The second,

BOX 8-1
Current Listing for Peripheral Arterial Disease

4.12 Peripheral arterial disease, as determined by appropriate medically acceptable imaging (see 4.00A3d, 4.00G2, 4.00G5, and 4.00G6), causing intermittent claudication (see 4.00G1) and one of the following:

A. Resting ankle/brachial systolic blood pressure ratio of less than 0.50.
OR
B. Decrease in systolic blood pressure at the ankle on exercise (see 4.00G7a and 4.00C16–4.00C17) of 50 percent or more of pre-exercise level and requiring 10 minutes or more to return to pre-exercise level.
OR
C. Resting toe systolic pressure of less than 30 mm Hg (see 4.00G7c and 4.00G8).
OR
D. Resting toe/brachial systolic blood pressure ratio of less than 0.40 (see 4.00G7c).

SOURCE: SSA, 2008.

4.12B, is applied when a claimant has intermittent claudication and the ABI is at 0.50 or higher (but rarely if it is 0.80 or higher). Sublisting 4.12B is met if there is intermittent claudication and systolic blood pressure at the ankle drops by half or more during a treadmill exercise test and does not recover for 10 minutes or longer.

The third and fourth sublistings were added when the PAD listing was revised in 2006. Sublisting 4.12C requires intermittent claudication and resting toe systolic blood pressure of less than 30 mm Hg (the normal range is 80 to 110), and sublisting 4.12D requires intermittent claudication and resting toe/brachial systolic blood pressure to be less than 0.40 (the normal range is greater than or equal to 0.7). The inclusion of toe pressures addressed the fact that the ankle blood pressure readings are not a valid measure of PAD in individuals with abnormally stiff ankle arteries because of medial arterial calcification or other causes.

The PAD listing must also be read in conjunction with part 4.00G, "Evaluating Peripheral Vascular Disease," of the introductory section to the cardiovascular system:

- The serious effects of PAD are delineated in 4.00G1 ("What is peripheral vascular disease?"): "you may have pain in your calf after walking a distance that goes away when you rest (intermittent claudication); at more advanced stages, you may have pain in your calf at rest or you may develop ulceration or gangrene."

- 4.00G2 ("How do we assess limitations resulting from PVD?") indicates that the Social Security Administration (SSA) will assess the claimant's limitations based on symptoms together with physical findings, Doppler studies, other appropriate noninvasive studies, or angiographic findings (the last if they are already in the medical record, because SSA will not pay for invasive tests due to risk and cost).
- 4.00G5 ("When will we purchase exercise Doppler studies for evaluating peripheral arterial disease?") outlines the policies regarding the purchase of exercise Doppler studies. SSA will pay for an exercise Doppler study if one has not been done or if it is needed to determine if the claimant meets sublisting 4.12B, and a disability determination services (DDS) medical consultant, "preferably one with experience in the care of patients with cardiovascular disease," determines the test would not be risky or would otherwise be contraindicated. SSA requires the exercise test to be performed on a treadmill at 2 mph on a 12 percent grade for up to 5 minutes. Blood pressures at the ankle are measured after exercise and the time required for the systolic blood pressure to return to or near to the preexercise level is determined.
- 4.00G6 ("Are there any other studies that are helpful in evaluating PAD?") lists recording ultrasound Doppler unit and strain-gauge plethysmography as additional tests useful in evaluating the severity of PAD, especially if there is small vessel disease or medial arterial calcification.
- 4.00G7 ("How do we evaluate PAD under 4.12?") and 4.00G8 ("How are toe pressures measured?") describe the acceptable techniques for taking systolic blood pressures at the ankle and toe and determining ankle-brachial and toe-brachial indexes.
- 4.00G9 ("How do we use listing 4.12 if you have had a peripheral graft?") says that current severity after peripheral grafting is based on Doppler studies measuring the flow of blood through the bypass vessel, not findings that precede the bypass surgery.

CONCLUSIONS AND RECOMMENDATIONS

The fundamental conclusion regarding evaluation of PAD disability is that hemodynamic measures such as the ABI do not adequately distinguish between individuals able to work and individuals unable to work. Individuals with an ABI less than 0.50, for example, will have a range of ability to function. Some individuals will be able to work despite intermittent claudication, and others will be unable even though they do not report typical symptoms of intermittent claudication. At the same time, some patients with PAD who have an ABI greater than 0.50 can have a severe walking impairment that limits their ability to work. Adopting more severe values, that is, an ABI less than 0.4, would make the PAD listing more specific, but would increase the number of false negatives, thus increasing the number of legitimate claimants having to go through Steps 4 and 5 to be allowed. Alternatively, adopting an ABI greater than 0.50 would be more sensitive and reduce the number of claims going through Steps 4 and 5, but there would be more false positives.

The basic recommendation for improving the PAD listing as an early screening tool is to supplement the medical diagnostic and severity requirements with evidence of severe functional limitations. Because PAD's path to disability is functional limitations on mobility, the committee recommends using the criteria for lower body disability used in the musculoskeletal listings. The committee also recommends some clarifications in and medical updates of listing 4.12.

Appropriate PAD Diagnostic Techniques

Listing 4.12 currently requires a diagnosis of PAD based on "appropriate medically acceptable imaging," which is defined in the introductory section to the cardiovascular system listings as a technique to diagnose and evaluate PAD that is widely accepted as accurate by the medical community.[5] The ACC/AHA PAD guidelines list a number of acceptable methods for diagnosis besides the ABI, including duplex ultrasound imaging, Doppler waveform analysis, CTA, MRA, and contrast angiography (Hirsch et al., 2006), which all have high sensitivity and specificity (Collins et al., 2007). In practice, however, a diagnosis of PAD is usually based on the ABI, and the other diagnostic methods are reserved for cases in which further evaluation is needed to make the diagnosis and determine appropriate medical management or to help guide decisions to intervene invasively.

Technically, the Doppler techniques used to determine ankle and toe blood pressures do not produce images. Similarly, the techniques used to record waveforms do not produce images. Also, although duplex ultrasonography images the leg arteries with B-mode ultrasound, it also measures flow velocity with pulsed Doppler, and the latter technique—which is not imaging—is often the main basis for a diagnosis of PAD.

[5] The actual wording is: "Appropriate medically acceptable imaging means that the technique used is the proper one to evaluate and diagnose the impairment and is commonly recognized as accurate for assessing the cited finding" (4.00A3d).

The committee was informed that SSA considers Doppler studies to be appropriate medically acceptable imaging. However, to eliminate confusion, the committee recommends that the phrase "appropriate medically acceptable imaging" in 4.12 be revised to say "appropriate medically acceptable testing." This revision would also be consistent with the ACC/AHA PAD guidelines, which also consider another nonimaging modality, treadmill exercise testing with or and without preexercise and postexercise ABIs, to be an appropriate diagnostic technique (see Recommendation 8-1a).

Appropriate PAD Symptom Requirements

Current listing 4.12 requires "intermittent claudication," which is calf pain that develops from walking that goes away soon after the claimant stops walking (4.00G1). Intermittent claudication is considered to be the classic symptom of PAD. It is an appropriate listing requirement because it is usually associated with severe functional limitations on ability to walk and climb stairs. However, other symptoms in the absence of intermittent claudication can also indicate inability to engage in any gainful activity. For example, some individuals with an ABI less than 0.50 experience atypical leg symptoms that are as disabling as symptoms of intermittent claudication (McDermott et al., 2001). In addition, individuals may apply to SSA for disability benefits with advanced-stage symptoms that have succeeded an earlier period of intermittent claudication. These include rest pain (i.e., constant leg pain), ulceration, or gangrene. These are appropriately mentioned in the introductory section to the cardiovascular system listings, but they are not in the PAD listing as an alternative to intermittent claudication.[6]

The committee understands that if a claimant has atypical leg pain attributable to PAD that limits walking, but meets the other requirements of 4.12 (e.g., an ABI less than 0.50), a finding of medical equivalence could be made. In this case, the atypical leg pain would substitute for the missing finding of "intermittent claudication." Similarly, if the claimant's PAD has already progressed beyond intermittent claudication to rest pain, ulcers, or gangrene, but otherwise satisfies the requirements of 4.12, a finding of medical equivalence would be possible.

The committee recommends that, rather than rely on equivalence, a broader set of symptoms be permitted to meet the listing than intermittent claudication alone (see Recommendation 8-1b).

[6] "If you have peripheral arterial disease, you may have pain in your calf after walking a distance that goes away when you rest (intermittent claudication); at more advanced stages, you may have pain in your calf at rest or you may develop ulceration or gangrene" (4.00G1).

Add Treatment Requirement

Treatments for PAD exist (described above) that reduce symptoms and increase mobility and quality of life. These include supervised physical rehabilitation, medications, and, if indicated, angioplasty or bypass surgery. The committee recommends that a requirement that the applicant be on a regimen of prescribed treatment be added to the listing (see Recommendation 8-1c).

PAD Severity Requirements

Listing 4.12 currently requires one of four test results: (1) an ABI less than 0.50, (2) a TBI less than 0.40, (3) a resting toe systolic pressure less than 30 mm Hg, or (4) a drop in resting ankle systolic pressure of at least 50 percent during exercise on a treadmill that requires at least 10 minutes to recover to the preexercise level.

The committee discussed the ABI values that currently meet the PAD listing. For evaluating disability, SSA strongly prefers clinical tests that are very sensitive (which would screen in the highest percentage of claimants unable to work as possible) and very specific (which would screen out as many individuals who can work as possible). As with all clinical screening tests, however, there is a trade-off between sensitivity and specificity. In this case, the higher the ABI, the more claimants unable to work will meet the Listings and be allowed, but also the more claimants who can work will be allowed. For example, if an ABI less than or equal to 0.90 met the listing, it would be highly sensitive because the vast majority of those with PAD and unable to work would be allowed. This gain would come at the cost of specificity, however, because many individuals with PAD who could work would be included. Similarly, if the listing required an ABI less than or equal to 0.10, the specificity would be very near, if not equal to, 100 percent, but the sensitivity would be very low, because only a small proportion of those unable to work would be allowed. There would be no false positives, but this would make the listing ineffective as an administrative device for speeding decisions on obvious allowances.

Because some individuals with an ABI less than 0.50 can work, the committee considered recommending a decrease in the ABI requirement in the PAD listing to less than 0.40. An ABI less than 0.40 is the point at which critical leg ischemia becomes a danger, potentially requiring an endovascular or surgical intervention soon, if not immediately, to prevent gangrene and amputation. Virtually everyone with this ABI score has severe leg pain and substantial muscle weakness, severely limiting mobility and stamina. Although this test result requirement would be very specific, the decrease in sensitivity would mean that more individuals who actually met the listing would not be allowed at Step 3 and would have to go through Steps 4 and 5 to be allowed. This would defeat the purpose of the Listings, which is to reduce the percentage of claimants going through Steps 4 and 5 who ultimately will be allowed.

The committee also discussed setting a higher ABI cut-off value, such as 0.70, at which point leg symptoms begin to be common. This would make the listing very sensitive, probably allowing most claimants truly unable to work because of PAD, and it would require fewer Step 4 and 5 determinations. However, it would also reduce specificity and allow more false positives, which would undermine the credibility of the disability program.

Unfortunately, the literature search found no studies of the sensitivity and specificity of an ABI less than 0.50 (or of any other ABI value) for predicting the functional status, however measured, nor of employment status, of working-age individuals. However, based on personal clinical observations by some committee members and logical extrapolation from studies of functional status of individuals with various ABI values, the committee recommends retaining the current ABI value of less than 0.50 to meet the listing, but requiring additional information about the functioning of the claimant (see Recommendation 8-1d).

Also, the PAD listing could be simplified by folding Criteria B, C, and D into a new, broader criterion, in which tests other than the ABI can be used to establish listing-level severity. These include the TBI, Doppler waveforms, duplex ultrasonography, MRA, CTA, contrast angiography, and graded treadmill tests. The basis for this change is the relative lack of evidence that toe pressures or changes in ankle pressure during exercise are predictive of functional status. The current introductory section to the cardiovascular system, which dates from 2006, notes that medical standards for evaluating exercise toe pressures do not exist, which is still the case. Given that TBI and toe systolic pressure results require interpretation by DDS medical consultants and consultative examiners, SSA might broaden as well the range of tests that can be used to establish listing-level severity (see Recommendation 8-1e). This criterion would apply to claimants with an ABI of 0.50 or greater or with evidence of medical calcification due to diabetes or other causes.

Addition of Functional Assessment of PAD

The committee concludes that an ABI less than 0.50 constitutes a reasonable trade-off between sensitivity and specificity, but it is not totally accurate. Although an ABI less than 0.50 is an indicator of severe PAD, and most individuals with that ABI will be unable to work because of immobility due to leg pain and muscle weakness, some individuals will be able to work. At the same time, some claimants with ABIs of 0.50 or more will be too functionally limited by pain and weakness to work. Therefore, an ABI less than 0.50 is neither 100 percent sensitive nor specific for inability to work.

The committee concludes that, to increase sensitivity without significantly decreasing specificity, the ABI and other clinical signs should be augmented with an assessment of function. PAD is disabling when it impinges on an individual's mobility and severely limits or precludes his or her ability to fulfill effectively normal life roles, including the ability to engage in gainful employment. This is equivalent to the requirement in the musculoskeletal system listings that a claimant be unable to ambulate effectively (Box 8-2). For consistency within the Listings, the committee recommends that SSA apply the same standard in evaluating PAD (see Recommendation 8-1f, below) or accept a history of three hospitalizations within a 12-month period as evidence of listing-level limitations on capacity to work.

BOX 8-2
1.00 Musculoskeletal System

B.2.b. What we mean by inability to ambulate effectively.

(1) Definition. Inability to ambulate effectively means an extreme limitation of the ability to walk; i.e., an impairment(s) that interferes very seriously with the individual's ability to independently initiate, sustain, or complete activities. Ineffective ambulation is defined generally as having insufficient lower extremity functioning . . . to permit independent ambulation without the use of a hand-held assistive device(s) that limits the functioning of both upper extremities.

(2) To ambulate effectively, individuals must be capable of sustaining a reasonable walking pace over a sufficient distance to be able to carry out activities of daily living. They must have the ability to travel without companion assistance to and from a place of employment or school. Therefore, examples of ineffective ambulation include, but are not limited to, the inability to walk without the use of a walker, two crutches or two canes, the inability to walk a block at a reasonable pace on rough or uneven surfaces, the inability to use standard public transportation, the inability to carry out routine ambulatory activities, such as shopping and banking, and the inability to climb a few steps at a reasonable pace with the use of a single hand rail. The ability to walk independently about one's home without the use of assistive devices does not, in and of itself, constitute effective ambulation.

SOURCE: SSA, 2008.

RECOMMENDATION 8-1. The requirement for diagnostic evidence of peripheral artery disease (PAD) should be based on appropriate medically acceptable testing, and evidence of listing-level PAD should be based on an ankle-brachial index (ABI) of less than 0.50 or other test results consistent with severe PAD, combined with a requirement that, despite prescribed treatment, (1) leg pain interferes with mobility consistent with the musculoskeletal system listings, or (2) there have been three hospitalizations due to PAD within a 12-month period. Specifically,

Recommendation 8-1a. The word *imaging* in the phrase "appropriate medically acceptable imaging" currently in 4.12 should be replaced by the word *testing* or other term broader than *imaging*, because nonimaging tests such as Doppler techniques are commonly used to diagnose PAD and also to assess its severity.

Recommendation 8-1b. The current requirement in listing 4.12 for the presence of *intermittent claudication* should be changed to require that "leg pain" caused by PAD be present because the definition of intermittent claudication excludes too many individuals with disabling leg symptoms.

Recommendation 8-1c. Listing 4.12 should require that the applicant be on a regimen of prescribed treatment because therapies exist that can improve functional capacity.

Recommendation 8-1d. Criterion A in listing 4.12—an ABI of less than 0.50—should be retained, coupled with a new requirement for evidence of a severe limitation, such as an extreme functional limitation on effective mobility or three hospitalizations for PAD within a 12-month period (see Recommendation 8-1f).

Recommendation 8-1e. Current criteria B, C, and D in listing 4.12 should be replaced by a new criterion B that an appropriate test or tests be consistent with severe PAD, when the ABI is 0.50 or greater or there is evidence of medial calcification of the ankle arteries. These tests should include the toe-brachial index, Doppler waveforms, duplex ultrasonography, magnetic resonance angiography, computed tomography angiography, contrast angiography, and graded treadmill tests. These test results should be coupled with a new requirement for evidence of a severe functional limitation on mobility or a history of three hospitalizations due to PAD within a 12-month period (see Recommendation 8-1f).

Recommendation 8-1f. Criterion A or new criterion B should be necessary but not sufficient to establish listing-level impairment unless there is also evidence of a severe limitation on mobility, for example, as defined in the musculoskeletal system listings (i.e., "inability to ambulate effectively") or there is a history of three hospitalizations due to PAD within a 12-month period.

REFERENCES

Allison, M. A., E. Ho, J. O. Denenberg, R. D. Langer, A. B. Newman, R. R. Fabsitz, and M. H. Criqui. 2007. Ethnic-specific prevalence of peripheral arterial disease in the United States. *American Journal of Preventive Medicine* 32(4):328–333.

Allison, M. A., V. Aboyans, T. Granston, M. M. McDermott, A. Kamineni, H. Ni, and M. H. Criqui. 2010. The relevance of different methods of calculating the ankle-brachial index: The multi-ethnic study of atherosclerosis. *American Journal of Epidemiology* 171(3):368–376. http://aje.oxfordjournals.org/cgi/reprint/171/3/368 (accessed June 4, 2010).

Amirhamzeh, M. M., J. H. Chant, J. L. Rees, L. J. Hands, R. J. Powell, and W. B. Campbell. 1997. A comparative study of treadmill tests and heel raising exercise for peripheral arterial disease. *European Journal of Vascular and Endovascular Surgery* 13(3):301–305.

Ankle Brachial Index Collaboration. 2008. Ankle brachial index combined with Framingham Risk Score to predict cardiovascular events and mortality: A meta-analysis. *Journal of the American Medical Association* 300(2):197–208. http://jama.ama-assn.org/cgi/reprint/300/2/197 (accessed June 4, 2010).

Belch, J. J. F., E. J. Topol, G. Agnelli, M. Bertrand, R. M. Califf, D. L. Clement, M. A. Creager, J. D. Easton, J. R. Gavin III, P. Greenland, G. Hankey, P. Hanrath, A. T. Hirsch, J. Meyer, S. C. Smith, F. Sullivan, M. A. Weber, and Prevention of Atherothrombotic Disease Network. 2003. Critical issues in peripheral arterial disease detection and management: A call to action. *Archives of Internal Medicine* 163(8):884. http://archinte.ama-assn.org/cgi/reprint/163/8/884 (accessed June 4, 2010).

Bowers, B. L., R. J. Valentine, S. I. Myers, A. Chervu, and G. P. Clagett. 1993. The natural history of patients with claudication with toe pressures of 40 mm Hg or less. *Journal of Vascular Surgery* 18(3):506–511. http://download.journals.elsevierhealth.com/pdfs/journals/0741-5214/PII074152149390269R.pdf (accessed June 4, 2010).

Brass, E. P., W. R. Hiatt, and S. Green. 2004. Skeletal muscle metabolic changes in peripheral arterial disease contribute to exercise intolerance: A point-counterpoint discussion. *Vascular Medicine* 9(6):293–301. http://vmj.sagepub.com/content/9/4/293.long (accessed July 28, 2010).

Brooks, B., R. Dean, S. Patel, B. Wu, L. Molyneaux, and D. K. Yue. 2001. TBI or not TBI: That is the question. Is it better to measure toe pressure than ankle pressure in diabetic patients? *Diabetic Medicine* 18(7):528–532. http://www3.interscience.wiley.com/cgi-bin/fulltext/118991958/PDFSTART (accessed June 4, 2010).

Carman, T. L., and B. B. Fernandez Jr. 2006. Contemporary management of peripheral arterial disease: II. Improving walking distance and quality of life. *Cleveland Clinic Journal of Medicine* 73(Suppl 4):S38–S44. http://www.ccjm.org/content/73/Suppl_4/S38.full.pdf (accessed June 4, 2010).

Collins, R., J. Burch, G. Cranny, R. Aguiar-Ibáñez, D. Craig, K. Wright, E. Berry, M. Gough, J. Kleijnen, and M. Westwood. 2007. Duplex ultrasonography, magnetic resonance angiography, and computed tomography angiography for diagnosis and assessment of symptomatic, lower limb peripheral arterial disease: Systematic review. *BMJ* 334(7606):1257. http://www.bmj.com/cgi/reprint/334/7606/1257 (accessed June 4, 2010).

Criqui, M. H., and J. Ninomiya. 2006. The epidemiology of peripheral arterial disease. In *Vascular medicine: A companion to Braunwald's heart disease*, edited by M. A. Creager, V. J. Dzau, and J. Loscalzo. Philadelphia, PA: Saunders. Pp. 223–238.

Criqui, M. H., A. Fronek, M. R. Klauber, E. Barrett-Connor, and S. Gabriel. 1985. The sensitivity, specificity, and predictive value of traditional clinical evaluation of peripheral arterial disease: Results from noninvasive testing in a defined population. *Circulation* 71(3):516–522. http://circ.ahajournals.org/cgi/reprint/71/3/516 (accessed June 4, 2010).

Criqui, M. H., M. J. Alberts, F. G. Fowkes, A. T. Hirsch, P. T. O'Gara, and J. W. Olin. 2008. Atherosclerotic Peripheral Vascular Disease Symposium II: Screening for atherosclerotic vascular diseases: Should nationwide programs be instituted? *Circulation* 118(25):2830–2836. http://circ.ahajournals.org/cgi/reprint/118/25/2830 (accessed June 4, 2010).

Dormandy, J., L. Heeck, and S. Vig. 1999. The natural history of claudication: Risk to life and limb. *Seminars in Vascular Surgery* 12(2):123–137.

Eberhardt, M. S., S. Saydah, R. Paulose-Ram, and M. Tao. 2005. Mobility limitation among persons aged ≥ 40 years with and without diagnosed diabetes and lower extremity disease—United States, 1999–2002. *Morbidity & Mortality Weekly Report* 54(46):1183–1186.

Gerhard-Herman, M., J. A. Beckman, and M. A. Creager. 2006. Vascular laboratory testing. In *Vascular medicine: A companion to Braunwald's heart disease*, edited by M. A. Creager, V. J. Dzau, and J. Loscalzo. Philadelphia, PA: Saunders. Pp. 146–165.

Girolami, B., E. Bernardi, M. H. Prins, J. W. Ten Cate, R. Hettiarachchi, P. Prandoni, A. Girolami, and H. R. Büller. 1999. Treatment of intermittent claudication with physical training, smoking cessation, pentoxifylline, or nafronyl: A meta-analysis. *Archives of Internal Medicine* 159(4):337–345. http://archinte.ama-assn.org/cgi/reprint/159/4/337 (accessed June 4, 2010).

Hiatt, W. R., D. Nawaz, J. G. Regensteiner, and K. F. Hossack. 1988. The evaluation of exercise performance in patients with peripheral vascular disease. *Journal of Cardiopulmonary Rehabilitation* 8(12):525–532.

Hiatt, W. R., J. G. Regensteiner, M. E. Hargarten, E. E. Wolfel, and E. P. Brass. 1990. Benefit of exercise conditioning for patients with peripheral arterial disease. *Circulation* 81(2):602–609. http://circ.ahajournals.org/cgi/reprint/81/2/602 (accessed June 4, 2010).

Hiatt, W. R., J. Goldstone, S. C. Smith Jr., M. McDermott, G. Moneta, R. Oka, A. B. Newman, and W. H. Pearce. 2008a. Atherosclerotic Peripheral Vascular Disease Symposium II: Nomenclature for vascular diseases. *Circulation* 118(25):2826–2829. http://circ.ahajournals.org/cgi/reprint/118/25/2826 (accessed June 4, 2010).

Hiatt, W. R., S. R. Money, and E. P. Brass. 2008b. Long-term safety of cilostazol in patients with peripheral artery disease: The CASTLE study (Cilostazol: A Study in Long-term Effects). *Journal of Vascular Surgery* 47(2):330–336. http://download.journals.elsevierhealth.com/pdfs/journals/0741-5214/PIIS0741521407016096.pdf (accessed June 4, 2010).

Hirsch, A. T., Z. J. Haskal, N. R. Hertzer, C. W. Bakal, M. A. Creager, J. L. Halperin, L. F. Hiratzka, W. R. Murphy, J. W. Olin, J. B. Puschett, K. A. Rosenfield, D. Sacks, J. C. Stanley, L. M. Taylor Jr., C. J. White, J. White, R. A. White, E. M. Antman, S. C. Smith Jr., C. D. Adams, J. L. Anderson, D. P. Faxon, V. Fuster, R. J. Gibbons, S. A. Hunt, A. K. Jacobs, R. Nishimura, J. P. Ornato, R. L. Page, and B. Riegel. 2006. ACC/AHA 2005 practice guidelines for the management of patients with peripheral arterial disease (lower extremity, renal, mesenteric, and abdominal aortic). *Circulation* 113(11):e463–e654. http://circ.ahajournals.org/cgi/reprint/113/11/e463 (accessed June 4, 2010).

Hirsch, A. T., H. Kalsi, and T. W. Rooke. 2007. Peripheral arterial diseases. In *Cardiovascular Medicine*, 3rd Ed., edited by J. T. Willerson, H. J. J. Wellens, J. N. Cohn, and

D. R. Holmes Jr. London: Springer, Pp. 1681–1703 (Chapter 78). http://www.springerlink.com/content/k44p86174748xl18/fulltext.pdf (accessed June 4, 2010).

Hobbs, S. D., and A. W. Bradbury. 2003. Smoking cessation strategies in patients with peripheral arterial disease: An evidence-based approach. *European Journal of Vascular and Endovascular Surgery* 26(4):341–347.

Jonason, T., and R. Bergström. 1987. Cessation of smoking in patients with intermittent claudication: Effects on the risk of peripheral vascular complications, myocardial infarction and mortality. *Acta Medica Scandinavica* 221(3):253–260.

Khan, N. A., S. A. Rahim, S. S. Anand, D. L. Simel, and A. Panju. 2006. Does the clinical examination predict lower extremity peripheral arterial disease? *Journal of the American Medical Association* 295(5):536–546. http://jama.ama-assn.org/cgi/reprint/295/5/536 (accessed June 4, 2010).

McDermott, M. M., K. Liu, J. M. Guralnik, S. Mehta, M. H. Criqui, G. J. Martin, and P. Greenland. 1998. The ankle brachial index independently predicts walking velocity and walking endurance in peripheral arterial disease. *Journal of the American Geriatrics Society* 46(11):1355–1362.

McDermott, M. M., M. H. Criqui, K. Liu, J. M. Guralnik, P. Greenland, G. J. Martin, and W. Pearce. 2000. Lower ankle/brachial index, as calculated by averaging the dorsalis pedis and posterior tibial arterial pressures, and association with leg functioning in peripheral arterial disease. *Journal of Vascular Surgery* 32(6):1164–1171. http://download.journals.elsevierhealth.com/pdfs/journals/0741-5214/PIIS0741521400653016.pdf (accessed June 4, 2010).

McDermott, M. M., P. Greenland, K. Liu, J. M. Guralnik, M. H. Criqui, N. C. Dolan, C. Chan, L. Celic, W. H. Pearce, J. R. Schneider, L. Sharma, E. Clark, D. Gibson, and G. J. Martin. 2001. Leg symptoms in peripheral arterial disease: Associated clinical characteristics and functional impairment. *Journal of the American Medical Association* 286(13):1599–1606. http://jama.ama-assn.org/cgi/reprint/286/13/1599 (accessed June 4, 2010).

McDermott, M. M., P. Greenland, K. Liu, J. M. Guralnik, L. Celic, M. H. Criqui, C. Chan, G. J. Martin, J. Schneider, W. H. Pearce, L. M. Taylor, and E. Clark. 2002. The ankle brachial index is associated with leg function and physical activity: The walking and leg circulation study. *Annals of Internal Medicine* 136(12):873–883. http://www.annals.org/content/136/12/873.full.pdf+html (accessed June 4, 2010).

McDermott, M. M., J. M. Guralnik, L. Tian, L. Ferrucci, K. Liu, Y. Liao, and M. H. Criqui. 2007. Baseline functional performance predicts the rate of mobility loss in persons with peripheral arterial disease. *Journal of the American College of Cardiology* 50(10):974–982. http://www.ncbi.nlm.nih.gov/pmc/articles/PMC2645658/pdf/nihms45550.pdf (accessed June 4, 2010).

McDermott, M. M., J. M. Guralnik, L. Tian, K. Liu, L. Ferrucci, Y. Liao, L. Sharma, and M. H. Criqui. 2009. Associations of borderline and low normal ankle-brachial index values with functional decline at 5-year follow-up: The WALCS (Walking and Leg Circulation Study). *Journal of the American College of Cardiology* 53(12):1056–1062.

McPhail, I. R., P. C. Spittell, S. A. Weston, and K. R. Bailey. 2001. Intermittent claudication: An objective office-based assessment. *Journal of the American College of Cardiology* 37(5):1381–1385. http://content.onlinejacc.org/cgi/reprint/37/5/1381.pdf (accessed June 4, 2010).

Mohler, E. R., III, D. Treat-Jacobson, M. P. Reilly, K. E. Cunningham, M. Miani, M. H. Criqui, W. R. Hiatt, and A. T. Hirsch. 2004. Utility and barriers to performance of the ankle-brachial index in primary care practice. *Vascular Medicine* 9(4):253–260. http://vmj.sagepub.com/cgi/reprint/9/4/253 (accessed June 4, 2010).

Norgren, L., W. R. Hiatt, J. A. Dormandy, M. R. Nehler, K. A. Harris, F. G. Fowkes, and TASC II Working Group. 2007. Inter-society consensus for the management of peripheral arterial disease (TASC II). *Journal of Vascular Surgery* 45(Suppl 1):S5–S67. http://download.journals.elsevierhealth.com/pdfs/journals/0741-5214/PIIS0741521406022968.pdf (accessed June 4, 2010).

Paulose-Ram, R., Q. Gu, M. Eberhardt, E. Gregg, L. Geiss, and M. Engelgau. 2005. Lower extremity disease among persons aged ≥ 40 years with and without diabetes—United States, 1999–2002. *Morbidity & Mortality Weekly Report* 54(45):1158–1160. http://www.cdc.gov/mmwr/preview/mmwrhtml/mm5445a4.htm (accessed June 4, 2010).

Pearson, T., G. Kukulka, and Z. Ur Rahman. 2009. Ankle brachial index measurement in primary care setting: How long does it take? *Southern Medical Journal* 102(11):1106–1110.

Peräkylä, T. K., M. Lepäntalo, R. Lassila, J. A. Pietilä, and O. Lindfors. 1994. Ability to work after arterial surgery for chronic incapacitating ischaemia of the lower limb in middle-aged patients. *European Journal of Surgery* 160(8):425–429.

Regensteiner, J. G., J. E. Ware Jr., W. J. McCarthy, P. Zhang, W. P. Forbes, J. Heckman, and W. R. Hiatt. 2002. Effect of cilostazol on treadmill walking, community-based walking ability, and health-related quality of life in patients with intermittent claudication due to peripheral arterial disease: Meta-analysis of six randomized controlled trials. *Journal of the American Geriatrics Society* 50(12):1939–1946. http://www3.interscience.wiley.com/cgi-bin/fulltext/121434226/PDFSTART (accessed June 4, 2010).

Regensteiner, J. G., W. R. Hiatt, J. R. Coll, M. H. Criqui, D. Treat-Jacobson, M. M. McDermott, and A. T. Hirsch. 2008. The impact of peripheral arterial disease on health-related quality of life in the Peripheral Arterial Disease Awareness, Risk, and Treatment: New Resources for Survival (PARTNERS) Program. *Vascular Medicine* 13(1):15–24. http://vmj.sagepub.com/cgi/reprint/13/1/15 (accessed June 4, 2010).

Rehring, T. F., B. G. Sandhoff, R. S. Stolcpart, J. A. Merenich, and H. W. Hollis Jr. 2005. Atherosclerotic risk factor control in patients with peripheral arterial disease. *Journal of Vascular Surgery* 41(5):816–822.

Rutherford, R. B., J. D. Baker, C. Ernst, K. W. Johnston, J. M. Porter, S. Ahn, and D. N. Jones. 1997. Recommended standards for reports dealing with lower extremity ischemia: Revised version. *Journal of Vascular Surgery* 26(3):517–538. http://download.journals.elsevierhealth.com/pdfs/journals/0741-5214/PIIS0741521497700454.pdf (accessed June 4, 2010).

Selvin, E., and A. T. Hirsch. 2008. Contemporary risk factor control and walking dysfunction in individuals with peripheral arterial disease: NHANES 1999–2004. *Atherosclerosis* 201(2):425–433. http://www.ncbi.nlm.nih.gov/pmc/articles/PMC2771432/pdf/nihms-82490.pdf (accessed June 4, 2010).

SSA (Social Security Administration). 2008. *Listing of impairments—Adult listings (Part A). Disability evaluation under Social Security (Blue Book).* http://www.socialsecurity.gov/disability/professionals/bluebook/AdultListings.htm (accessed July 22, 2010).

Watson, L., B. Ellis, and G. C. Leng. 2008. Exercise for intermittent claudication. *Cochrane Database Systematic Reviews* 8(4):CD000990.

9

Chronic Venous Insufficiency

This chapter recommends revisions of the chronic venous insufficiency (CVI) listing (4.11) in the following areas: documentation of the presence of CVI, criteria for establishing the severity of CVI, and appropriate therapy and duration of therapy for CVI. The listing should require documentation that the visible leg abnormalities assumed to be CVI are caused by underlying venous disease. The listing should require documentation of venous reflux or obstruction using the current diagnostic standard—that is, duplex ultrasound. The terminology for skin changes in the lower leg secondary to CVI should be updated. The trial period of therapy in attempting to heal a venous ulcer should be longer. Three hospitalizations within a year for CVI should meet the functional limitation criterion, consistent with other listings.

DESCRIPTION

Chronic venous insufficiency (CVI) is a common disease and cause of debility in the United States. It can be defined as a pathological condition of the skin and subcutaneous tissue secondary to prolonged stasis of venous blood flow (Fowkes, 1996). CVI often may be associated with changes in skin pigmentation due to venous hypertension, and venous ulceration of the skin can occur. Physical manifestations include trophic changes, such as hyperpigmentation, induration, lipodermatosclerosis, and venous ulcers (Criqui et al., 2003). Leg symptoms associated with CVI include aching, itching, heaviness, fatigue, and swelling (Langer et al., 2005).

EPIDEMIOLOGY

In the United States, 3 to 4 percent of the population suffer from CVI (Coon et al., 1973). Approximately 1.5 percent of adults will be affected by venous ulceration. In 2007, more than 500,000 individuals in the United States had venous stasis ulcers.

Risk factors for CVI include older age, family history, multiple pregnancies, standing occupation, obesity in females, history of leg trauma, and prior deep venous thrombosis (Adhikari et al., 2000; Criqui et al., 2007). The annual incidence of varicose veins in the Framingham study was 2.6 percent in women and 1.9 percent in men. The prevalence of changes in skin pigmentation varied between 3 and 13 percent in the population. The presence of active or healed ulcers varied between 1.0 and 2.7 percent.

DIAGNOSTIC CRITERIA AND METHODS

CVI is often diagnosed by a visual inspection of the lower limbs to identify the presence of characteristic trophic changes of the skin, such as hyperpigmentation, edema, and ulcers (Criqui et al., 2003). Duplex ultrasound has become the standard for diagnosing the underlying venous reflux or obstruction, and is a procedure that is noninvasive and highly accurate (Neglen and Raju, 1992). The duplex ultrasound examination can detect reflux, or reverse flow of venous blood through a valve, and the probe can detect incompressibility of a vein, indicating obstruction from a prior blood clot. Other diagnostic techniques include contrast venography and plethysmography (Meissner et al., 2007).

Visible changes in the lower extremity consistent with CVI should not be assumed to be caused by CVI without documentation of venous reflux or obstruction (Criqui et al., 2003). Other conditions, such as right heart failure, can produce leg edema. In addition, distal leg swelling can reflect impaired lymphatic rather than venous drainage, a condition known as lymphedema. Lymphedema can be congenital, postinfectious, or posttraumatic, or can result from cancer or other surgery (Rockson, 2010). It is associated with functional limitations and reduced quality of life comparable to that reported by patients with venous leg ulcers (Augustin et al., 2005). There is no listing for lymphedema but the current introductory section of the cardiovascular system stipulates that it can medically equal the CVI listing in severity. Nevertheless, the committee believes that an accurate diagnosis should be made before granting disability for lymphedema.

Seven clinical categories have been developed to help clinicians understand and categorize the nature of chronic peripheral venous disease (see Table 9-1). The etiology of these disorders may be described as congenital, primary (i.e., not associated with an identifiable mechanism of venous dys-

TABLE 9-1 Clinical Classification of Chronic Venous Disease (CVD)

	Class
No signs of venous disease	C_0
Telangiectasias or reticular veins	C_1
Varicose veins	C_2
Edema	C_3
Skin changes secondary to CVD without ulceration	C_4
C_{4a}—Pigmentation or eczema	
C_{4b}—Lipodermatosclerosis or atrophie blanche	
Healed venous ulcer	C_5
Active venous ulcer	C_6

NOTE: The 0–6 clinical classification in this table is part of the CEAP (Clinical-Etiologic-Anatomic-Pathophysiologic) classification system developed by an international ad hoc committee of the American Venous Forum and is widely used in clinical research on CVD. In this classification system, chronic venous insufficiency indicates more severe disease. "The term 'chronic venous insufficiency' implies a functional abnormality of the venous system, and is usually reserved for more advanced disease, including edema (C3), skin changes (C4), or venous ulcers (C5–C6)" (Eklöf et al., 2004:1249).
SOURCE: Eklöf et al., 2004.

function), or secondary (i.e., the result of an antecedent event, usually an episode of acute deep venous thrombosis).

TREATMENT

Effective preventive and curative treatments for CVI are currently limited. The recurrent nature of the disease places the cost of care at more than $1 billion annually.

The main treatment for CVI and venous ulceration is compression stockings, leg elevation, and intensive skin care (Korn et al., 2002). An extensive review of clinical trials indicates that compression stocking therapy increases healing of ulcers; multicomponent systems are more effective than single component systems; and multicomponent systems containing elastic are more effective than those with largely inelastic components (O'Meara et al., 2009).

Some drugs have shown efficacy in helping ulcer healing, including pentoxifylline (Jull et al., 2007). Various surgical interventions have also shown efficacy in many patients (White and Ryjewski, 2005).

DISABILITY

CVI is associated with pain, physical function and mobility limitations, and depression and social isolation. Assessments of quality of life correlate directly with the severity of disease (Comerota, 2009; Kaplan et al., 2003). In addition to the discomfort caused by CVI, patients require leg elevation and avoidance of prolonged sitting or standing, which can impair participation in activities of daily living and instrumental activities of daily living.

CURRENT LISTING

Currently, the listing is for CVI of a lower extremity, with incompetency or obstruction of the deep venous system *and* either extensive brawny edema *or* superficial varicosities, stasis dermatitis, and recurrent or persistent ulceration that has not healed despite 3 or more months of treatment (Box 9-1).

CONCLUSIONS AND RECOMMENDATION

CVI results from either venous reflux or obstruction. The committee suggests replacing the outmoded term *incompetency* with *reflux*. The listing should also require the presence of symptoms as well as evidence, ideally by duplex ultrasound examination, of venous reflux or obstruction.

The requirement that reflux or obstruction should be in the deep venous system should be revised to refer to the *venous system* more generally, including the superficial, perforating, and deep veins, because research

BOX 9-1
Current Listing for Chronic Venous Insufficiency

4.11 Chronic venous insufficiency of a lower extremity with incompetency or obstruction of the deep venous system and one of the following:

A. Extensive brawny edema (see 4.00G3) involving at least two-thirds of the leg between the ankle and knee or the distal one-third of the lower extremity between the ankle and hip.

OR

B. Superficial varicosities, stasis dermatitis, and either recurrent ulceration or persistent ulceration that has not healed following at least 3 months of prescribed treatment.

SOURCE: SSA, 2008.

shows that disease of the superficial and perforator veins can also cause CVI and associated disability (Shami et al., 1993).

The listing should require documentation of reflux or obstruction with duplex or equivalent diagnostic techniques.

The committee recommends that the current (A) criterion, "extensive brawny edema," should be changed to trophic skin changes below the knee consistent with severe CVI, such as brawny edema, hyperpigmentation, or lipodermatosclerosis, that is not responsive to compression therapy. The current (B) criteria should be limited to recurrent or persistent venous ulcers. "Superficial varicosities" should be deleted because alone they are not indicative of CVI. "Stasis dermatitis" should also be deleted because this is a generic term referring to the trophic changes suggested for the new (A) listing above. Requiring a minimum of 6 months or more of unsuccessful prescribed therapy in attempting to heal a venous ulcer is a more definitive criterion than a 3-month trial. Finally, a third criterion (C) should be added: three hospitalizations for CVI within a year.

RECOMMENDATION 9-1. Listing 4.11 should be revised to require symptoms attributed to chronic venous insufficiency (CVI) as well as reflux or obstruction in the venous system, documented by duplex ultrasound or comparable technique. The documented symptomatic venous reflux or obstruction should be coupled with a requirement of the following:

- **Trophic changes of skin below the knee consistent with severe chronic venous insufficiency (e.g., hyperpigmentation, lipodermatosclerosis, brawny edema) and unresponsive to compression therapy;**

OR

- **Recurrent or persistent venous ulceration that has not been responsive to prescribed treatment for at least 6 months;**

OR

- **Three hospitalizations for CVI during a 12-month period.**

Also, if the committee's recommendations are adopted, the current introductory text to the cardiovascular system relevant to the current listing 4.11 would need to be revised. For example, the discussion of trophic changes required in the listing, which currently includes only brawny edema, should also include hyperpigmentation and lipodermatosclerosis.

REFERENCES

Adhikari, A., M. H. Criqui, V. Wooll, J. O. Deneberg, A. Fronek, R. D. Langer, and M. Klauber. 2000. The epidemiology of venous diseases. *Phlebology* 15(1):2–18.

Augustin, M., F. Bross, E. Foldi, W. Vanscheidt, and I. Zschocke. 2005. Development, validation and clinical use of the FLQA-I, a disease-specific quality of life questionnaire for patients with lymphedema. *Vasa* 34(1):31–35.

Comerota, A. J. 2009. Treatment of chronic venous disease of the lower extremities: What's new in guidelines? *Phlebolymphology* 16(4):313–320. http://www.phlebolymphology.org/2009/11/treatment-of-chronic-venous-disease-of-the-lower-extremities (accessed June 14, 2010).

Coon, W. W., P. W. Willis III, and J. B. Keller. 1973. Venous thromboembolism and other venous disease in the Tecumseh Community Health Study. *Circulation* 48(4):839–846. http://circ.ahajournals.org/cgi/reprint/48/4/839 (accessed June 14, 2010).

Criqui, M. H., M. Jamosmos, A. Fronek, J. O. Denenberg, R. D. Langer, J. Bergan, and B. A. Golomb. 2003. Chronic venous disease in an ethnically diverse population: The San Diego Population Study. *American Journal of Epidemiology* 158(5):448–456. http://aje.oxfordjournals.org/cgi/reprint/158/5/448 (accessed July 2, 2010).

Criqui, M. H., J. O. Denenberg, J. Bergan, R. D. Langer, and A. Fronek. 2007. Risk factors for chronic venous disease: The San Diego Population Study. *Journal of Vascular Surgery* 46(2):331–337. http://www.ncbi.nlm.nih.gov/pmc/articles/PMC2023874/pdf/nihms28091.pdf (accessed July 2, 2010).

Eklöf, B., R. B. Rutherford, J. J. Bergan, P. H. Carpentier, P. Gloviczki, R. L. Kistner, M. H. Meissner, G. L. Moneta, K. Myers, F. T. Padberg, M. Perrin, C. V. Ruckley, P. C. Smith, and T. W. Wakefield. 2004. Revision of the CEAP classification for chronic venous disorders: Consensus statement. *Journal of Vascular Surgery* 40(6):1248–1252. http://download.journals.elsevierhealth.com/pdfs/journals/0741-5214/PIIS0741521404012777.pdf (accessed June 14, 2010).

Fowkes, F. G. R. 1996. Epidemiology of chronic venous insufficiency. *Phlebology* 11(1):2–5.

Jull, A., B. Arroll, V. Parag, and J. Waters. 2007. Pentoxifylline for treating venous leg ulcer. *Cochrane Database of Systematic Reviews* 3(CD001733).

Kaplan, R. M., M. H. Criqui, J. O. Denenberg, J. Bergan, and F. Fronek. 2003. Quality of life in patients with chronic venous disease: San Diego Population Study. *Journal of Vascular Surgery* 37(5):1047–1053. http://download.journals.elsevierhealth.com/pdfs/journals/0741-5214/PIIS0741521402753093.pdf (accessed July 2, 2010).

Korn, P., S. T. Patel, J. A. Heller, J. S. Deitch, K. V. Krishnasastry, H. L. Bush, and K. C. Kent. 2002. Why insurers should reimburse for compression stockings in patients with chronic venous stasis. *Journal of Vascular Surgery* 35(5):950–957. http://download.journals.elsevierhealth.com/pdfs/journals/0741-5214/PIIS0741521402801021.pdf (accessed July 2, 2010).

Langer, R. D., E. Ho, J. O. Denenberg, A. Fronek, M. Allison, and M. H. Criqui. 2005. Relationships between symptoms and venous disease: The San Diego Population Study. *Archives of Internal Medicine* 165(12):1420–1424. http://archinte.ama-assn.org/cgi/content/full/165/12/1420 (accessed June 30, 2010).

Meissner, M. H., G. Moneta, K. Burnand, P. Gloviczki, J. M. Lohr, F. Lurie, M. A. Mattos, R. B. McLafferty, G. Mozes, R. B. Rutherford, F. Padberg, and D. S. Sumner. 2007. The hemodynamics and diagnosis of venous disease. *Journal of Vascular Surgery* 46(Suppl S):4S–24S. http://download.journals.elsevierhealth.com/pdfs/journals/0741-5214/PIIS0741521407015297.pdf (accessed June 14, 2010).

Neglen, P., and S. Raju. 1992. A comparison between descending phlebography and duplex Doppler investigation in the evaluation of reflux in chronic venous insufficiency:

A challenge to phlebography as the "gold standard." *Journal of Vascular Surgery* 16(5):687–693. http://download.journals.elsevierhealth.com/pdfs/journals/0741-5214/PII074152149290222T.pdf (accessed July 2, 2010).

O'Meara, S., N. A. Cullum, and E. A. Nelson. 2009. Compression for venous leg ulcers. *Cochrane Database of Systematic Reviews* 1(CD000265).

Rockson, S. G. 2010. Current concepts and future directions in the diagnosis and management of lymphatic vascular disease. *Vascular Medicine* 15(3):223–231.

Shami, S. K., S. Sarin, T. R. Cheatle, J. H. Scurr, and P. D. Smith. 1993. Venous ulcers and the superficial venous system. *Journal of Vascular Surgery* 17(3):487–490.

SSA (Social Security Administration). 2008. *Listing of impairments—Adult listings (Part A). Disability evaluation under Social Security (Blue Book).* http://www.socialsecurity.gov/disability/professionals/bluebook/AdultListings.htm (accessed July 22, 2010).

White, J. V., and C. Ryjewski. 2005. Chronic venous insufficiency. *Perspectives in Vascular Surgery and Endovascular Therapy* 17(4):319–327.

10

Congenital Heart Disease

This chapter includes a recommendation that evaluation for disability due to congenital heart disease be divided into four age groupings consistent with the changed timing of surgery for these defects and the developmental capacities of these age groups; criteria for evaluating functional impairment for each age group; a recommendation that one form of congenital heart disease of great severity meet the listing without additional evaluation of functional limitation; and a recommendation that all persons with congenital heart disease being evaluated for disability have information included in their applications about comorbidities, specifically any learning disability, cognitive impairment, depression, and anxiety.

DESCRIPTION

Congenital heart disease is an umbrella term that covers all heart defects present at birth, including dozens of defects that may occur singly or in combination. The abnormal structure of the cardiac chambers, valves, or great vessels in patients with congenital heart disease alters the normal pattern of blood flow. Additionally, individuals with congenital heart disease may develop cardiac complications such as arrhythmias, heart failure, and valve insufficiency, even after surgical correction of the structural abnormalities. In the 1980s, survival to 1 year of age of all individuals born with congenital heart defects was 81 percent (Ferencz et al., 1993), but by 2003 this had improved to 92 percent (Tennant et al., 2010).

Surgery is the mainstay of treatment for congenital heart disease, and the expected results can be classified as follows:

- *Curative*: Patients with these conditions rarely have long-term sequelae after surgical correction in childhood. These conditions are patent ductus arteriosus, secundum atrial defect, and uncomplicated ventricular septal defect.
- *Reparative*: Patients with these defects are improved after corrective surgery, yet have lifelong sequelae, and some proportion will have significant late impairment. These defects are aortic stenosis, atrioventricular canal, coarctation of the aorta, partial anomalous pulmonary venous return, pulmonary stenosis, tetralogy of Fallot, total anomalous pulmonary venous return, d-transposition of the great arteries, and l-transposition (also called congenital corrected transposition of the great arteries).
- *Palliative*: Surgery in these patients (if done) does not fully correct the underlying defect, so they are likely to have significant lifelong impairment of function. These defects are Eisenmenger syndrome, hypoplastic left heart syndrome, malaligned atrioventricular canal with single ventricle repair, single ventricle, tricuspid atresia, and unrepaired cyanotic heart disease.

EPIDEMIOLOGY

Eight out of 1,000 infants are born with congenital heart disease. Of these, approximately 25 percent require immediate surgical or catheter-based intervention (Ferencz et al., 1993). Even with treatment, the lifespan of individuals with congenital heart disease is limited compared with their peers; 89.5 percent of individuals with congenital heart disease are alive at age 20, but for some diagnoses (e.g., truncus arteriosus and single ventricle), the survival is much poorer (Tennant et al., 2010). Survival in individuals with congenital heart disease who reach adulthood is reduced (Verheugt et al., 2010). Death is commonly due to heart failure or sudden death, and risk is increased by arrhythmia, endocarditis, myocardial infarction, and pulmonary hypertension.

In 2000, 1 million adults in the United States were living with congenital heart disease. An estimated half of them had relatively simple residual disease, one quarter had moderately complex residual disease, and one quarter had severe residual disease (Warnes et al., 2001). However, functional disability is not limited to those with "severe" disease, as even an individual with "simple" disease may be disabled due to a complication.

DIAGNOSTIC CRITERIA AND METHODS

The diagnosis of congenital heart disease is made by physical examination, echocardiography, magnetic resonance imaging, cardiac computed tomography, cardiac catheterization, and open-heart surgery. The ICD-9 diagnosis codes indicating congenital heart disease fall primarily between 745.0 and 747.9. Distinguishing among the various congenital heart disease defects can be difficult, and accurate diagnosis can require special expertise and training. Children with congenital heart disease are best evaluated, when possible, in pediatric cardiology centers and by echocardiographic centers certified in congenital heart disease. Adults with congenital heart disease are best evaluated by specialized centers devoted to the evaluation and treatment of such adults. These centers are recommended for their ongoing care (Warnes et al., 2008).

CONSIDERATION OF NONCARDIAC CONGENITAL ANOMALIES

The evaluation of disability status in individuals with congenital heart disease is further complicated by the presence of concomitant noncardiac congenital abnormalities in about 20 percent of cases (e.g., diGeorge syndrome and Down syndrome, among others). Individuals with congenital heart disease also have a higher prevalence of neuropsychiatric disorders, including learning disabilities, cognitive impairment, depression, and anxiety.

TREATMENT

Recent Advances

Surgical intervention for congenital heart disease began in the mid-1960s and was first applied to infants in the mid-1970s. Advances in surgical techniques have continued since that time. These include the development of staged palliation for hypoplastic left heart syndrome. Catheter-based treatment is also evolving rapidly, permitting the placement of valves and closure of atrial and ventricular defects percutaneously in some patients. Drug treatments for the complications of congenital heart disease have also advanced, including the development of medications for pulmonary hypertension (Eisenmenger syndrome) and better drug treatments for heart failure and arrhythmias.

Side Effects of Treatments

With improvement in infant surgery and palliation of more complex lesions, the number of survivors of congenital heart disease has increased and the population of children and adults with congenital heart disease in the United States has grown.

Residual defects after surgical repair may contribute to functional impairment (Perloff and Warnes, 2001: adapted from information presented in Table 2). They can be classified as follows:

- *Valvular*: Mitral or tricuspid insufficiency, pulmonary insufficiency, mitral stenosis
- *Ventricular*
    - Ventricular inversion, atrial baffling of blood flow
    - Hypertrophy
    - Abnormal systolic or diastolic function
- *Vascular*: Abnormal venous connections
- *Prosthetic*: Synthetic conduits, artificial valves

Even when surgical treatment corrects the abnormal anatomy, patients may still have late complications and sequelae. The incidence of atrial arrhythmias increases with age: up to 40 percent of adults with congenital heart disease may have atrial arrhythmias by age 50 (Bouchardy et al., 2009). Pulmonary vascular resistance may be increased as a result of longstanding left-to-right shunting.

Trends in Morbidity and Mortality

Survival improved for infants to 90 percent by the 1990s, but longterm survival remains diminished compared with the general population. With extended lifespan after surgery, more late sequelae of congenital heart disease are evident among adults.

DISABILITY

Congenital Heart Disease and Work/Effort

In one European database, 59 percent of adults with complex congenital heart disease had paid employment, compared with 76 percent of patients with mild, complex congenital heart disease. The employment rate among adults with complex disease was significantly less than the general population (Kamphuis et al., 2002). Learning disabilities, depression, and syndromic comorbidities may also impair the ability of individuals with congenital heart disease to hold gainful employment.

Other conditions that may affect overall functional status among congenital heart patients include developmental abnormalities, mental retardation, growth retardation, somatic abnormalities (auditory, dental, facial, musculoskeletal), central nervous system abnormalities, seizures, visual abnormalities, and medical disorders (e.g., renal insufficiency or liver cirrhosis).

Congenital Heart Disease and Functional Limitation

Children

Prior to cardiac surgery many children are unable to feed normally, requiring frequent prolonged or enteral feedings. Children may lack normal muscle strength and, consequently, may have delayed development. They may be unable to attend day care because of weakness or intolerance to respiratory infections. Infants may require home monitoring of heart rate, respiratory rate, daily weight, and pulse oximetry prior to surgery, compromising their ability to function (Kugler et al., 2009). Some infants have additional noncardiac congenital abnormalities that contribute to medical morbidity or developmental delay.

Following cardiac surgery, children may have variable degrees of disability. At school age, 11 to 17 percent of children who have had an operation for their congenital heart disease have significant limitations in adaptive behavior, socialization, communication skills, and daily living skills (Majnemer et al., 2008). Even after arterial switch operation for transposition of the great arteries, one of the surgical procedures thought to be most successful, one quarter of children were functionally impaired 15 years later. Psychosocial deficits are common (Williams et al., 2003).

Patients who have had only palliative surgery typically have severe lifelong functional limitations. Individuals born with single ventricles, for instance, have exercise capacity of only 50 to 60 percent of what is normal for their ages (Reybrouck and Mertens, 2005), and older individuals are more functionally impaired than younger individuals. Exercise capacity is also decreased in many other complex congenital heart diseases and declines at repeat testing (Manlhiot et al., 2009; Samman et al., 2008; Weipert et al., 1997).

Persons with congenital heart disease may be limited in school or work ability by intrinsic or extrinsic factors. Intrinsic factors may include arrhythmia, chronic heart failure, depression, learning disability, and pulmonary hypertension. Extrinsic factors may include intolerance of lifting weight, intolerance of heat or humidity, lack of stamina, and decreased aerobic capacity. Many patients with congenital heart disease have restrictive lung disease in addition to chronic heart disease (Lubica, 1996).

Neuropsychiatric symptoms (fears, depression, or anxiety) have been identified in 40 to 50 percent of children and adults with complex congenital heart disease (Bromberg et al., 2003; Cohen et al., 2007; Gupta et al., 1998; Karsdorp et al., 2007; Kovacs et al., 2009; Loup et al., 2009; McCrindle et al., 2006; Norozi et al., 2006.; Spijkerboer et al., 2007; Toren and Horesh, 2007).

Functional limitation in older children and adults with congenital heart disease may be assessed objectively by exercise testing with measurement of maximal oxygen consumption. Effort can be measured by the respiratory exchange ratio. Although measured exercise capacity correlates with perceived quality of life, children and adults with congenital heart disease tend to report greater exercise capacity than would be judged by peak exercise performance (Hager and Hess, 2005).

Age-Related Issues in Evaluation

The functional consequences of congenital heart disease change as children grow into adolescence and adulthood. In addition, surgery alters the natural history of disease in both predictable and unpredictable ways.

Surgery is the mainstay of treatment for congenital heart disease, but the timing and extent of surgery varies according to the specific defect. Most congenital heart defects are now repaired in infancy, certainly by age 1. Single ventricle defects, however, are repaired with staged surgery, using a sequence of several procedures over the first 2 to 3 years of life. Other defects that can be corrected in a single procedure are occasionally delayed until the child reaches a defined size or age.

After the completion of planned corrective surgery, a patient with congenital heart disease may be restored to full functional capacity (e.g., after "curative" procedures) or have residual function limitations. These are best assessed after about 6 months of recovery from the last planned operation.

Growth and development continues through childhood and may alter functional capabilities. The functional status of patients should be relatively stable by age 12, at which time children can cooperate sufficiently to undergo exercise testing. Reevaluation of patients with congenital heart disease at this age can establish their longer-term capacities and facilitate educational and vocational planning. Functional limitations may develop at any age, however, due to the development of arrhythmia, heart failure, endocarditis, or pulmonary hypertension, among other problems.

See Figures 10-1 through 10-4 for documentation of congenital heart defects likely to require surgery, from diagnosis of significant heart disease in infancy or childhood through age 12 to adult.

CURRENT LISTINGS

The current listings for children and adults are found in Boxes 10-1 (children) and 10-2 (adults).

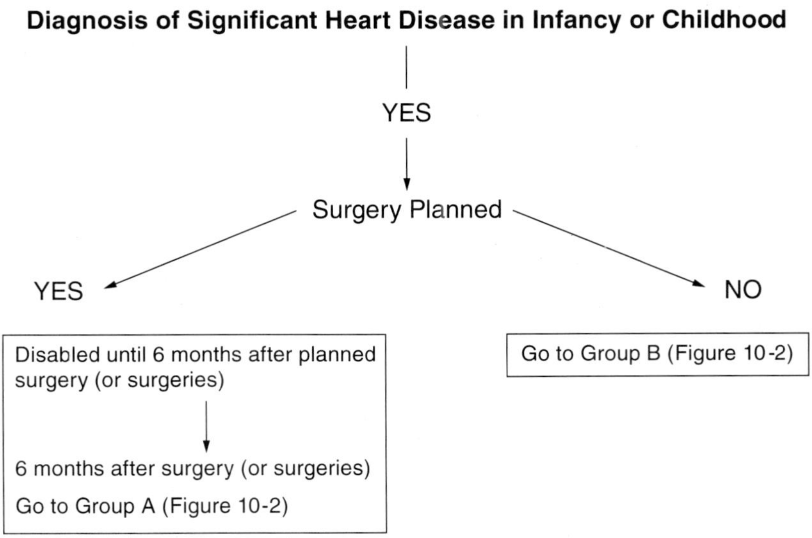

FIGURE 10-1 Documentation of congenital heart defect likely to require surgery, diagnosis of significant heart disease in infancy or childhood.

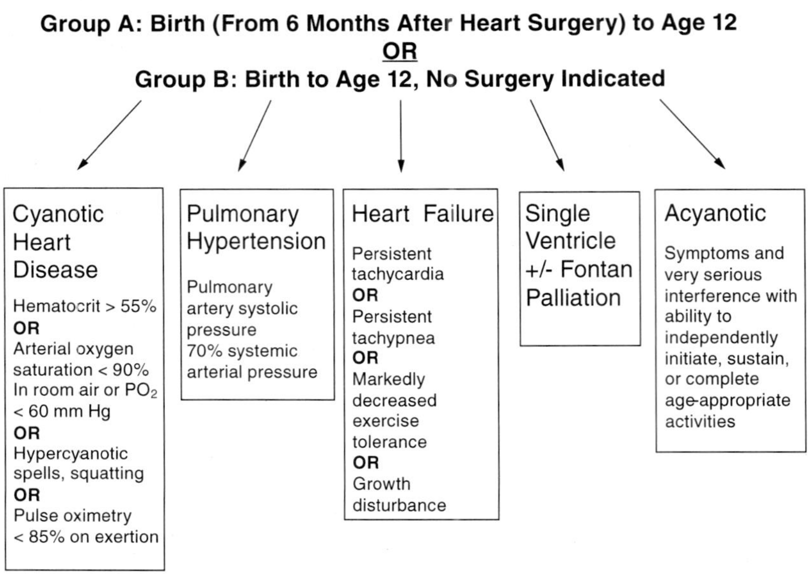

FIGURE 10-2 Documentation of congenital heart defect likely to require surgery, disabled by Groups A and B, birth to age 12.

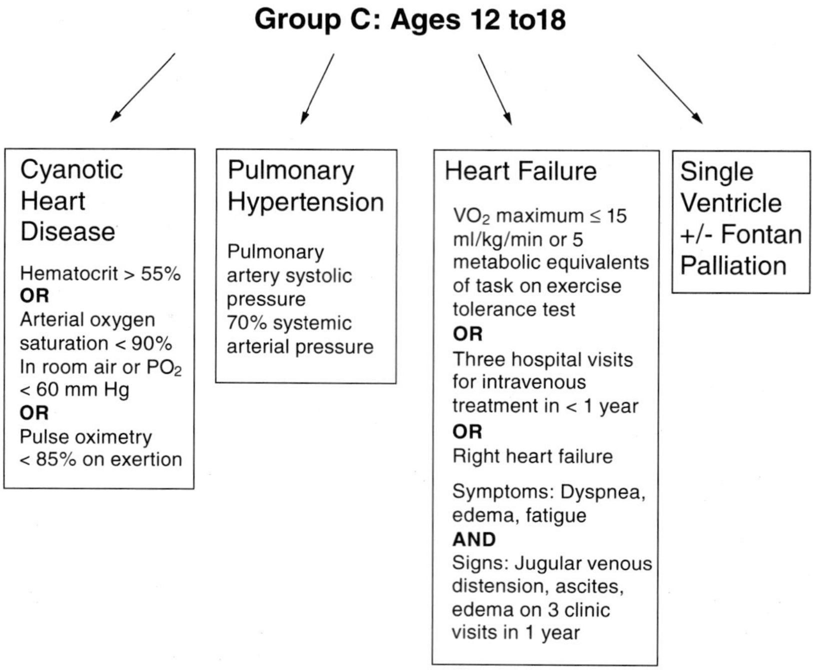

FIGURE 10-3 Documentation of congenital heart defect, disabled by Group C, ages 12 to 18.

CONCLUSIONS AND RECOMMENDATIONS

All Individuals

RECOMMENDATION 10-1. Learning disabilities, cognitive impairment, and associated noncardiac congenital anomalies are frequent comorbidities for individuals with congenital heart disease. Disability evaluators should be trained to understand the effects of these comorbidities to better evaluate if a combination of impairments, no one of which meets a listing, equals a listing.

RECOMMENDATION 10-2. Assessment of disability in children should account for the natural history of congenital heart disease and patterns of development by dividing children into three age/treatment groups:

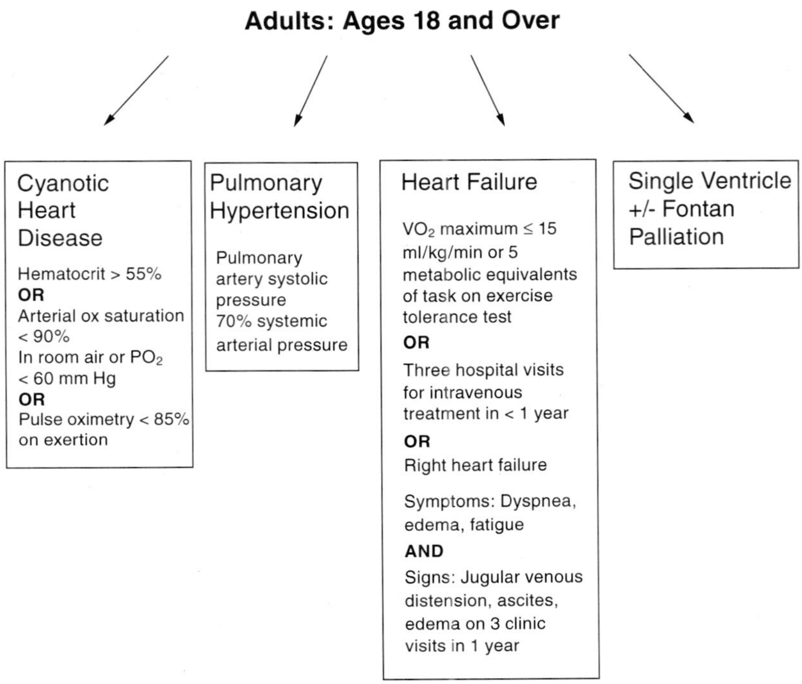

FIGURE 10-4 Documentation of congenital heart defect disabled as adults, ages 18 and over.

Group A: Infants prior to and for 6 months after definitive cardiac surgery;
Group B: Children from 6 months after definitive surgery until age 12 and children from birth onward for whom surgery is not indicated; and
Group C: Children age 12 and older.

RECOMMENDATION 10-3. Infants with a medically confirmed diagnosis of cardiac malformation requiring open-heart surgery should be considered disabled until 6 months after definitive corrective surgery. A diagnosis of significant cardiac disease and documentation of a surgical plan or surgical event should be sufficient evidence of disability.

RECOMMENDATION 10-4. Children from 6 months after definitive cardiac surgery until their 12th birthday and children from birth

BOX 10-1
Current Congenital Heart Disease Listing for Children

104.06 Congenital heart disease, documented by appropriate medically acceptable imaging (see 104.00A3d) or cardiac catheterization, with one of the following:

A. Cyanotic heart disease, with persistent, chronic hypoxemia as manifested by:

1. Hematocrit of 55 percent or greater on two evaluations 3 months or more apart within a consecutive 12-month period (see 104.00A3e); or
2. Arterial O_2 saturation of less than 90 percent in room air, or resting arterial PO_2 of 60 Torr or less; or
3. Hypercyanotic spells, syncope, characteristic squatting, or other incapacitating symptoms directly related to documented cyanotic heart disease; or
4. Exercise intolerance with increased hypoxemia on exertion.

OR

B. Secondary pulmonary vascular obstructive disease with pulmonary arterial systolic pressure elevated to at least 70 percent of the systemic arterial systolic pressure.

OR

C. Symptomatic acyanotic heart disease, with ventricular dysfunction interfering very seriously with the ability to independently initiate, sustain, or complete activities.

OR

D. For infants under 12 months of age at the time of filing, with life-threatening congenital heart impairment that will require or already has required surgical treatment in the first year of life, and the impairment is expected to be disabling (because of residual impairment following surgery, or the recovery time required, or both) until the attainment of at least 1 year of age, consider the infant to be under disability until the attainment of at least age 1; thereafter, evaluate impairment severity with reference to the appropriate listing.

SOURCE: SSA, 2008b.

BOX 10-2
Current Congenital Heart Disease Listing for Adults

4.06 Symptomatic congenital heart disease (cyanotic or acyanotic), documented by appropriate medically acceptable imaging (see 4.00A3d) or cardiac catheterization, with one of the following:

A. Cyanosis at rest, and:

1. Hematocrit of 55 percent or greater; or

2. Arterial O_2 saturation of less than 90 percent in room air, or resting arterial PO_2 of 60 Torr or less.

OR

B. Intermittent right-to-left shunting resulting in cyanosis on exertion (e.g., Eisenmenger's physiology) and with arterial PO_2 of 60 Torr or less at a workload equivalent to 5 METs or less.

OR

C. Secondary pulmonary vascular obstructive disease with pulmonary arterial systolic pressure elevated to at least 70 percent of the systemic arterial systolic pressure.

SOURCE: SSA, 2008a.

onward for whom surgery is not indicated, with congenital heart disease documented by appropriate medically acceptable imaging or cardiac catheterization, with one of the following criteria should be considered disabled:

A. Cyanotic heart disease, with persistent, chronic hypoxemia as manifested by:

1. Hematocrit of 55 percent or greater; or
2. Arterial O_2 saturation of less than 90 percent in room air, or resting arterial PO_2 of 60 Torricelli or less; or
3. Hypercyanotic spells, syncope, characteristic squatting, or other incapacitating symptoms directly related to documented cyanotic heart disease; or
4. Exercise intolerance with increased hypoxemia on exertion measured by pulse oximetry.

OR

B. Secondary pulmonary vascular obstructive disease with pulmonary arterial systolic pressure elevated to at least 70 percent of the systemic arterial systolic pressure determined by echocardiography or right heart catheterization;

OR

C. Symptomatic acyanotic heart disease interfering seriously with the ability to independently initiate, sustain, or complete activities;

OR

D. Chronic heart failure manifested by:

1. Persistent tachycardia at rest (see Table I[1]); or
2. Persistent tachypnea at rest (see Table II[2]); or
3. Markedly decreased exercise tolerance; or
4. Growth disturbance with:

    a. An involuntary weight loss or failure to gain weight at an appropriate rate for age, resulting in a fall of 15 percentiles from an established growth curve (on the current Centers for Disease Control and Prevention [CDC] growth chart), which is currently present (see 104.00A3f) and has persisted for 2 months or longer; or
    b. An involuntary weight loss or failure to gain weight at an appropriate rate for age, resulting in a fall to below the third percentile from an established growth curve (on the current CDC growth chart), which is currently present (see 104.00A3f) and has persisted for 2 months or longer.

[1] See Table 1, Section 104.02, Chronic Heart Failure. For tachycardia at rest, apical heart rate: under age 1, 150 beats per minute; ages 1 through 3, 130 beats per minute; ages 4 through 9, 120 beats per minute; ages 10 through 15, 110 beats per minute; and over age 15, 100 beats per minute (SSA, 2008b).

[2] See Table II, Tachypnea at Rest, Section 104.02, Chronic Heart Failure. For tachypnea at rest, respiratory rate, under age 1, over 40 breaths per minute; ages 1 through 5, over 35 breaths per minute; ages 6 through 9, over 30 breaths per minute; and over age 9, over 25 breaths per minute (SSA, 2008b).

RECOMMENDATION 10-5. Children age 12 and older should be considered disabled if they have congenital heart disease documented by appropriate medically acceptable imaging or cardiac catheterization, with one of the following criteria:

A. Cyanosis at rest, and:

1. Hematocrit of 55 percent or greater; or
2. Arterial O_2 saturation of less than 90 percent in room air, or resting arterial PO_2 of 60 Torricelli (Torr) or less.

OR

B. Intermittent right-to-left shunting resulting in cyanosis on exertion (e.g., Eisenmenger's physiology) as determined by pulse oximetry and with arterial PO_2 of 60 Torr or less or pulse oximetry 85 percent or less at a workload equivalent to 5 metabolic equivalents of task (METs) or less;

OR

C. Secondary pulmonary vascular obstructive disease with pulmonary arterial systolic pressure elevated to at least 70 percent of the systemic arterial systolic pressure determined by echocardiography or cardiac catheterization;

OR

D. Single ventricle, including hypoplastic left heart syndrome, double inlet left ventricle, and Fontan operation for single ventricle;

OR

E. Chronic heart failure manifested by:

1. Exercise capacity with maximal oxygen consumption less than 15 ml/kg/min or work load less than 5 METs; or
2. Three hospitalizations or emergency room visits with use of intravenous medications for heart failure management in 1 year; or
3. Evidence of right heart failure manifested by:

a. Symptoms of dyspnea, edema, or exercise intolerance; and
b. Jugular venous distension, hepatomegaly, ascites, and/or dependent edema on three clinic visits in 1 year.

RECOMMENDATION 10-6. Adults with a medically confirmed diagnosis of congenital heart disease should be considered disabled if they also demonstrate one of the following:

A. Cyanosis at rest, and:

1. Hematocrit of 55 percent or greater; or
2. Arterial O_2 saturation of less than 90 percent in room air, or resting arterial PO_2 of 60 Torricelli (Torr) or less;

OR

B. Intermittent right-to-left shunting resulting in cyanosis on exertion (e.g., Eisenmenger's physiology) as determined by pulse oximetry and with arterial PO_2 of 60 Torr or less or pulse oximetry 85 percent or less at a workload equivalent to 5 metabolic equivalents of task (METs) or less;

OR

C. Secondary pulmonary vascular obstructive disease with pulmonary arterial systolic pressure elevated to at least 70 percent of the systemic arterial systolic pressure determined by echocardiography or right heart catheterization;

OR

D. Single ventricle including hypoplastic left heart syndrome, double inlet left ventricle, and Fontan operation for single ventricle;

OR

E. Diagnosis of congenital heart disease and chronic heart failure manifested by:

1. Exercise capacity with maximal oxygen consumption less than 15 ml/kg/min or work load less than 5 METs; or

2. **Three hospitalizations or emergency room visits with intravenous medication administration for heart failure management in 1 year; or**
3. **Evidence of right heart failure manifested by:**

    a. **Symptoms of dyspnea, edema, or exercise intolerance; and**
    b. **Jugular venous distension, hepatomegaly, ascites, and dependent edema on three clinic visits in 1 year.**

REFERENCES

Bouchardy, J., J. Therrien, L. Pilote, R. Ionescu-Ittu, G. Martucci, N. Bottega, and A. J. Marelli. 2009. Atrial arrhythmias in adults with congenital heart disease. *Circulation* 120(17):1679–1686.

Bromberg, J. I., P. J. Beasley, E. J. D'Angelo, M. Landzberg, and D. R. DeMaso. 2003. Depression and anxiety in adults with congenital heart disease: A pilot study. *Heart & Lung* 32(2):105–110.

Cohen, M., D. Mansoor, H. Langut, A. Lorber. 2007. Quality of life, depressed mood, and self-esteem in adolescents with heart disease. *Psychosomatic Medicine* 69(4):313–318.

Ferencz, C., J. D. Rubin, C. A. Loffredo, and C. M. Magee. 1993. *Epidemiology of congenital heart disease: The Baltimore-Washington Infant Study, 1981–1989*. Mount Kisco, NY: Futura Publishing Company.

Gupta, S., R. M. Giuffre, S. Crawford, and J. Waters. 1998. Covert fears, anxiety and depression in congenital heart disease. *Cardiology in the Young* 8(4):491–499.

Hager, A., and J. Hess. 2005. Comparison of health related quality of life with cardiopulmonary exercise testing in adolescents and adults with congenital heart disease. *Heart* 91(4):517–520.

Kamphuis, M., T. Vogels, J. Ottenkamp, E. E. Van Der Wall, S. P. Verloove-Vanhorick, and H. W. Vliegen. 2002. Employment in adults with congenital heart disease. *Archives of Pediatrics & Adolescent Medicine* 156(11):1143–1148.

Karsdorp, P. A., W. Everaerd, M. Kindt, and B. J. M. Mulder. 2007. Psychological and cognitive functioning in children and adolescents with congenital heart disease: A meta-analysis. *Journal of Pediatric Psychology* 32(5):527–541.

Kovacs, A. H., A. S. Saidi, E. A. Kuhl, S. F. Sears, C. Silversides, J. L. Harrison, L. Ong, J. Colman, E. Oechslin, and R. P. Nolan. 2009. Depression and anxiety in adult congenital heart disease: Predictors and prevalence. *International Journal of Cardiology* 137(2):158–164.

Kugler, J. D., R. H. Beekman III, G. L. Rosenthal, K. J. Jenkins, T. S. Klitzner, G. R. Martin, S. R. Neish, and C. Lannon. 2009. Development of a pediatric cardiology quality improvement collaborative: From inception to implementation. From the Joint Council on Congenital Heart Disease Quality Improvement Task Force. *Congenital Heart Disease* 4(5):318–328.

Loup, O., C. von Weissenfluh, B. Gahl, M. Schwerzmann, T. Carrel, and A. Kadner. 2009. Quality of life of grown-up congenital heart disease patients after congenital cardiac surgery. *European Journal of Cardio-Thoracic Surgery* 36(1):105–111.

Lubica, H. 1996. Pathologic lung function in children and adolescents with congenital heart defects. *Pediatric Cardiology* 17(5):314–315.

Majnemer, A., C. Limperopoulos, M. Shevell, C. Rohlicek, B. Rosenblatt, and C. Tchervenkov. 2008. Developmental and functional outcomes at school entry in children with congenital heart defects. *Journal of Pediatrics* 153(1):55–60.

Manlhiot, C., S. Knezevich, E. Radojewski, G. Cullen-Dean, W. G. Williams, and B. W. McCrindle. 2009. Functional health status of adolescents after the Fontan procedure—Comparison with their siblings. *Canadian Journal of Cardiology* 25(9):e294–e300.

McCrindle, B. W., R. V. Williams, P. D. Mitchell, D. T. Hsu, S. M. Paridon, A. M. Atz, J. S. Li, J. W. Newburger, and Pediatric Heart Network Investigators. 2006. Relationship of patient and medical characteristics to health status in children and adolescents after the Fontan procedure. *Circulation* 113(8):1123–1129.

Norozi, K., M. Zoege, R. Buchhorn, A. Wessel, and S. Geyer. 2006. The influence of congenital heart disease on psychological conditions in adolescents and adults after corrective surgery. *Congenital Heart Disease* 1(6):282–288.

Perloff, J. K., and C. A. Warnes. 2001. Challenges posed by adults with repaired congenital heart disease. *Circulation* 103:2637–2643.

Reybrouck, T., and L. Mertens. 2005. Physical performance and physical activity in grown-up congenital heart disease. *European Journal of Cardiovascular Prevention & Rehabilitation* 12(5):498–502.

Samman, A., M. Schwerzmann, O. H. Balint, D. Tanous, A. Redington, J. Granton, S. C. Siu, and C. K. Silversides. 2008. Exercise capacity and biventricular function in adult patients with repaired tetralogy of Fallot. *American Heart Journal* 156(1):100–105.

Spijkerboer, A. W., W. A. Helbing, A. J. J. C. Bogers, R. T. Van Domburg, F. C. Verhulst, and E. M. W. J. Utens. 2007. Long-term psychological distress, and styles of coping, in parents of children and adolescents who underwent invasive treatment for congenital cardiac disease. *Cardiology in the Young* 17(6):638–645.

SSA (Social Security Administration). 2008a. *Listing of impairments—Adult listings (Part A). Disability evaluation under Social Security (Blue Book).* http://www.socialsecurity.gov/disability/professionals/bluebook/AdultListings.htm (accessed July 22, 2010).

SSA. 2008b. *Listing of impairments—Childhood listings (Part B). Disability evaluation under Social Security (Blue Book).* http://www.socialsecurity.gov/disability/professionals/bluebook/ChildhoodListings.htm (accessed July 22, 2010).

Tennant, P. W., M. S. Pearce, M. Bythell, and J. Rankin. 2010. 20-year survival of children born with congenital anomalies: A population-based study. *Lancet* 375(9715):649–656.

Toren, P., and N. Horesh. 2007. Psychiatric morbidity in adolescents operated in childhood for congenital cyanotic heart disease. *Journal of Paediatrics and Child Health* 43(10):662–666.

Verheugt, C. L., C. S. P. M. Uiterwaal, E. T. van der Velde, F. J. Meijboom, P. G. Peiper, A. P. J. van Dijk, H. W. Vliegen, D. E. Grobbee, and B. J. M. Mulder. 2010. Mortality in adult congenital heart disease. *European Heart Journal* 31(10):1220–1229.

Warnes, C. A., R. Liberthson, G. K. Danielson Jr, A. Dore, L. Harris, J. I. E. Hoffman, J. Somerville, R. G. Williams, and G. D. Webb. 2001. Task Force 1: The changing profile of congenital heart disease in adult life. *Journal of the American College of Cardiology* 37(5):1170–1175.

Warnes, C. A., R. G. Williams, T. M. Bashor, J. S. Child, H. M. Connolly, J. A. Dearani, P. del Nido, J. W. Fasules, T. P. Graham Jr, Z. M. Hijazi, S. A. Hunt, M. E. King, M. J. Landzberg, P. D. Miner, M. J. Radford, E. P. Walsh, and G. D. Webb. 2008. ACC/AHA 2008 guidelines for the management of adults with congenital heart disease: A report of the American College of Cardiology/American Heart Association Task Force on Practice Guidelines (Writing Committee to Develop Guidelines on the Management of Adults With Congenital Heart Disease) developed in collaboration with the American Society of Echocardiography, Heart Rhythm Society, International Society for Adult Congenital

Heart Disease, Society for Cardiovascular Angiography and Interventions, and Society of Thoracic Surgeons. *Journal of the American College of Cardiology* 52(23):e143–e263.

Weipert, J., W. Koch, J. C. Haehnel, and H. Meisner. 1997. Exercise capacity and mid-term survival in patients with tricuspid atresia and complex congenital cardiac malformations after modified Fontan-operation. *European Journal of Cardio-Thoracic Surgery* 12(4):574–580.

Williams, W. G., B. W. McCrindle, D. A. Ashburn, R. A. Jonas, C. Mavroudis, E. H. Blackstone, and the Congenital Heart Surgeon's Society. 2003. Outcomes of 829 neonates with complete transposition of the great arteries 12-17 years after repair. *European Journal of Cardio-Thoracic Surgery* 24(1):1–9.

11

Pulmonary Hypertension

In this chapter, the committee recommends that a new listing in the cardiovascular system listings be created to address pulmonary hypertension. Pulmonary hypertension, which is incurable despite treatment, is associated with functional limitations and significantly increases patient mortality. Most patients will meet criteria for disability based on the condition generally being fairly advanced at the time of diagnosis.

DESCRIPTION

The right side of the heart collects venous blood from the body and pumps it into the lungs, where oxygen is taken up from inspired air and carbon dioxide is released in the expired air. This critical circulation of blood through the vessels of the lungs—the pulmonary arteries, capillaries, and veins—normally occurs at much lower pressures than blood flow through the systemic circulation to the rest of the body. The normal pulmonary artery systolic pressure is 20 mm Hg or less, and the normal mean (average) pulmonary artery pressure is 12 mm Hg. A number of disease processes affect the pulmonary circulation and increase the pressure levels in the pulmonary arteries and right ventricle. If these pressure elevations are sufficiently severe or sustained, right-sided heart failure may develop.

Pulmonary hypertension is present when the pulmonary artery pressures are elevated above normal. The term applies particularly to diseases that affect the small pulmonary arteries and markedly increase their resistance to blood flow. Pulmonary hypertension of this type may be of unknown cause (so-called primary pulmonary hypertension) or secondary to conditions, such as connective tissue disease, sarcoidosis, and certain inherited conditions. Pulmonary hypertension may develop as the result of chronic pulmonary thromboembolism. The condition may also develop secondary to lung disease or hypoxemia, such as chronic obstructive pulmonary disease, interstitial lung disease, and obstructive sleep apnea. Pulmonary hypertension secondary to lung disease is termed *cor pulmonale* (cor pulmonale is not discussed further because disability criteria are established in the pulmonary disease listings). Pulmonary hypertension is a relatively common complication of left-sided heart disease, such as mitral valvular disease or cardiomyopathy, or due to congenital heart disease. Pulmonary hypertension that develops as a secondary manifestation of another primary form of heart disease should be evaluated using the disability criteria established for the primary disease, and so is not discussed further in this chapter.

Pulmonary hypertension is associated with high mortality and with marked functional limitations. The condition is often quite advanced at the time of diagnosis, laɪgely because its symptoms are nonspecific and the diagnosis is difficult to make.

EPIDEMIOLOGY

Pulmonary hypertension is an uncommon disease with an estimated prevalence of 2 per million in the United States. Women are affected much more often than men, and the typical age at the time of diagnosis is between 30 and 50. The disease is associated with genetic markers (mutations and polymorphisms in the Type II bone morphogenic protein receptor), and with the use of appetite suppressants.

DIAGNOSTIC CRITERIA AND METHODS

The definitive method for the diagnosis of pulmonary hypertension is a right heart catheterization with hemodynamic measurements.

Right Heart Catheterization

Pressures in the pulmonary artery, right ventricle, and right atrium can be measured directly during a right heart catheterization. Cardiac output and pulmonary capillary wedge pressure should also be measured to characterize fully the state of the pulmonary vessels.

Pulmonary hypertension is considered present when the mean pulmonary artery pressure is greater than 25 mm Hg at rest. Pulmonary arterial hypertension is a more specific diagnostic term that requires a pulmonary capillary wedge pressure of 15 mm Hg or less with a pulmonary vascular resistance of greater than 3 Wood units (mm Hg/liters/minute) in the setting of an elevated mean pulmonary artery pressure (McLaughlin et al., 2009).

Doppler Echocardiography

Most patients with pulmonary hypertension have some degree of regurgitation of the tricuspid valve. The velocity of tricuspid regurgitation can be measured using Doppler echocardiography, and this can then be used to estimate the systolic pulmonary artery pressure. This estimated pressure correlates with the measured pressure, but the mean pulmonary artery pressure, the pulmonary capillary wedge pressure, and the pulmonary vascular resistance cannot be estimated with echocardiography.

Other Diagnostic Methods

The chest radiograph and the 12-lead electrocardiogram are commonly abnormal among patients with pulmonary hypertension, but are neither sensitive nor specific diagnostic markers. No biomarker has yet been established to be useful for the diagnosis of pulmonary hypertension.

Functional Assessment

The distance a patient can walk in 6 minutes (the "6-minute walk test") has been used in many clinical trials to assess efficacy of treatment, but it is not commonly used in clinical practice. Although age and gender-based community norms have not been established for the 6-minute walk test, walking 500 meters or more in 6 minutes is considered normal.

Cardiopulmonary exercise testing can establish objectively the functional work capacity of the patient by establishing the patient's anaerobic threshold and maximum oxygen uptake with exercise. However, formal exercise testing is used infrequently among patients with pulmonary hypertension.

TREATMENT

In 2009, the American College of Cardiology Foundation and American Heart Association issued an expert consensus document on pulmonary hypertension that reviewed in detail the recent advances in treatment (McLaughlin et al., 2009).

Patients with pulmonary artery hypertension are advised to avoid heavy physical exertion or isometric exercise, which may lead to loss of consciousness. Continuous intravenous infusion of prostacyclin analogs improves functional status and survival in patients with primary pulmonary hypertension. Other prostanoid drugs that are easier to administer have subsequently been developed (treprostinil, iloprost) and have promise for the treatment of primary pulmonary hypertension. Endothelin receptor antagonists (bosentan, sitaxsentan, ambrisentan) and phosphodiesterase inhibitors (sildenafil, tadalafil) also improve the symptoms and functional status of patients with pulmonary arterial hypertension. Severe cases of pulmonary hypertension can be treated with heart-lung transplantation.

Secondary forms of pulmonary hypertension may be treated by addressing the root cause of the disorder. Chronic pulmonary embolism may be treated surgically with pulmonary thromboendarterectomy in selected patients.

Recent Advances

Several new drug therapies have been developed over the past decade, with particular interest in the endothelin receptor antagonists and phosphodiesterase inhibitors.

Side Effects of Treatment

Continuous intravenous therapy with epoprostenol carries the risk of infection and difficulties of maintaining access for the drug. All drugs used to lower pulmonary artery pressures may also lower systemic blood pressures. Endothelin antagonists may cause liver damage.

DISABILITY

Functional Limitations

Patients with pulmonary hypertension have been shown to have marked limitations on standard functional status measures, such as the RAND Short-Form 36 scales (Chen et al., 2008; Rubenfire et al., 2009). Patients with pulmonary hypertension also have had evidence of reduced functional capacity on standard heart failure measures, such as the Minnesota Living with Heart Failure Scale (Zlupko et al., 2008).

Work Disability

Patients with pulmonary hypertension may be unable to work because of either functional limitations or their use of continuous intravenous treatment.

CURRENT LISTING

Pulmonary hypertension has no current listing. The current listing for cor pulmonale from the respiratory system listings (3.00) is:

3.09 *Cor pulmonale secondary to chronic pulmonary vascular hypertension.* Clinical evidence of cor pulmonale (documented according to 3.00G) with:

A. Mean pulmonary artery pressure greater than 40 mm Hg,
or
B. Arterial hypoxemia. Evaluate under the criteria in 3.02C2 (SSA, 2008).

CONCLUSIONS AND RECOMMENDATION

Pulmonary hypertension is associated with functional limitations to exercise, and it significantly increases patient mortality. Pulmonary hypertension can be treated with drugs, but such treatment does not cure the disease. Because the disease is generally at a fairly advanced stage by the time of diagnosis, most patients with pulmonary hypertension will meet criteria for disability (Figure 11-1).

RECOMMENDATION 11-1. The Social Security Administration should establish a new listing in the cardiovascular system for pul-

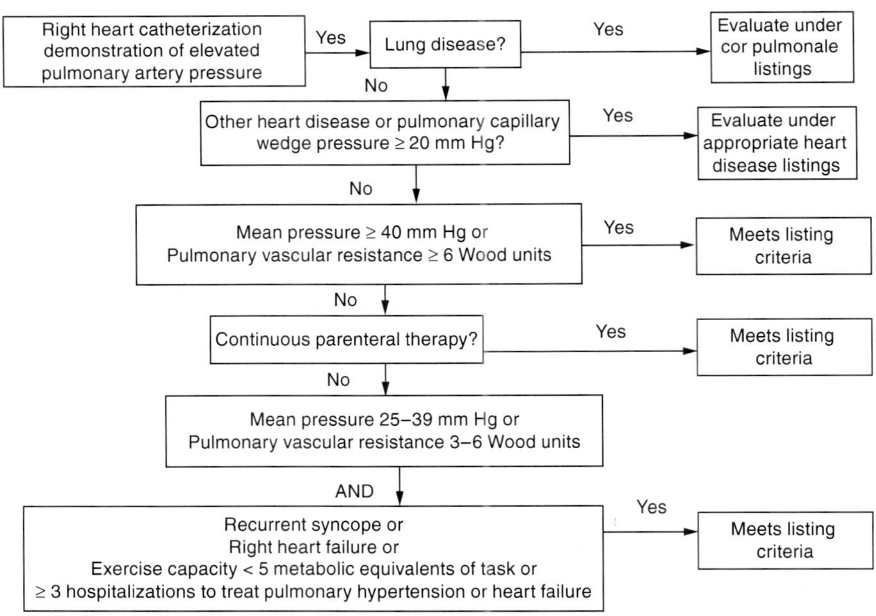

FIGURE 11-1 Meeting criteria for disability due to pulmonary hypertension.

monary hypertension. The new listing should allow claimants with pulmonary hypertension documented by right heart catheterization to meet the listing if (A) there is evidence of severe pulmonary hypertension OR (B) there is evidence of moderate pulmonary hypertension AND of marked functional limitations.

A. Evidence of severe pulmonary hypertension, which is associated with severe functional limitation, includes any of the following:

- Mean pulmonary artery pressure of 40 mm Hg or greater; or
- Pulmonary vascular resistance of 6 Wood units (mm Hg per liter per minute) or greater; or
- Continuous parenteral therapy with prostacyclin analogs.

OR

B. Evidence of moderate pulmonary hypertension, which imposes severe functional limitation on many but not all individuals, includes any of the following:

- Recurrent syncope secondary to pulmonary hypertension; or
- Right heart failure (same criteria as for heart failure listing); or
- Mean pulmonary artery pressure between 25 and 39 mm Hg; or
- Pulmonary vascular resistance above 3 and below 6 Wood units.

AND

Evidence of marked functional disability provided by either of the following:

- An exercise capacity of less than 5 metabolic equivalents of task; or
- Three or more hospital admissions within a consecutive 12-month period to treat right heart failure or pulmonary hypertension.

REFERENCES

Chen, H., D. B. Taichman, and R. L. Doyle. 2008. Health-related quality of life and patient-reported outcomes in pulmonary arterial hypertension. *Proceedings of the American Thoracic Society* 5(5):623–630.

McLaughlin, V. V., S. L. Archer, D. B. Badesch, R. J. Barst, H. W. Farber, J. R. Lindner, M. A. Mathier, M. D. McGoon, M. H. Park, R. S. Rosenson, L. J. Rubin, V. F. Tapson, and J. Varga. 2009. ACC/AHA 2009 expert consensus document on pulmonary hypertension: A report of the American College of Cardiology Foundation Task Force on Expert Consensus Documents and the American Heart Association developed in collaboration with the American College of Chest Physicians, the American Thoracic Society, Inc., and the Pulmonary Hypertension Association. *Journal of the American College of Cardiology* 53(17):1573–1619.

Rubenfire, M., G. Lippo, B. D. Bodini, F. Blasi, L. Allegra, and E. Bossone. 2009. Evaluating health-related quality of life, work ability, and disability in pulmonary arterial hypertension: An unmet need. *Chest* 136(2):597–603.

SSA (Social Security Administration). 2008. *Listing of impairments—Adult listings (Part A). Disability evaluation under Social Security (Blue Book).* http://www.socialsecurity.gov/disability/professionals/bluebook/AdultListings.htm (accessed July 22, 2010).

Zlupko, M., M. O. Harhay, R. Gallop, J. Shin, C. Archer-Chicko, R. Patel, H. I. Palevsky, and D. B. Taichman. 2008. Evaluation of disease-specific health-related quality of life in patients with pulmonary arterial hypertension. *Respiratory Medicine* 102(10):1431–1438.

12

Valvular Heart Disease

The chapter on valvular heart disease (VHD) adds new listings specific to VHD. The awarding of disability is appropriate for all patients with severe symptomatic aortic stenosis and for other types of severe VHD associated with severe symptomatic impairment. Disease severity is determined by the echocardiogram and functional impairment by a careful history and physical examination and in some cases exercise testing.

DESCRIPTION

Valvular heart disease (VHD) is characterized by damage to or a congenital defect in one or more heart valves: mitral, aortic, tricuspid, and pulmonary. Heart valves have a single function: to permit unobstructed forward blood flow through the heart. Damaged or defective valves can cause two types of problems: either they fail to open properly (a condition called stenosis) impeding blood flow, or they leak (a condition called regurgitation) permitting back flow. Regurgitation occurs because a valve does not close tightly, which allows blood to flow back into the previous chamber from where it came. Mitral regurgitation is most often due to prolapse, a condition in which the valve leaflets bulge into the left atrium during a heartbeat. Stenosis occurs when the heart valve cannot fully open because the valve flaps, or ring, have become thick, stiff, or fused together, preventing sufficient supply of blood to flow through the valve.

Valve conditions may be congenital, arise from inflammation, or occur due to complications from infections. Mild or moderate disease is usually asymptomatic at first, but due to the progressive and degenerative nature of the disease, may eventually become severe and lead to heart failure and death if left untreated. In general, VHD is related to aging. Prevalence is increasing as the U.S. population ages and lives longer. Aortic stenosis is the most common valve disease in the United States, followed by mitral regurgitation, aortic regurgitation, and mitral stenosis.

Symptoms of VHD in decreasing frequency include shortness of breath or dyspnea, chest pain and palpitations, and syncope or near syncope. Because nearly all patients with severe disease will present with one of these symptoms, VHD can usually be evaluated using the algorithms for these symptom categories described in Figure 12-1.

DIAGNOSTIC CRITERIA AND METHODS

Two simple principles govern the management of VHD and the probability that a patient is disabled from it: the presence of symptoms and the severity of the lesion. Table 12-1 presents the categories of disease severity for each valve lesion. In general, but with rare exceptions, only severe disease is capable of causing symptoms and disability. VHD should be diagnosed based on clinical evaluation of the patient and assessment by

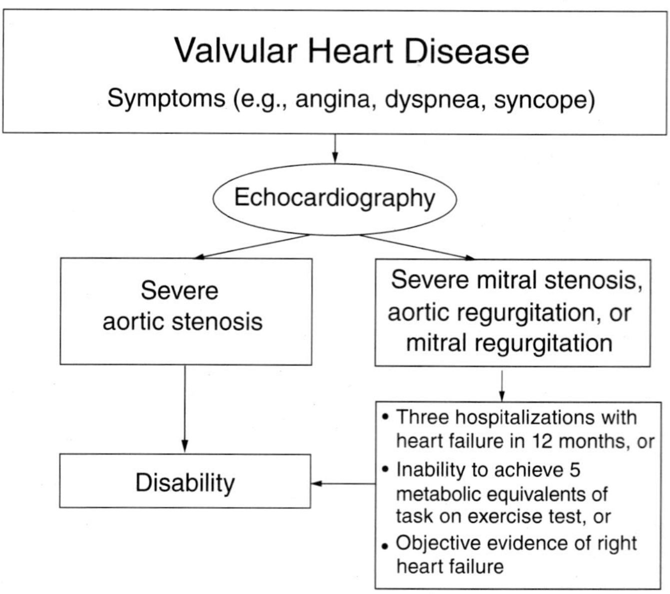

FIGURE 12-1 Determining listing-level disability for claimants with valvular heart disease.

TABLE 12-1 Characterization of Severe Valve Disease

Aortic Stenosis			
	Mild	Moderate	Severe
Jet velocity (m per second)	< 3.0	3.0–4.0	> 4.0
Mean gradient (mm Hg)	< 2.5	25–40	> 40
Valve area (cm^2)	> 1.5	1.0–1.5	< 1.0
Valve area index (cm^2 per m^2)			< 0.6
Mitral Stenosis			
	Mild	Moderate	Severe
Mean gradient (mm Hg)	< 5	5–10	> 10
Pulmonary artery systolic pressure (mm Hg)	< 30	30–50	> 50
Valve area (cm^2)	> 1.5	1.0–1.5	< 1.0
Aortic Regurgitation			
	Mild	Moderate	Severe
Qualitative			
Angiographic grade	1+	2+	3–4+
Color Doppler jet width	Central jet, width < 25% of LVOT	More than mild but no signs of severe AR	Central jet, width > 65% LVOT
Doppler vena contracta width (cm)	< 0.3	0.3–0.6	> 0.6
Quantitative (catheterization or echocardiography)			
Regurgitant volume (ml per beat)	< 30	30–59	≥ 60
Regurgitant fraction (%)	< 30	30–49	≥ 50
Regurgitant orifice area (cm^2)	< 0.10	0.10–0.29	≥ 0.30
Additional Essential Criteria			
Left ventricular size			Increased
Mitral Regurgitation			
	Mild	Moderate	Severe
Qualitative			
Angiographic grade	1+	2+	3–4+
Color Doppler jet area	Small, central jet (< 4 cm^2 or < 20% LA area)	Signs of MR more than mild present but no criteria for severe MR	Vena contracta width > 0.7 cm with large central MR jet (area > 40% of LA area) or with a wall impinging jet of any size, swirling in LA
Doppler vena contracta width (cm)	< 0.3	0.3–0.69	≥ 0.70

continued

TABLE 12-1 Continued

Mitral Regurgitation (*continued*)			
Quantitative (catheterization or echocardiography)			
Regurgitant volume (ml per beat)	< 30	30–59	≥ 60
Regurgitant fraction (%)	< 30	30–49	≥ 50
Regurgitant orifice area (cm^2)	< 0.20	0.2–0.39	≥ 0.40
Additional Essential Criteria			
Left atrial size			Enlarged
Left ventricular size			Enlarged

NOTE: AR = aortic regurgitation; LA = left atrial/atrium; LVOT = left ventricular outflow tract; MR = mitral regurgitation.
SOURCE: Bonow et al., 2006:e14. Reprinted with permission from Elsevier.

echocardiography (see Table 12-1). Obtaining detailed information about patients' related symptoms while reviewing their medical histories is important to confirm the presence of possible comorbidities or detect possible VHD in asymptomatic patients.

Diagnosis by echocardiography is the standard technique by which to confirm VHD, as well as determine disease severity and prognosis. Echocardiography evaluates valve structure and function (Bonow et al., 2006).

TREATMENT

There are no effective long-term medical therapies for severe VHD. Valve replacement or repair performed either surgically or by catheter intervention are the only effective therapies. Mortality risk with such intervention ranges from 1 to 20 percent and can be as high as 30 percent depending on circumstances, including the presence of other cardiac conditions, the skill of the surgeon, age of the patient, and the presence of a host of comorbidities including lung, kidney, and neurological disease.

DISABILITY

Approximately 8 million Americans have some form of VHD. Approximately 800,000 patients have valve disease that becomes serious enough to warrant some level of disability. Of those, roughly 80,000 a year undergo heart surgery to repair or replace defective valves.

Once it is determined that the patient has severe symptomatic VHD, the algorithm in Figure 12-1 should be used to determine disability. Aortic stenosis is treated separately from the other lesions because symptomatic severe aortic stenosis is universally fatal if untreated (usually within 5 years or less of onset of symptoms) and is an automatic indication for disability unless aortic valve replacement is performed. Patients with this condition should not perform manual work, because it is possible that they could experience sudden death on the job.

CONCLUSIONS AND RECOMMENDATIONS

Severe symptomatic VHD leads to heart failure and death if left untreated and may be the cause of serious disability. Disability is determined on the basis of the presence of severe anatomic valve disease determined by echocardiography or other appropriate medical imaging and the symptoms caused by it. The committee concludes it is reasonable to provide disability at the listing level to symptomatic patients with severe valve disease, including aortic stenosis, mitral stenosis, aortic regurgitation, and mitral regurgitation.

Unlike other cardiac impairments, determining disability using measurements of functional criteria is not advised for symptomatic individuals with severe aortic stenosis, because there is risk to the patient in performing exercise tests. Furthermore, the severity of disease for patients with severe symptomatic aortic stenosis is sufficient to grant disability at the listing level without other indications of functional limitation, such as evidence of related heart failure.

RECOMMENDATION 12-1. Provide a listing-level pathway to disability for symptomatic claimants with objective evidence via echocardiogram or other appropriate medically acceptable imaging of severe aortic stenosis, characterized by mean gradient greater than 40 mm Hg, jet velocity greater than 4.0 m/sec, valve area less than 1.0 cm^2, and valve area index less than 0.6 cm^2/m^2.

Severe mitral stenosis, aortic regurgitation, or mitral regurgitation may also warrant disability at the listing level, but these patients must demonstrate functional limitation in addition to an objective diagnosis of severity. Functional limitation may be demonstrated by repeated hospitalizations with heart failure, or an inability to achieve 5 metabolic equivalents of task on an exercise test, or objective evidence of right heart failure in the patient's medical record. Individuals with moderate or mild valve disease may still be disabled by their impairment, however, but the committee agrees these impairments would not warrant disability at the listing level.

RECOMMENDATION 12-2. Provide a listing-level pathway to disability for symptomatic claimants with objective evidence via echocar-

diogram or other appropriate medically acceptable imaging of severe mitral stenosis, aortic regurgitation, or mitral regurgitation and demonstrated functional limitation. Objective evidence is measured by one of the following:

- **Severe mitral stenosis characterized by mean gradient greater than 10 mm Hg, pulmonary artery systolic pressure greater than 50 mm Hg, and valve area less than 1.0 cm^2; or**
- **Severe aortic regurgitation characterized by regurgitant volume greater than or equal to 60 ml/beat, and regurgitant orifice area greater than or equal to 50 cm^2, and increased left ventricular size; or**
- **Severe mitral regurgitation characterized by regurgitant volume greater than or equal to 60 ml/beat or regurgitant fraction greater than or equal to 50 percent, and regurgitant orifice area greater than or equal to 0.40 cm^2, and enlarged left atrial size and enlarged left ventricular size.**

Functional limitation(s) from severe mitral stenosis, aortic regurgitation, or mitral regurgitation would be demonstrated by one of the following:

- **Three hospitalizations with heart failure in 12 months; or**
- **Inability to achieve 5 metabolic equivalents of task on an exercise test; or**
- **Objective evidence of right heart failure.**

Unlike many diseases such as chronic lung disease or certain cancers, treatment for VHD can have a dramatic improving effect on a patient's functional status. For example, an individual may undergo medical testing revealing results that meet the recommended listing, but then receive treatment and on further testing, no longer meet the disability criteria at the listing level. The most common example of this scenario for VHD would be valve replacement or repair. An applicant with evidence of severe symptomatic valve disease may undergo surgery with complete resolution of symptoms and no functional limitations. Therefore, the committee concludes that any applicant applying for disability who has undergone valve surgery should be reassessed at a minimal duration of 3 months following the procedure, as the individual's functional status may have changed significantly.

REFERENCE

Bonow, R. O., B. A. Carabello, K. Chatterjee, A. C. de Leon, D. P. Faxon, M. D. Freed, W. H. Gaasch, B. W. Lytle, R. A. Nishimura, P. T. O'Gara, R. A. O'Rourke, C. M. Otto, P. M. Shah, and J. S. Shanewise. 2006. ACC/AHA 2006 guidelines for the management of patients with valvular heart disease: A report of the American College of Cardiology/American Heart Association Task Force on Practice Guidelines. *Journal of the American College of Cardiology* 48(3):e1–e148.

13

Arrhythmias

The previous arrhythmia listing should be revised to focus on arrhythmias (i.e., tachycardias and bradycardias) rather than on their symptoms (i.e., syncope and near syncope), which can be caused not only by arrhythmias but also by other etiologies. This chapter recommends that the listing be met if recurrent episodes of tachycardia or bradycardia cause syncope, near syncope, or other debilitating symptoms that very seriously limit the ability of the claimant to independently initiate, sustain, or complete activities of daily living or instrumental activities of daily living.

DESCRIPTION

An arrhythmia is an abnormal change in the regular beat of the heart and may include irregular heartbeats, skipped beats, rapid heartbeats (tachycardia), or slow heartbeats (bradycardia) (Libby et al., 2008). Arrhythmias are characterized by the location of their origin in the heart and the symptoms the patient experiences when the arrhythmia occurs. Arrhythmias originating in the upper chambers of the heart (the atria) are called atrial or supraventricular arrhythmias. Arrhythmias originating in the lower chambers of the heart (the ventricles) are called ventricular arrhythmias. Atrial and ventricular arrhythmias can occur in individuals with or without other cardiac disorders (Zipes et al., 2006). Bradycardia may be due to abnormalities of initiation of the heart beat or of transmission of electrical impulses within the heart. The latter are called conduction disturbances. In general, ventricular arrhythmias that are associated with structural heart diseases and genetic disorders can lead to the most serious and potentially life-threatening and disabling conditions.

Arrhythmias may manifest in a variety of ways, and some patients with arrhythmias are asymptomatic. Others may experience palpitations (pounding sensations in the chest), chest discomfort, dyspnea, syncope, or near syncope (Libby et al., 2008). Syncope, sometimes called "fainting," is defined as a sudden loss of consciousness and postural tone with spontaneous recovery. Near syncope is a period of altered consciousness. Since syncope is complete loss of consciousness, it is not merely a feeling of light-headedness, momentary weakness, or dizziness. Cardiac syncope is due to inadequate blood flow to the brain from any cardiac cause, such as obstruction of flow or disturbance in rhythm or conduction resulting in inadequate cardiac output (Grubb and Olshansky, 1998). Determining the cause of syncope can be difficult, as there are several cardiac and noncardiac disturbances that may lead to loss of consciousness (Grubb and Olshansky, 1998).

Cardiac syncope may be caused by bradycardia, tachycardia, valve disease, or myocardial disease leading to hypotension. Cardiac syncope may also be due to nonarrhythmic causes, such as vasovagal syncope (mediated by discharge of the vagus nerve) that is purely vasodepressor (hypotensive) with no cardioinhibitory (bradycardic) component, an extremely rare condition. Noncardiac causes of loss of consciousness include epilepsy and pseudoseizures from psychiatric disease (Grubb and Olshansky, 1998). Since syncope is a symptom and not a disease, it is important to identify accurately its underlying cause. Due to the multiple causes of syncope, it is important to recognize that only syncope in association with arrhythmias is discussed here.

Types of Arrhythmias

Bradycardia is defined as a heart rate of less than 60 beats per minute and requires treatment if accompanied by symptoms, which may include fatigue, lethargy, nausea, shortness of breath, mental confusion, dizziness, and near syncope or syncope (Grubb and Olshansky, 1998). A diagnosis of bradycardia in the absence of symptoms is rarely an indication for treatment, for example, the implantation of a pacemaker. Symptoms drive the need for intervention.

Tachycardias, sometimes called tachyarrhythmias, may be supraventricular or ventricular in origin. Supraventricular arrhythmias may be often highly symptomatic but are rarely life threatening (Wood et al., 2010). Examples include atrioventricular nodal reentrant tachycardia (AVNRT), atrioventricular reentrant tachycardia (AVRT) in association with the Wolff-Parkinson-White syndrome, atrial flutter, and atrial fibrillation. The latter is the most common arrhythmia in older populations, since its prevalence increases with age (Fuster et al., 2006; Go et al., 2001; Miyasaka et al., 2006). Atrial fibrillation is especially important because its consequences cause significant morbidity and mortality. All the aforementioned arrhythmias are treatable with drug or catheter ablation therapy; success rates are dependent on the particular arrhythmia. Catheter ablation involves the placement of wires (catheters) into the heart (or sometimes on its surface) through which energy is delivered that destroys the origin of the targeted arrhythmia, or interrupts the circuit supporting the arrhythmia. Ablation is considered a first-line therapy for AVNRT, AVRT, and atrial flutter. Indeed, when patients are given the choice between drug therapy and ablation, they most commonly choose the latter, because ablation has demonstrated success rates of 95 percent or more. Since AVNRT, AVRT, and atrial flutter are usually curable by this technique, they are rarely disabling.

Ventricular arrhythmias may occur in isolation or in association with structural heart disease and genetic abnormalities. Like supraventricular arrhythmias, ventricular arrhythmias that occur in the setting of a structurally normal heart and in the absence of genetic disease are generally not life threatening although they may be debilitating. Most are treatable by drug therapy, and many are curable with catheter ablation. The most common ventricular arrhythmias requiring treatment are those that occur in association with coronary artery disease. They are responsible for cardiac arrest and sudden cardiac death, which are not chronic conditions (although cardiac arrest may result in a chronic cardiovascular or other condition).

EPIDEMIOLOGY

Supraventricular arrhythmias other than atrial fibrillation and atrial flutter are most common in the young. The incidence of atrial fibrillation increases with age, approximately doubling with each decade of life, and is an independent risk factor for death. In U.S. Air Force recruits the incidence is 0.04 percent, and by age 75 years it is 11.6 percent (Cairns and Connolly, 1991). The Anticoagulation and Risk Factors in Atrial Fibrillation Study predicted that the number of patients with atrial fibrillation in the United States is likely to increase 2.5-fold in the next 50 years as a consequence of the aging of the population, from approximately 2.3 million in the early 2000s to 5.6 million by the year 2050 (Go et al., 2001). A more recent study projected the number of persons with atrial fibrillation in the United States might exceed 10 million by 2050 (Miyasaka et al., 2006).

Based on data from the Resuscitation Outcomes Consortium, 295,000 out-of-hospital cardiac arrests occur annually in the United States (Lloyd-Jones et al., 2009). Approximately 60 percent of sudden cardiac deaths are treated by emergency medical services, and 31 percent of out-of-hospital cardiac arrest patients receive bystander cardiopulmonary resuscitation. Most unexpected cardiac deaths are thought to be secondary to a ventricular arrhythmia, and about 80 percent of out-of-hospital cardiac arrests occur in private or residential settings. The incidence of nonfatal ventricular arrhythmias is not well defined, although in practice they are not uncommon. The incidence of arrhythmias due to congenital disease is highly dependent on the particular genetic mutation. The long QT syndrome occurs in about 1 in 3,000 individuals, but the risk is highly dependent on the individual patient's history and location of the genetic mutation (Libby et al., 2008).

DIAGNOSTIC CRITERIA AND METHODS

Minimal required documentation for diagnosing arrhythmias includes either an electrocardiogram (ECG) recording, for example from an ambulatory (Holter) monitor or from an emergency medical service unit dispatched to a cardiac arrest victim, or a 12-lead ECG. Such tracings define the origin of the arrhythmia (supraventricular or ventricular), enable risk stratification, and direct therapy. Some arrhythmias may be recorded during exercise testing, and in this case the test can be used to diagnose the arrhythmia, determine functional status independent of the arrhythmia, and sometimes determine appropriate therapy.

TREATMENT

Patients with arrhythmias can either be observed closely, or treated with drugs, catheter ablation, a pacemaker, an implantable cardioverter defibrillator (ICD), or a combination. ICDs are devices that can stimulate the heart as a pacemaker to treat bradycardia (and heart failure), or terminate ventricular tachyarrhythmias with either shocks or special pacing techniques (Epstein et al., 2008). The appropriate choice of therapy will depend on the particular arrhythmia, consequences of the arrhythmia (symptoms and blood pressure, for example), patient preference, and sometimes job requirements. Depending on the arrhythmia, efficacy of treatment is variable. Ventricular arrhythmias may be treated by drug therapy, catheter ablation, and ICDs, the latter being the mainstay of therapy when they occur in patients with structural heart disease (e.g., coronary artery disease, cardiomyopathy, genetic heart diseases).

Advances in Treatment

Few new antiarrhythmic drugs have been approved by the Food and Drug Administration in the past decade. The major advances in arrhythmia treatment have been in device and catheter-based therapies. Pacemakers have become reliable and effective treatments for bradycardia. ICDs can be implanted either in patients who have been resuscitated from a life-threatening ventricular arrhythmia or in patients at high risk for a life-threatening ventricular arrhythmia. The efficacy of catheter ablation depends on the targeted arrhythmia and the type of energy source that is used. The field of ablation is rapidly advancing with new technologies becoming available each year.

Effects of Treatment

No medical treatment is devoid of risk. Drugs may cause toxic reactions, some of which can be permanent, including organ toxicity. Some antiarrhythmic drugs can even cause cardiac arrest in susceptible individuals. Catheter ablation offers the possibility of curing some arrhythmias, but carries risks, including injury to blood vessels leading to the heart, damage to the heart itself, and sometimes the need for a pacemaker. As noted, pacemakers are remarkably effective for the treatment of bradycardia, and the only therapy available other than withdrawing bradycardia-causing drugs. Similarly, ICDs are extremely effective in resuscitating cardiac arrest, and in some instances can use pacing techniques to terminate ventricular arrhythmias without resorting to shock therapy. ICDs, however, do not prevent arrhythmias and thus may not prevent syncope. Furthermore, shocks are painful. Finally, all implantable devices carry the risks of complications related to implantation itself (i.e., an invasive procedure) and to infection and malfunction. Any of these complications may be life threatening.

DISABILITY

There are no generally accepted criteria to determine disability from arrhythmia. The origin of the arrhythmia, associated symptoms, and the environment of a particular occupation establish an individual's disability status. Syncope may or may not be disabling depending on its etiology, frequency, and unique factors specific to an individual. Similarly, the same arrhythmia may be disabling for one person and not for another depending on associated symptoms. In short, the consequences, severity, and frequency of symptoms due to arrhythmia are what determine disability.

The presence of comorbid depression and anxiety in patients may contribute to the disabling effects of arrhythmias. For example, patients experiencing anxiety due to the unpredictable nature of the associated symptoms of their arrhythmias, such as episodes of syncope, may avoid engaging in usual activities.

When ventricular arrhythmias are recurrent and cause syncope, especially if they are unresponsive to drug or other treatment, disability may be warranted. Furthermore, having an ICD may be a contraindication for working in certain professions in which sudden, unexpected loss of consciousness could cause injury or death to either the patient or others. For example, having an ICD implanted precludes certification for a Department of Transportation commercial motor vehicle license (Blumenthal et al., 2002, 2007).

Although it may sometimes be difficult to determine the cause of an arrhythmia, identification of the etiology of the arrhythmia is essential to properly treating the symptomatic patient. Disability of patients impaired as a consequence of arrhythmia may be based on either the arrhythmia diagnosis itself, or on its underlying cause. For example, a patient who has survived myocardial infarction, which itself may or may not be disabling, could be disabled on the basis of an arrhythmia if the latter is recurrent, or uncontrolled or unresponsive to therapy.

The Social Security Administration (SSA) currently reviews applicants' disability claims for arrhythmias based on specific diagnostic and clinical criteria. These criteria were most recently updated in 2006. A relatively low number of cardiovascular allowances are made using the current arrhythmias impairment code. Generally, listing-level decisions have been fairly stable with a slight increase in allowances across the past decade. The set of disability criteria at the listing-level (see Box 13-1) evaluates claimants for disability with recurrent arrhythmias with uncontrolled and recurrent episodes of cardiac syncope or near syncope documented by a resting or ambulatory (Holter) ECG or other appropriate medically acceptable tests. The claimant's syncope or near syncope must either be unresponsive to

BOX 13-1
Current Listing for Recurrent Arrhythmias

4.05 Recurrent arrhythmias, not related to reversible causes, such as electrolyte abnormalities or digitalis glycoside or antiarrhythmic drug toxicity, resulting in uncontrolled (see 4.00A3f), recurrent (see 4.00A3c) episodes of cardiac syncope or near syncope (see 4.00F3b), despite prescribed treatment (see 4.00B3 if there is no prescribed treatment), and documented by resting or ambulatory (Holter) electrocardiography, or by other appropriate medically acceptable testing, coincident with the occurrence of syncope or near syncope (see 4.00F3c).

SOURCE: SSA, 2008.

treatment (claimants not receiving ongoing treatment may be required to undergo a consultative examination paid for by SSA or be found disabled if there is another impairment or impairments that combine with the arrhythmia to equal the severity of a listing). The claimant's arrhythmia cannot be attributed to reversible causes, such as electrolyte abnormalities or digitalis glycoside or antiarrhythmic drug toxicity, as arrhythmias due to reversible causes are likely to respond to treatment.

CONCLUSIONS AND RECOMMENDATION

After review of the most recent medical literature and related American College of Cardiology/American Heart Association treatment and practice guidelines, the committee determined the arrhythmias listing should be revised to allow claimants to meet the listing with objective diagnosis of recurrent (as defined by SSA) episodes of tachycardia or bradycardia, that cause cardiac syncope, near syncope, or other debilitating symptoms, confirmed by ECG or other appropriate medically acceptable testing. A documented arrhythmia should be coincident with the occurrence of symptoms that very seriously limit the patient's ability to independently initiate, sustain, or complete activities of daily living or instrumental activities of daily living. Furthermore, the arrhythmia and symptoms must occur despite prescribed treatment. As with the current listing, claimants' medical records should show the arrhythmia is not related to a reversible cause.

RECOMMENDATION 13-1. Revise listing 4.05 to define arrhythmias as recurrent episodes of tachycardia or bradycardia documented by electrocardiography or other appropriate medically acceptable testing; that cause cardiac syncope, near syncope, or other debilitating symptoms; are not due to a reversible cause; do not respond to prescribed treatment; and very seriously limit the ability to independently initiate, sustain, or complete activities of daily living or instrumental activities of daily living.

REFERENCES

Blumenthal, R., J. Braunstein, H. Connolly, A. E. Epstein, B. J. Gersh, and E. H. Wittles. 2002. *Cardiovascular Advisory Panel guidelines for the medical examination of commercial motor vehicle drivers*. McLean, VA: U.S. Department of Transportation, Federal Motor Carrier Safety Administration.

Blumenthal, R. S., A. E. Epstein, and R. E. Kerber. 2007. *Cardiovascular disease and commercial motor vehicle driver safety (expedited review)*. McLean, VA: Department of Transportation: Federal Motor Carrier Safety Administration.

Cairns, J. A., and S. J. Connolly. 1991. Nonrheumatic atrial fibrillation. Risk of stroke and role of antithrombotic therapy. *Circulation* 84:469–481.

Epstein, A. E., J. P. DiMarco, K. A. Ellenbogen, N. A. Estes, R. A. Freedman, L. S. Gettes, G. Gregoratos, A. M. Gillinov, S. C. Hammill, D. L. Hayes, M. A. Hlatky, L. K. Newby, R. L. Page, M. H. Schoenfeld, M. J. Silka, L. W. Stevenson, and M. O. Sweeney. 2008. Guidelines for device-based therapy of cardiac rhythm abnormalities: A report of the American College of Cardiology/American Heart Association Task Force on Practice Guidelines (Writing Committee to Revise the ACC/AHA/NASPE 2002 Guideline Update for Implantation of Cardiac Pacemakers and Antiarrhythmia Devices). *Journal of the American College of Cardiology* 51:e1–e62.

Fuster, V., L. E. Ryden, D. S. Cannom, H. J. Crijns, A. B. Curtis, K. A. Ellenbogen, J. L. Halperin, J.-Y. Le Heuzey, G. N. Kay, J. E. Lowe, S. B. Olsson, E. N. Prystowsky, J. L. Tamargo, and S. Wann. 2006. ACC/AHA/ESC 2006 guidelines for the management of patients with atrial fibrillation: A report of the American College of Cardiology/American Heart Association Task Force on Practice Guidelines and the European Society of Cardiology Committee for Practice Guidelines (Writing Committee to Revise the 2001 Guidelines for the Management of Patients with Atrial Fibrillation). Developed in collaboration with the European Heart Rhythm Association and the Heart Rhythm Society. *Journal of the American College of Cardiology* 48(4):e149–e246.

Go, A. S., E. M. Hylek, K. A. Phillips, Y. Chang, L. E. Henault, J. V. Selby, and D. E. Singer. 2001. Prevalence of diagnosed atrial fibrillation in adults: National implications for rhythm management and stroke prevention: The Anticoagulation and Risk Factors in Atrial Fibrillation (ATRIA) Study. *Journal of the American Medical Association* 285(18):2370–2375.

Grubb, B. P., and B. Olshansky. 1998. *Syncope: Mechanisms and management.* 1st ed. Armonk, NY: Futura Publishing Co.

Libby, P., R. O. Bonow, D. P. Zipes, and D. L. Mann. 2008. *Braunwald's heart disease: A textbook of cardiovascular medicine.* 8th ed. St. Louis, MO: W. B. Saunders.

Lloyd-Jones, D., R. Adams, M. Carnethon, G. De Simone, T. B. Ferguson, K. Flegal, E. Ford, K. Furie, A. Go, K. Greenlund, N. Haase, S. Hailpern, M. Ho, V. Howard, B. Kissela, S. Kittner, D. Lackland, L. Lisabeth, A. Marelli, M. McDermott, J. Meigs, D. Mozaffarian, G. Nichol, C. O'Donnell, V. Roger, W. Rosamond, R. Sacco, P. Sorlie, R. Stafford, J. Steinberger, T. Thom, S. Wasserthiel-Smoller, N. Wong, J. Wylie-Rosett, and Y. Hong, for the American Heart Association Statistics Committee Stroke Statistics Subcommittee. 2009. Heart disease and stroke statistics—2009 update: A report from the American Heart Association Statistics Committee and Stroke Statistics Subcommittee. *Circulation* 119(3):e21–e181.

Miyasaka, Y., M. E. Barnes, B. J. Gersh, S. S. Cha, K. R. Bailey, W. P. Abhayaratna, J. B. Seward, and T. S. M. Tsang. 2006. Secular trends in incidence of atrial fibrillation in Olmsted County, Minnesota, 1980 to 2000, and implications on the projections for future prevalence. *Circulation* 114(2):119–125.

SSA (Social Security Administration). 2008. *Listing of impairments—Adult listings (Part A). Disability evaluation under Social Security (Blue Book).* http://www.socialsecurity.gov/disability/professionals/bluebook/AdultListings.htm (accessed July 22, 2010).

Wood, K. A., A. L. Stewart, B. J. Drew, M. Melvin, M. M. Scheinman, and E. S. Froelicher. 2010. Patient perception of symptoms and quality of life following ablation in patients with supraventricular tachycardia. *Heart & Lung* 39(1):12–20.

Zipes, D. P., A. J. Camm, M. Borggrefe, A. E. Buxton, B. Chaitman, M. Fromer, G. Gregoratos, G. Klein, A. J. Moss, R. J. Myerburg, S. G. Priori, M. A. Quinones, D. M. Roden, M. J. Silka, C. Tracy, S. C. Smith Jr., A. K. Jacobs, C. D. Adams, E. M. Antman, J. L. Anderson, S. A. Hunt, J. L. Halperin, R. Nishimura, J. P. Ornato, R. L. Page, B. Riegel, J.-J. Blanc,

A. Budaj, V. Dean, J. W. Deckers, C. Despres, K. Dickstein, J. Lekakis, K. McGregor, M. Metra, J. Morais, A. Osterspey, J. L. Tamargo, and J. L. Zamorano. 2006. ACC/AHA/ESC 2006 guidelines for management of patients with ventricular arrhythmias and the prevention of sudden cardiac death: A report of the American College of Cardiology/American Heart Association Task Force and the European Society of Cardiology Committee for Practice Guidelines (Writing Committee to Develop Guidelines for Management of Patients with Ventricular Arrhythmias and the Prevention of Sudden Cardiac Death). *Journal of the American College of Cardiology* 48(5):e247–e346.

14

Aneurysm or Dissection of the Aorta and Peripheral Arteries

The recommendations in this chapter concern definitions, the specification of disabling symptoms and signs, and a fuller set of predisposing conditions. Aneurysm as well as dissection should be specified because they can occur separately. The dilation of aneurysms can cause pain, and both aneurysms and dissections can reduce or cut off blood flow to vital organs, including the heart, lungs, brain, viscera, and limbs. According to clinical guidelines, limits on severe physical exertion and heavy lifting may be prescribed to prevent an aneurysm from rupturing or dissecting. Connective tissue disorders, including Marfan, Loeys-Dietz, Ehlers-Danlos, and Turner syndromes, may weaken the aortic and other vessel walls and need intervention at an earlier stage.

DESCRIPTION

The aorta is the largest artery in the body and is divided into four parts: the aortic root (originating at the heart), the ascending aorta (rising to the head), the aortic arch, and the descending aorta (descending along the spine through the chest and upper abdomen before splitting into two branches, one into each leg). The peripheral arteries and other vessels extending from the aorta deliver freshly oxygenated blood throughout the entire body (Hiratzka et al., 2010; O'Gara, 2003). The aorta is composed of three layers: (1) the inner intimal lining, (2) the medial layer containing connective tissue interspersed with smooth muscle cells, and (3) the outer adventitial shell of connective tissue composed of collagen as well as very small blood vessels (the vasovasorum) that provide nutrients to the vessel wall.

An aneurysm may occur when a blister or bulge develops in weak areas of the aorta or peripheral arteries that expand under constant pressure from flowing blood. When the bulge grows to 50 percent or greater than the normal size of the vessel, it is classified as an aneurysm (Hiratzka et al., 2010; O'Gara, 2003). Modest arterial dilation that is less than 150 percent of the normal vessel dimension is commonly defined as vascular "ectasia." Aneurysms can occur in the aorta as well as peripheral vessels such as the popliteal artery (the vessel behind the knee) or small vessels in the brain (sometimes referred to as "berry aneurysms"). Untreated, most aneurysms may grow to sizes that pose a major risk of rupture. A ruptured aortic aneurysm is a life-threatening event, making early detection and medical management important to avoid death. Similarly, a ruptured small-vessel aneurysm in the brain can cause a fatal hemorrhagic stroke or result in long-term neurological deficits.

The histopathology of aortic aneurysm and dissection is characterized by degeneration of the muscle or medial layer of the aortic wall as well as disruption of elastic fibers and increased deposition of connective tissue components such as proteoglycans. The former use of the term *cystic medial necrosis* is now recognized as a misnomer that inaccurately describes the progressive loss of smooth muscle cells in the aortic aneurysm. In most cases of aneurysmal disease, the process of medial degeneration is associated with a superimposed atherosclerotic lesion.

Aortic dissection occurs with a "tear" or disruption within the degenerated medial layer of the aorta, involving bleeding within and along the aortic wall. Dissection may occur without the presence of an aneurysm (Hiratzka et al., 2010). Genetic disorders such as Marfan and Loeys-Dietz syndromes affect the composition and function of the aorta such that individuals are predisposed to aneurysm formation and dissection at early ages.

An aortic dissection should be distinguished from an "intramural hematoma," which lacks evidence of blood flow in a false lumen channel within the medial layer or evidence of a blood channel connection to the vessel lumen through an intimal tear. Intramural hematomas typically occur in the descending aorta of elderly individuals and are postulated to arise from a rupture of the small vessels in the outer layer that feed the aortic wall (the vasovasorum).

EPIDEMIOLOGY, NATURAL HISTORY, AND TYPES OF AORTIC ANEURYSMS

Abdominal aortic aneurysms (AAAs), involving the infradiaphragmatic abdominal area, are the most common type of aneurysms. In addition, aneurysms may occur in various peripheral arteries such as subclavian, popliteal, or cerebral vessels. Approximately 15,000 deaths occur every year in the United States due to AAAs. Risk factors include cigarette smoking, high blood pressure, family history of AAA in the first-degree male relative (e.g., father, brother), and signs of cholesterol buildup in other parts of the body. AAAs are more common in men than in women and typically occur after age 50 (O'Gara, 2003).

Aneurysms originating in the descending thoracic aorta (TA) occur in 5.9 to 10.4 per 100,000 person-years and rupture at a rate of 3.5 per 100,000 person-years. The incidence of TA aneurysms is estimated to be increasing and is now approximately 10.4 cases per 100,000 person-years. Most TA aneurysms are associated with atherosclerosis and medial layer degeneration. Risk factors for development of TA aneurysms include hypertension and smoking.

It is important to recognize that the size of the normal aorta increases with age and is affected by factors such as gender and body weight. Because the aorta gradually tapers along its course, it is critically important for measurements of aortic dimension to be localized precisely in defining abnormal vessel dimensions or determining rates of expansion. Studies have documented that the risk of death due to rupture and dissection of the aorta is directly associated with the size of the aorta. Accordingly, the guidelines for recommending prophylactic aortic repair are based on aortic dimensions in which the risks of complications are deemed to outweigh the risks of the reparative procedure (Conrad and Cambria, 2008; Davies et al., 2002; Elefteriades, 2002; Lobato and Puech-Leão, 1998). The rate of growth appears to increase as descending TA aneurysms become larger, further increasing the risk of rupture (Davies et al., 2002; Elefteriades, 2002; Lobato and Puech-Leão, 1998). The average rate of expansion of TA aneurysms is estimated to be 0.10 to 0.42 cm/year. This ongoing expansion of aneurysms serves as the basis for clinical practice guidelines that recommend annual noninvasive imaging tests to evaluate aortic dimension, such as a computed tomography (CT) or magnetic resonance imaging (MRI) scan.

Associated Conditions

Although the most common causes of aortic aneurysms are related to underlying atherosclerosis and medial degeneration, a variety of pathological processes can produce similar aneurysmal changes observed on an imaging study (e.g., CT scan). There are forms of congenital heart disease such as a bicuspid aortic valve that predispose patients to aortic dilation. Similarly, inflammatory conditions can predispose to aneurysm formation, such as giant cell arteritis, Takayasu arteritis, and Behçet disease. Under rare circumstances, aneurysms can be caused by infections due to viruses, bacteria, fungi, spirochetes (i.e., syphilis), or tubercles bacilli (i.e., tuberculosis). Aneurysms due to infectious causes have been variously described as "mycotic aneurysms" or more recently as either an "infected aneurysm" or "infectious aortitis."

Some forms of aortic disease are clustered in families and are due to genetic mutations that are either inherited from parents or occur de novo. Marfan syndrome is a genetic connective tissue disease that results from mutations in the fibrillin gene and is characterized by a high predisposition to aortic disease as well as cardinal clinical features affecting the eye (e.g., ectopia lentis, causing dislocation of the lens of the eye) and musculoskeletal system (e.g., joint laxity and dural ectasia). Nearly all patients with Marfan syndrome will eventually develop aortic disease and typically require ongoing annual surveillance of the status of their heart and aortic disease. In addition, patients with Marfan syndrome can exhibit other cardiovascular conditions, such as mitral regurgitation secondary to mitral valve prolapse or aortic regurgitation secondary to distortion of the valve cusps due to aortic dilation.

Loeys-Dietz syndrome results from mutations in the transforming growth factor receptor Type I or II genes and is characterized by the triad of arterial tortuousity and aneurysms, hypertelorism (wide-set eyes), and bifid uvula or cleft palate. These patients also have a spectrum of other features that overlap with the Marfan syndrome (e.g., joint laxity, dural ectasia) as well as features that are distinctly different from Marfan syndrome (e.g., presence of bifid uvula; translucent, easily bruised skin; or absence of ectopia lentis). Patients with Loeys-Dietz syndrome exhibit arterial tortuousity most commonly observed in the vessels of the head and neck, but this can also occur in other vessels. The vascular disease in these patients is particularly aggressive, with a mean age of death of 26 years. Children with prominent craniofacial features and severe systemic manifestations of Loeys-Dietz syndrome often exhibit more severe aortic disease. Accordingly, the American College of Cardiology/American Heart Association (ACC/AHA) guidelines recommend prophylactic repair once the aortic diameter exceeds the 99th percentile for age and the aortic valve annulus reaches 1.8 to 2.0 cm in children. Patients who undergo vascular repair remain at risk to develop additional vascular lesions at other sites. It is recommended that patients undergo annual surveillance of the vasculature by noninvasive imaging modalities (e.g., MRI) (Hiratzka et al., 2010).

In addition to Marfan and Loeys-Dietz syndromes, there are other heritable forms of aortic disease, such as Ehlers-Danlos and Turner syndromes, that remain to be further characterized as well-defined genetic diseases with vascular features.

DIAGNOSTIC CRITERIA AND METHODS

The ACC/AHA *2010 Guidelines for the Diagnosis and Management of Patients with Thoracic Aortic Disease* recommend an aneurysm be identified by imaging techniques. The size of aortic aneurysm and the extent of aortic dissection can be visualized by several modalities, including helical CT, MRI, angiography, and echocardiogram/ultrasound. A previously diagnosed aneurysm or dissection should be reimaged at least every year or when symptoms develop to determine if enlargement has occurred (Hiratzka et al., 2010).

TREATMENT

The treatment for aortic aneurysms may involve surgical or endovascular repair of the weakened arterial wall. Endovascular aneurysm repair (EVAR) now accounts for 56 percent of repairs in patients with AAA. Surgical repair of TA aneurysms is less successful than AAAs and can be associated with a significant risk of morbidity and mortality. Therefore, most guidelines weigh the risk of rupture and complications related to the size of the aortic dilation relative to the risks of the surgical repair. There appears to be increasing use of EVAR for AAA and some small TA aneurysms in the descending aorta.

Acute dissection involving the ascending thoracic aorta typically requires urgent surgical repair. Acute dissection involving the descending thoracic aorta can often be managed with medical treatment in the absence of significant compromise to vital organs.

Patients with TA aneurysms should have a long-term medical treatment regimen designed to achieve stringent control of cardiovascular risk factors such as hypertension, dyslipidemia, and tobacco exposure. Drugs that block the beta-adrenergic receptor are most clearly indicated for all patients with Marfan syndrome and aortic aneurysm to reduce the rate of aortic dilation and the risk of complications. Recent evidence supports the adjunctive use of drugs that block the angiotensin receptor as an additional means of reducing the rate of aortic dilation in patients with Marfan syndrome.

ACC/AHA guidelines currently recommend prophylactic surgical repair for asymptomatic patients with various forms of aortic disease, such as degenerative thoracic aneurysm, chronic aortic dissection, and mycotic aneurysm with an ascending aorta or aortic sinus diameter of 5.5 cm or greater. In certain subsets of high-risk patients with aortic disease, earlier intervention at smaller aortic dimensions (4 to 5 cm depending on the condition) is recommended. These patients include those with aortic disease and genetic predispositions (e.g., Marfan, Loeys-Dietz, Turner, and Ehlers-Danlos syndromes) or certain associated disorders (bicuspid aortic valve).

Patients who exhibit a rapid rate of increase in aortic dimensions (greater than 0.5 cm/year) are at increased risk of complications and should also be considered for earlier prophylactic repair at TA dimensions less than 5.5 cm (Hiratzka et al., 2010).

DISABILITY

In addition to the acute, catastrophic symptoms that result from arterial rupture, aneurysms and aortic dissections can also produce a variety of chronic debilitating symptoms. For example, aortic dilation may compromise the normal function of the aortic valve and produce chronic aortic regurgitation that eventually results in heart failure. An arterial aneurysm can compress a peripheral nerve and induce neuropathic pain, numbness, or limb weakness, which could impair a patient's functional capacity. An aneurysm could be the source of a blood clot that travels to the brain to cause a stroke or travels to the leg to cause critical limb ischemia. An aortic dissection may chronically disrupt the blood flow to vital organs such as the digestive tract or spinal cord and thereby result in pain syndromes or organ dysfunction that could compromise the capacity of a patient to engage in gainful employment.

Although surgical and endovascular repair of aortic disease is often successful enough to restore the individual to a good functional status, aortic surgery can be complicated by long-term sequelae such as spinal cord injury or kidney failure that could result in chronic disabling symptoms (Hiratzka et al., 2010).

Overall, most of the chronic debilitating symptoms related to aneurysms or aortic dissection are secondary to its effects on impairing blood flow to vital organs (i.e., tissue ischemia) or direct mechanical effects (i.e., compression) that compromise the function of vital organs. Accordingly, the disability listings related to aortic disease will most likely be met by reference to specific listings of the vital organ affected by the aortic disease.

In defining the criteria for abnormal aortic dilation, it must be recognized that the diameter of the aorta varies by several patient characteristics including age, sex, and weight (see Table 14-1). In addition to absolute size criteria, an abnormal aortic dilation may be defined by the relative relationship between the size of the ascending aorta and the descending aorta. Assessing these relative differences in dimensions may be particularly helpful in evaluating abnormal aortic dilation in children.

CONCLUSIONS AND RECOMMENDATIONS

The current listing for aneurysm (Listing 4.10, Aneurysm of aorta or major branches) is met if patients have an aneurysm of the aorta or major

TABLE 14-1 Normal Adult Thoracic Aortic Diameters

Thoracic Aorta	Range of Reported Mean (cm)	Reported SD (cm)	Assessment Method
Root (female)	3.50–3.72	0.38	CT
Root (male)	3.63–3.91	0.38	CT
Ascending (female, male)	2.86	N/A	CXR
Mid-descending (female)	2.45–2.64	0.31	CT
Mid-descending (male)	2.39–2.98	0.31	CT
Diaphragmatic (female)	2.40–2.44	0.32	CT
Diaphragmatic (male)	2.43–2.69	0.27–0.40	CT, arteriography

NOTE: cm = centimeters; CT = computed tomography; CXR = chest x-ray; SD = standard deviation.
SOURCE: Hiratzka et al., 2010.

branches, due to any cause, demonstrated by medical imaging and uncontrolled by treatment (see Box 14-1). The most common and appropriate management of symptomatic cases involves surgical or endovascular treatment of the aneurysm or dissection. In high-risk patients with aortic disease and/or a genetic predisposition to aneurysm formation or aortic dissection (e.g., Marfan syndrome), the standard medical management may include substantial restrictions in physical activity in adults and children with asymptomatic aortic aneurysms or dissections. The prescribed treatment may include limitations on strenuous physical exertion or heavy lifting that may have implications on the capacity to perform certain activities of gainful employment.

BOX 14-1
Current Listing for Aneurysm of Aorta or Major Branches

4.10 Aneurysm of aorta or major branches, due to any cause (e.g., atherosclerosis, cystic medial necrosis, Marfan syndrome, trauma), demonstrated by appropriate medically acceptable imaging, with dissection not controlled by prescribed treatment (see 4.00H6).

SOURCE: SSA, 2008.

The committee concludes that the medical record should provide documentation of the aneurysm or dissection by imaging studies (e.g., CT, MRI) that are accompanied by evidence of impairment due to chronic debilitating symptoms resulting from the effects of the aneurysm or dissections on the heart, brain, peripheral nerves, or limbs. The Social Security Administration should reference other appropriate listings for the criteria for evaluating impairments on these related systems or organs.

RECOMMENDATION 14-1. Revise listing (4.10) to require the presence of chronic disabling symptoms due to the aneurysm or dissection. Disabling symptoms may be the result of the functional impairment to the heart, brain, peripheral nerves, or limbs due to the aneurysm or dissection. Claimants should be evaluated under the appropriate related cardiovascular listings or listings for other body systems if necessary.

The committee reviewed the current introductory text (i.e., the preamble) relevant to current listing 4.10 and recommended revisions to the text. These revisions will provide disability examiners with clear instructions for reviewing the medical records of patients with aneurysms or dissections and making appropriate evaluations of disability claims.

RECOMMENDATION 14-2. Revise the introductory text to the cardiovascular system to account for the following changes:

- **Include the term *dissection* in the primary description of the condition (i.e., aneurysm or dissection);**
- **Develop the definitions for aneurysm and dissection to include: An aneurysm is a bulge in the aorta or a peripheral artery. A dissection of the aorta or its branches occurs when the inner lining of the artery is "torn" and begins to separate from the rest of the arterial wall. An aneurysm or dissection may compromise organ function and produce symptoms by the compression of other structures in the tissue or body compartment or induce ischemia by compromising the flow of blood to the heart, kidneys, brain, or other organs;**
- **Revise the effects of aneurysm or dissection to include: An aneurysm or dissection can cause heart failure, renal (kidney) failure, or neurological complications. If an aneurysm or dissection is present, there must be one or more of these associated symptomatic conditions; the condition(s) are evaluated using the appropriate associated listings; and**

- **Revise the diagnostic criteria of Marfan syndrome to include: There is no specific laboratory test to diagnose Marfan syndrome, although the mutation in the gene that causes it has been defined. The diagnosis is generally made by medical history, including family history and physical examination including an evaluation of the musculoskeletal features, a slit-lamp eye examination, and a heart test(s), such as an echocardiogram. In some cases, a genetic analysis may be useful, but such analyses may not provide any additional helpful information. Include a description of Loeys-Dietz syndrome as another example of a genetic disorder with increased risk of aortic aneurysm and/or dissection affecting both children and adults.**

REFERENCES

Conrad, M. F., and R. P. Cambria. 2008. Contemporary management of descending thoracic and thoracoabdominal aortic aneurysms: Endovascular versus open. *Circulation* 117(6):841–852.

Davies, R. R., L. J. Goldstein, M. A. Coady, S. L. Tittle, J. A. Rizzo, G. S. Kopf, and J. A. Elefteriades. 2002. Yearly rupture or dissection rates for thoracic aortic aneurysms: Simple prediction based on size. *Annals of Thoracic Surgery* 73(1):17–28.

Elefteriades, J. A. 2002. Natural history of thoracic aortic aneurysms: Indications for surgery, and surgical versus nonsurgical risks. *Annals of Thoracic Surgery* 74(5):S1877–S1880.

Hiratzka, L. F., G. L. Bakris, J. A. Beckman, R. M. Bersin, V. F. Carr, D. E. Casey Jr., K. A. Eagle, L. K. Hermann, E. M. Isselbacher, E. A. Kazerooni, N. T. Kouchoukos, B. W. Lytle, D. M. Milewicz, D. L. Reich, S. Sen, J. A. Shinn, L. G. Svensson, and D. M. Williams. 2010. 2010 ACCF/AHA/AATS/ACR/ASA/SCA/SCAI/SIR/STS/SVM guidelines for the diagnosis and management of patients with thoracic aortic disease: A report of the American College of Cardiology Foundation/American Heart Association Task Force on Practice Guidelines, American Association for Thoracic Surgery, American College of Radiology, American Stroke Association, Society of Cardiovascular Anesthesiologists, Society for Cardiovascular Angiography and Interventions, Society of Interventional Radiology, Society of Thoracic Surgeons, and Society for Vascular Medicine. *Circulation* 121(13):e266–e369.

Lobato, A. C., and P. Puech-Leão. 1998. Predictive factors for rupture of thoracoabdominal aortic aneurysm. *Journal of Vascular Surgery* 27(3):446–453.

O'Gara, P. T. 2003. Aortic aneurysm. *Circulation* 107(6):e43–e45.

SSA (Social Security Administration). 2008. *Listing of impairments—Adult listings (Part A). Disability evaluation under Social Security (Blue Book).* http://www.socialsecurity.gov/disability/professionals/bluebook/AdultListings.htm (accessed July 22, 2010).

15

Comorbidities

Many individuals with a severe cardiovascular impairment, such as heart failure, coronary artery disease, or peripheral vascular disease, have chronic comorbid conditions, such as depression or diabetes, that further reduce their capacity to work. It would be efficient for the Social Security Administration (SSA), and beneficial for claimants with chronic comorbidities, to recognize claimants whose cardiovascular impairment is not severe enough to meet a listing, but who are unable to work because of the combined effect of their impairments, and to allow them at Step 3.

This chapter reviews the current state of knowledge about the extent of cardiovascular comorbidities and their effects on functional capacity. It also reviews SSA policies and procedures for evaluating claimants with multiple impairments at Step 3. The committee has no recommendations on revising these policies and procedures. Evaluating the effect of comorbidities in applying the Listings cannot be reduced to a predetermined formula and therefore should be determined by the judgment of the adjudicators. The committee intends the information in this chapter to better inform those decisions.

EXTENT OF COMORBIDITIES

Multiple morbidities are common and, generally, the more morbidities, the greater the likelihood of disability. An analysis of data from the 2005 Behavioral Risk Factor Surveillance System found that the prevalence of disability among U.S. adults ages 50 to 64 was 26.3 percent. It was much higher among those with chronic conditions, however—between 1.9 and

4.5 times higher depending on the condition. Adults with multiple chronic conditions were 42.9 times more likely to have a disability than those without comorbidities (Zhao et al., 2009).[1]

Depression and Anxiety

Depression and anxiety can cause profound functional impairment. Major depressive disorder produces impairment in functioning as severe as other chronic medical illnesses, including cardiovascular disease (Hays et al., 1995; Kessler et al., 2003; Ormel et al., 2008; Papakostas, 2009). The World Health Organization reports that depression is the leading cause of years lost due to disability for both men and women worldwide, and projects that depression and heart disease will be the two leading causes of disability in developed countries in the next decade (WHO, 2008). When major psychiatric and medical disorders co-occur, the proportion of disability attributable to psychiatric comorbidity is often greater than that attributable to the medical illness (Kessler et al., 2003).

Having even a few depression symptoms can contribute significantly to functional impairment and disability, although the level of impairment increases with the severity of depression (Papakostas, 2009; Spertus et al., 2000). Mild levels of anxiety may actually encourage adherence to the cardiac treatment regimen and more attentiveness to potentially fatal symptoms of heart disease; whereas moderate to severe anxiety is likely to contribute to cardiac disability, excessive medical service use, and an increased risk of further cardiac morbidity and even mortality (Frasure-Smith and Lespérance, 2008; Shen et al., 2008; Shibeshi et al., 2007). Of the two, depression is more difficult to detect, and therefore less likely to be treated or even documented in medical records. Also, substantially more research has been done on depression than anxiety or other mental disorders. Therefore, depression will be considered here in some detail, followed by a short review of research on anxiety and coronary heart disease (CHD).

Epidemiology of Depression

Depression is common in patients with cardiovascular disease. For example, at any point in time about 15 to 20 percent of patients with docu-

[1] The definition of disability in the Behavioral Risk Factor Surveillance System (BRFSS) is different from, i.e., less severe than, the Social Security Administration's definition. The latter pertains to individuals unable to engage in any substantial gainful activities, while the BRFSS classifies respondents as disabled if they answer "yes" to either of two questions: "Are you limited in any way in any activities because of physical, mental, or emotional problems?" or "Do you now have any health problem that requires you to use special equipment, such as a cane, a wheelchair, a special bed, or a special telephone?" (CDC, 2010).

mented CHD have major depression, and another 20 percent have at least a few symptoms of depression (Carney and Freedland, 2008). The prevalence rates are similarly high in patients with heart failure (Jiang et al., 2007; Norra et al., 2008), peripheral artery disease (McDermott et al., 2003; Ruo et al., 2007; Smolderen et al., 2008), and other forms of cardiovascular disease (Goodwin et al., 2009). Depressed patients with cardiovascular disease have a higher rate of hospitalization, experience more frequent cardiac symptoms, have more physical impairment and functional decline, are less likely to attend cardiac rehabilitation, are slower in returning to work following a myocardial infarction, and are twice as likely to suffer a second heart attack or to die, compared with those without depression symptoms (Beck et al., 2001; Carney and Freedland, 2008; deJonge et al., 2006; Frasure-Smith and Lespérance, 2006, 2008; Ladwig et al., 1994; Lane et al., 2001; McDermott et al., 2003; Ruo et al., 2007; Soderman et al., 2003; Spertus et al., 2000).

Despite its prevalence, associated functional impairment, and risk for morbidity and mortality, depression often goes undetected. In some cases this occurs because patients consider depression to be a normal part of having heart disease and they do not report it to their physician. Others may be too embarrassed to admit to feeling depressed, especially if they were not depressed before developing heart disease. In addition, many physicians do not ask about symptoms of depression. Consequently, depression status may not be known or mentioned in a patient's medical record.

Diagnostic Methods

The standard criteria for diagnosing depression are included in the *Diagnostic and Statistical Manual* (DSM-IV-TR) of the American Psychiatric Association (APA, 2000). A major depressive episode requires the presence of five or more depressive symptoms. These symptoms must persist for at least 2 weeks and cause clinically significant distress or functional impairment to meet the diagnostic criteria. Symptoms of depression include dysphoric mood, loss of interest in usual activities, poor concentration, difficulty in falling asleep or sleeping too much, poor appetite or overeating, feeling tired or fatigued, feeling like a failure, moving or speaking very slowly or feeling restless, and thoughts of death or suicide.

Dysthymia is a less symptomatic but chronic form of depression that is often associated with low self-esteem. Dysthymia is not diagnosed unless dysphoric mood and two or more additional depressive symptoms have been present for at least 2 years. In some cases, a major depressive episode is superimposed on dysthymia, a condition known as "double depression."

Treatment of Depression

A variety of medications and other methods may be used to treat depression when it is identified. None of these treatment options has been shown to be more effective than the others. Patients whose depression fails to respond to one type of antidepressant, for example, may improve with another, or with a combination of drugs or other treatments. Roughly half of all patients with major depression, with or without cardiovascular disease, show at least some improvement in depression symptoms with treatment, and remission is achieved in about 20 to 30 percent of cases (Rush et al., 2008).

In addition to antidepressants, specific forms of evidence-based psychotherapy, including cognitive behavior therapy and interpersonal psychotherapy, have been shown to be as effective as medications, especially for patients with mild to moderate depression. Psychotherapy can also be helpful for severe depression, but usually in combination with antidepressant medications. For more severe depression that does not respond to medications, electroconvulsive therapy may be considered with proper precautions. In addition, experimental treatments for depression may be available in some communities.

Although about half of patients treated for depression will show significant improvement; if residual symptoms remain after the patient has been treated for depression, functional impairment is likely to persist (Papakostas, 2009). Furthermore, even after remission of depression, a complete functional recovery may take months to occur, and some patients may be unable to function outside of a highly supportive environment during that time.

Generalized Anxiety Disorder

Approximately 24 to 31 percent of patients with CHD exhibit symptoms of anxiety. A recent cohort analysis from the Heart and Soul Study found that patients with stable CHD and generalized anxiety disorder had a 62 percent higher risk of cardiovascular events such as myocardial infarction, stroke, or death than CHD patients without anxiety symptoms, after controlling for factors such as demographics, major depressive disorder, other comorbid conditions, cardiac disease severity, and medication use (Martens et al., 2010).

Diabetes

The prevalence of diabetes mellitus (DM) increases with age. Of U.S. adults ages 45 to 64, 11.6 percent have DM, as do 2.9 percent of those ages 20 to 44 and 0.4 percent of those ages 0 to 19. Some individuals with a cardiovascular disease have comorbid DM, which is often associated with worse cardiovascular outcomes. For example, National Health and Nutrition Examination Survey (NHANES) data for the years 1999 to 2004 on adults ages 40 and older show that 24 percent of those who had peripheral artery disease (PAD) also had CHD, and 18 percent who had CHD also had PAD. NHANES data also show that adults ages 40 to 59 with lower extremity disease (LED) who also have DM are much more likely to have mobility limitations. Specifically, 15.6 percent of those with LED, but not DM, had mobility limitations, 29.6 percent with both LED and DM had mobility limitations, while 6 percent of those with neither LED nor DM had mobility limitations (Eberhardt et al., 2005).[2] A study of a cohort of PAD patients found that PAD progressed significantly on average during 4.6 years of follow-up and that progression was independently associated with DM, among other factors (Bird et al., 1999).

A study of residents of Olmstead County, Minnesota, who experienced a validated incident of myocardial infarction (MI) from 1979 to 1989 found that 19 percent of those whose MI occurred during the period 1994 to 1998 had DM (compared with 15 percent during the period 1979 to 1983), and those with diabetes had a lower survival rate 5 years post-MI (Gandhi et al., 2006). An earlier Minnesota Heart Survey study found that 26 percent of women and 17 percent of men hospitalized for an MI in 1985 had comorbid DM (Sprafka et al., 1991).

Franklin et al. (2004) compared patients who had suffered an acute coronary event who had DM with those who did not. Approximately 25 percent of the patients with ST-segment elevation myocardial infarction, non-ST-segment elevation myocardial infarction, and unstable angina (21, 26, and 25 percent, respectively) had DM. Compared with patients without DM, they had more coronary risk factors and comorbidities, and they were more likely to experience heart failure, renal failure, cardiogenic shock, or death in the hospital.

Chronic Obstructive Pulmonary Disease and Other Respiratory Diseases

Chronic obstructive pulmonary disease (COPD) is a progressive disease that contributes to significant morbidity and mortality in the United States. Cigarette smoking is the leading cause of COPD. As the prevalence of individuals who smoke declines due to public health initiatives, incidence of COPD is expected to similarly decline over time.

---

[2] Lower extremity disease includes peripheral artery disease and peripheral neuropathy. Mobility limitations are defined as the inability to perform activities of daily living or walk one-quarter mile or climb 10 steps without resting.

Symptoms of the disease include cough with mucus, shortness of breath, fatigue, frequent respiratory infections, and wheezing. Patients may be prescribed steroid inhalers to treat associated symptoms; however, there is no curative treatment for COPD, and, therefore, the combined effects of a comorbid cardiovascular disease may lead to disability. One of the leading causes of death among patients with COPD is comorbid heart failure. In a cohort study of 1,927 patients, patients with COPD had a 194 percent increase in the risk of heart failure after adjustment for age and sex, and a 194 percent increase in the risk of death after adjustment for age and sex, compared with patients without COPD (García Rodríguez et al., 2010).

Obesity

Obesity is an increasingly prevalent metabolic disorder in the United States. Heredity and environment both contribute to the development of obesity. Genes are thought to explain obesity in 30 to 70 percent of cases. High-fat diets and low levels of physical exercise are likely the conditions that most lead to overweight and eventual obesity. Overweight and obesity contribute to comorbidities, including a number of cardiovascular conditions such as arrhythmia, coronary heart disease, and heart failure (Eckel, 1997).

Defining obesity continues to be controversial, and ultimately depends on the individual. Body mass index (BMI) is the most common measurement for determining overweight and obesity, and is defined as weight (kilograms) divided by height in meters squared (kg/m^2). However, a BMI-based definition of obesity does not consider the distribution of body fat across the body frame. Substantial evidence now indicates that an increased waist circumference, or waist-to-hip ratio, predicts comorbidities and mortality from obesity (Eckel, 1997).

Obesity and Ischemic Heart Disease

The relationship between obesity and ischemic heart disease has been viewed as indirect, or through channels related to both diseases, such as hypertension, dyslipidemia, or non-insulin-dependent diabetes mellitus. Insulin resistance and accompanying hyperinsulinemia are typically associated with these comorbidities (Reaven, 1988). Although most of the comorbidities associating obesity and ischemia increase in a positive relationship with BMI, they also relate to body fat distribution. However, long-term longitudinal studies indicate that obesity also predicts coronary atherosclerosis independently (Garrison and Castelli, 1985; Manson et al., 1995; Rabkin et al., 1977).

Obesity and Heart Failure

Diastolic dysfunction is common in obese individuals. When obesity is present, but systemic hypertension is absent, left ventricular volume is often increased, but wall stress usually remains normal. However, in obese patients without hypertension, increases in stroke volume and cardiac output, as well as diastolic dysfunction, are seen. These changes in the left ventricle are related to sudden death in obese patients. Increased left ventricular volume and wall stress, increased stroke volume, and cardiac output are seen as commonly in systemic hypertension as in patients with obesity (Alpert and Hashimi, 1993; Messerli and Aepfelbacher, 1995).

A study examined 22 patients with severe obesity postmortem and reported dilated cardiomyopathy as the most frequent condition associated with sudden death (Duflou et al., 1995). Dilated cardiomyopathies, presumably with concomitant cardiac arrhythmias, may be the most common cause of sudden death in patients with severe obesity. The prolonged QT interval[3] also seen in obesity may predispose patients to such arrhythmias (Frank et al., 1986).

Obesity may also lead to changes in the right heart, eventually leading to right heart failure. The pathophysiology is related to sleep apnea or the obesity hypoventilation syndrome, both of which produce pulmonary hypertension and right ventricular hypertrophy, dilatation, and progressive dysfunction. All these conditions may lead to right heart failure (Menashe et al., 1965).

EVALUATING COMORBIDITIES AT THE LISTINGS STEP

Current Policies and Procedures

According to current SSA policy, claimants may be allowed at Step 3 of the sequential evaluation process on the basis that their impairment medically equals a listing if they have "a combination of impairments, no one of which meets a listing, but the findings related to these impairments are at least of equal medical significance to those of a listed impairment." SSA also may find medical equivalence in two other ways:

- The claimant's impairment is described in a listing, but it does not exhibit one or more of the findings specified in the particular listing, or it exhibits all of the findings, but one or more of them is not as severe as specified in the listing, and there are other findings

[3] The QT interval is the time from the electrocardiogram Q wave to the end of the T wave corresponding to electrical systole. http://www.medilexicon.com/medicaldistionary.php?t=45242 (accessed July 16, 2010).

related to the impairment that are at least of equal medical significance to the required criteria.
- The claimant's impairment is not described in a listing, but it exhibits findings that are closely analogous to a listed impairment, and these findings are at least of equal medical significance to that listed impairment.

In 2008, more than one-third of the adult cardiovascular Step 3 allowances were based on medical equivalence rather than meeting a listing.[4] Medical equivalency accounted for 30 to 50 percent of the listing-based allowances, with the exception of heart transplant.[5] More than 90 percent of heart transplantation Step 3 allowances were based on meeting the heart transplantation listing, probably because it is easy to ascertain objectively that a heart transplant occurred.

For children under age 18 who have a severe impairment or impairments that do not meet or medically equal a listing, SSA will determine whether the impairment or impairments functionally equal the Listings. This functional equivalence process, which applies to children only, is described in Chapter 2 of this report. For adults who have a severe impairment or impairments that do not meet or medically equal a listing, SSA will evaluate the functional limitations resulting from their impairments at Step 4 and, if necessary, Step 5 of the disability decision process, which is also described in Chapter 2.

CONCLUSION

The current procedure to determine if one or more comorbidities combine with a severe cardiovascular impairment to produce a case equaling or exceeding a listing-level impairment relies on the judgment of a medical or psychological consultant or other adjudicator. If the criteria for meeting a listing are complex and technical, as are the criteria for cardiovascular listings, an adjudicator may decide to forgo Step 3 and proceed to Steps 4 and 5, relying on the residual functional capacity evaluation to decide the claim, a process that requires more time and resources.

The committee considered whether to recommend a more objective decision-making procedure, such as adopting criteria for meeting the heart failure listing that included (1) an ejection fraction between 30 and 35 per-

---

[4] Medical or psychological consultants from the various disability determination services have the overall responsibility for determining medical equivalence in initial and reconsideration decisions.

[5] The data on Step 3 allowances based on medical equivalence do not distinguish among the three bases for medical equivalency, so it is uncertain how many or what share of allowances were based on a combination of impairments equal to the severity of a listed impairment.

cent *and* (2) a diagnosis of severe depression, but could find no evidence that this combination invariably results in inability to work. However, SSA is in a good position to ascertain the impact of comorbidities by analyzing patterns in cases it has decided. Taking the example above, SSA could analyze a sample of disability claims with heart failure as the primary impairment to examine the relationship with comorbidities, such as depression. If, for example, 95 percent or more of claims with a diagnosis of major depression and certain ejection fraction values are allowed at Step 5, SSA could consider creating a listing criterion for major depression in combination with those ejection fraction values. Alternatively, SSA could provide more focused training to adjudicators on how to evaluate equivalency at Step 3 in such cases. These points are addressed further in the Chapter 16 discussion of research opportunities for improving the Listings.

REFERENCES

Alpert, M. A., and M. W. Hashimi. 1993. Obesity and the heart. *American Journal of the Medical Sciences* 306(2):117–123.

APA (American Psychiatric Association). 2000. *Diagnostic and statistical manual of mental disorders,* 4th ed., text revision (DSM-IV-TR). Washington, DC: American Psychiatric Association.

Beck, C. A., L. Joseph, P. Belisle, and L. Pilote. 2001. Predictors of quality of life 6 months and 1 year after acute myocardial infarction. *American Heart Journal* 142(2):271–279.

Bird, C. E., M. H. Criqui, A. Fronek, J. O. Denenberg, M. R. Klauber, and R. D. Langer. 1999. Quantitative and qualitative progression of peripheral arterial disease by non-invasive testing. *Vascular Medicine* 4(1):15–21.

Carney, R. M., and K. E. Freedland. 2008. Depression in patients with coronary heart disease. *American Journal of Medicine* 121(11 Suppl 2):S20–S27.

CDC (Centers for Disease Control and Prevention). 2010. *Behavioral Risk Factor Surveillance System 2010 Questionnaire.* http://www.cdc.gov/brfss/questionnaires/pdf-ques/2010brfss.pdf (accessed August 23, 2010).

deJonge, P., T. A. Spijkerman, R. H. van den Brink, and J. Ormel. 2006. Depression after myocardial infarction is a risk factor for declining health related quality of life and increased disability and cardiac complaints at 12 months. *Heart* 92(1):32–39.

Duflou, J., R. Virmani, I. Rabin, A. Burke, A. Farb, and J. Smialek. 1995. Sudden death as a result of heart disease in morbid obesity. *American Heart Journal* 130(2):306–313.

Eberhardt, M. S., S. Saydah, R. Paulose-Ram, and M. Tao. 2005. Mobility limitation among persons aged ≥ 40 years with and without diagnosed diabetes and lower extremity disease—United States, 1999–2002. *Morbidity and Mortality Weekly Report* 54(46):1183–1186. http://www.cdc.gov/ mmwr/PDF/wk/mm5446.pdf (accessed July 16, 2010).

Eckel, R. H. 1997. Obesity and heart disease: A statement for healthcare professionals from the nutrition committee, American Heart Association. *Circulation* 96(9):3248–3250. http://circ.ahajournals.org/cgi/content/full/96/9/3248 (accessed August 4, 2010).

Frank, S., J. A. Colliver, and A. Frank. 1986. The electrocardiogram in obesity: Statistical analysis of 1,029 patients. *Journal of the American College of Cardiology* 7(2):295–299.

Franklin, K., R. J. Goldberg, F. Spencer, W. Klein, A. Budaj, D. Brieger, M. Marre, P. G. Steg, N. Gowda, J. M. Gore, and GRACE Investigators. 2004. Implications of diabetes in patients with acute coronary syndromes. The Global Registry of Acute Coronary Events.

Archives of Internal Medicine 164(13):1457–1463. http://archinte.ama-assn.org/cgi/reprint/164/13/1457 (accessed July 16, 2010).

Frasure-Smith, N., and F. Lespérance. 2006. Recent evidence linking coronary heart disease and depression. *Canadian Journal of Psychiatry* 51:730–737.

Frasure-Smith, N., and F. Lespérance. 2008. Depression and anxiety as predictors of 2-year cardiac events in patients with stable coronary artery disease. *Archives of General Psychiatry* 65(1):62–71. http://archpsyc.ama-assn.org/cgi/reprint/65/1/62 (accessed October 8, 2010).

Gandhi, G. Y., V. L. Roger, K. R. Bailey, P. J. Palumbo, J. E. Ransom, and C. L. Leibson. 2006. Temporal trends in prevalence of diabetes mellitus in a population-based cohort of incident myocardial infarction and impact of diabetes on survival. *Mayo Clinic Proceedings* 81(8):1034–1040. http://www.mayoclinicproceedings.com/content/81/8/1034.full.pdf+html (accessed July 16, 2010).

García Rodríguez, L. A., M. A. Wallander, E. Martín-Merino, and S. Johansson. 2010. Heart failure, myocardial infarction, lung cancer and death in COPD patients: A UK primary care study. *Respiratory Medicine,* May 17. Epub ahead of print. http://www.ncbi.nlm.nih.gov/pubmed/20483577 (accessed July 12, 2010).

Garrison, R. J., and W. P. Castelli. 1985. Weight and thirty-year mortality of men in the Framingham Study. *Annals of Internal Medicine* 103(6 Pt 2):1006–1009.

Goodwin, R. D., K. W. Davidson, and K. Keyes. 2009. Mental disorders and cardiovascular disease among adults in the United States. *Journal of Psychiatric Research* 43(3):239–246.

Hays, R. D., K. B. Wells, C. D. Sherbourne, W. Rogers, and K. Spritzer. 1995. Functioning and well-being outcomes of patients with depression compared with chronic general medical illnesses. *Archives of General Psychiatry* 52(1):11–19.

Jiang, W., M. Kuchibhatla, G. L. Clary, M. S. Cuffe, E. J. Christopher, J. D. Alexander, R. M. Califf, R. R. Krishnan, and C. M. O'Connor. 2007. Relationship between depressive symptoms and long-term mortality in patients with heart failure. *American Heart Journal* 154(1):102–108.

Kessler, R. C., J. Ormel, O. Demler, and P. E. Stang. 2003. Comorbid mental disorders account for the role impairment of commonly occurring chronic physical disorders: Results from the National Comorbidity Survey. *Journal of Occupational and Environmental Medicine* 45(12):1257–1266.

Ladwig, K. H., G. Roll, G. Breithardt, T. Budde, and M. Borggrefe. 1994. Post-infarction depression and incomplete recovery 6 months after acute myocardial infarction. *Lancet* 343(8888):20–23.

Lane, D., D. Carroll, C. Ring, D. G. Beevers, and G. Y. Lip. 2001. Predictors of attendance at cardiac rehabilitation after myocardial infarction. *Journal of Psychosomatic Research* 51(3):497–501.

Manson, J. E., W. C. Willett, M. J. Stampfer, G. A. Colditz, D. J. Hunter, S. E. Hankinson, C. H. Hennekens, and F. E. Speizer. 1995. Body weight and mortality among women. *New England Journal of Medicine* 333(11):677–685.

Martens, E. J., P. de Jonge, B. Na, B. E. Cohen, H. Lett, and M. A. Whooley. 2010. Scared to death? Generalized anxiety disorder and cardiovascular events in patients with stable coronary heart disease: The Heart and Soul Study. *Archives of General Psychiatry* 67(7):750–758.

McDermott, M. M., P. Greenland, J. M. Guralnik, K. Liu, M. H. Criqui, W. H. Pearce, C. Chan, J. Schneider, L. Sharma, L. M. Taylor, A. Arseven, M. Quann, and L. Celic. 2003. Depressive symptoms and lower extremity functioning in men and women with peripheral arterial disease. *Journal of General Internal Medicine* 18(6):461–467.

Menashe, V. D., C. Farrehi, and M. Miller. 1965. Hypoventilation and cor pulmonale due to chronic upper airway obstruction. *Journal of Pediatrics* 67:198–203.

Messerli, F. H., and F. C. Aepfelbacher. 1995. Hypertension and left-ventricular hypertrophy. *Cardiology Clinics* 13(4):549–557.

Norra, C., E. C. Skobel, M. Arndt, and P. Schauerte. 2008. High impact of depression in heart failure: Early diagnosis and treatment options. *International Journal of Cardiology* 125(2):220–231.

Ormel, J., M. Petukhova, S. Chatterji, S. Aguilar-Gaxiola, J. Alonso, M. C. Angermeyer, E. J. Bromet, H. Burger, K. Demyttenaere, G. de Girolamo, J. M. Haro, I. Hwang, E. Karam, N. Kawakami, J. P. Lépine, M. E. Medina-Mora, J. Posada-Villa, N. Sampson, K. Scott, T. B. Ustun, M. Von Korff, D. R.Williams, M. Zhang, and R. C. Kessler. 2008. Disability and treatment of specific mental and physical disorders across the world. *British Journal of Psychiatry* 192(5):368–375.

Papakostas, G. I. 2009. Major depressive disorder: Psychosocial impairment and key considerations in functional improvement. *American Journal of Managed Care* 15(11 Suppl): S316–S321. http://www.ajmc.com/media/pdf/A269_09decPapakostasS316to321.pdf (accessed August 23, 2010).

Rabkin, S. W., F. A. Mathewson, and P. H. Hsu. 1977. Relation of body weight to development of ischemic heart disease in a cohort of young North American men after a 26 year observation period: The Manitoba Study. *American Journal of Cardiology* 39(3):452–458.

Reaven, G. M. 1988. Banting lecture: Role of insulin resistance in human disease. *Diabetes* 37(12):1595–1607.

Ruo, B., K. Liu, L. Tian, J. Tan, L. Ferrucci, J. M. Guralnik, and M. M. McDermott. 2007. Persistent depressive symptoms and functional decline among patients with peripheral arterial disease. *Psychosomatic Medicine* 69(5):415–424.

Rush, A. J., J. Kilner, M. Fava, S. R. Wisniewski, D. Warden, A. A. Nierenberg, and M. H. Trivedi. 2008. Clinically relevant findings from STAR*D. *Psychiatric Annals* 38(3): 188–193.

Shen, B. J., Y. E. Avivi, J. F. Todaro, A. Spiro III, J. P. Laurenceau, K. D. Ward, and R. Niaura. 2008. Anxiety characteristics independently and prospectively predict myocardial infarction in men: The unique contribution of anxiety among psychologic factors. *Journal of the American College of Cardiology* 51(2):113–119.

Shibeshi, W. A., Y. Young-Xu, and C. M. Blatt. 2007. Anxiety worsens prognosis in patients with coronary artery disease. *Journal of the American College of Cardiology* 49(20):2021–2027.

Smolderen, K. G., A. E. Aquarius, J. de Vries, O. R. Smith, J. F. Hamming, and J. Denollet. 2008. Depressive symptoms in peripheral arterial disease: A follow-up study on prevalence, stability, and risk factors. *Journal of Affective Disorders* 110(1–2):27–35.

Soderman, E., J. Lisspers, and O. Sundin. 2003. Depression as a predictor of return to work in patients with coronary artery disease. *Social Science & Medicine* 56(1):193–202.

Spertus, J. A., M. McDonnell, C. L. Woodman, and S. D. Fihu. 2000. Association between depression and worse disease-specific functional status in outpatients with coronary artery disease. *American Heart Journal* 140(1):105–110.

Sprafka, J. M., G. L. Burke, A. R. Folsom, P. G. McGovern, and L. P. Hahn. 1991. Trends in prevalence of diabetes mellitus in patients with myocardial infarction and effect of diabetes on survival: The Minnesota Heart Survey. *Diabetes Care* 14(7):537–543.

WHO (World Health Organization). 2008. *The global burden of disease: 2004 update.* Geneva, Switzerland: WHO Press. http://www.who.int/healthinfo/global_burden_disease/2004_report_update/en/index.html (accessed August 3, 2010).

Zhao, G., E. S. Ford, C. Li, J. E. Crews, and A. H. Mokdad. 2009. Disability and its correlates with chronic morbidities among U.S. adults aged 50 ≤ 65 years. *Preventive Medicine* 48(2):117–121.

16

Future Directions for Improving the Listings

In the course of its work, the committee encountered a number of knowledge gaps in evaluating the effectiveness of the cardiovascular listings. The gaps would be reduced, and the listings improved, by research in four areas, discussed in the following sections.

POLICY ISSUES

If health insurance reform increases access to health services, and if increased access helps ensure that tests and other procedures Social Security cannot provide because of high cost or risk, such as catheterization, are regularly performed, the cardiovascular listings could be revised to require such tests and other procedures to meet the Listings. Also, increased access may reduce the rate of decline in an individual's health and the resultant inability to work caused by some impairments to the point that a listing is no longer needed. The Social Security Administration (SSA) should support research on the disability-related effects of health insurance reform, which are currently uncertain, to improve program planning and future updates of the Listings—not just the cardiovascular listings.

PROGRAMMATIC ISSUES

In evaluating the impact of the current Listings and alternatives for revising them, the committee had many questions that will be brought up the next time they are revised. Many of these questions could be addressed with data that SSA already produces routinely or could obtain from a sample of case files.

One important lack of information the committee faced consistently was the dearth of data on the relationship between severity of anatomical impairment or other markers in the medical record with the likelihood that a claimant with those characteristics are allowed, first at Step 3, then at Step 5. SSA itself has programmatic data that could be used to address this question. For example, a sample of Step 5 allowances for a specific impairment could be analyzed retrospectively to see if there is a common feature in the medical record. If so, that feature could be made a listing-level criterion and thus allow these claimants more quickly. Currently, for example, an ejection fraction of 30 percent or less with certain symptoms or signs or very serious limitations on activities of daily living meets the heart failure listing, and an ankle-brachial index (ABI) less than 0.50 meets the peripheral artery disease (PAD) listing. An analysis of claims process data could find that functionally limited claimants with heart failure with an ejection fraction of 35 percent are nearly always allowed at Step 5, or that claimants with PAD with an ABI of 0.55 are invariably allowed at Step 5, and the listings could be revised accordingly. Similar analyses could be done of allowances that equal a listing; for example, if the rate of allowances equaling the listing for a particular impairment was increasing unexpectedly, the research might find that the medical community has adopted a new test to diagnose or determine the severity of the condition, and that test could be added to the listing so claimants could more easily and reliably be allowed at Step 3.

Another critical area where research is needed is on the effects of comorbidities that claimants with a cardiovascular impairment often have. Again, SSA has data that can be analyzed to illuminate the impact of these effects. A research project along these lines was suggested in the conclusion of Chapter 15. The project would track the percentage of claims of heart failure with a diagnosis of major depression and various ejection fraction cutoff points, for example, 35 and 40 percent, that are allowed at Step 5. If the rate is very high for any of these cutoff points, that is, 95 percent or higher, SSA could create a listing criterion for major depression in combination with that specific ejection fraction value.

SSA could also pretest the impact of a proposed change in a listing by prospectively comparing a sample of claims while going through the regular process. The committee was pleased to learn that since the release of the 2007 Institute of Medicine report on improving the Social Security disability decision process (IOM, 2007), SSA has engaged a National Institutes of Health group in conducting such analyses of disability program data. Analyses of the use of the Listings are being done within SSA's Office of Disability Programs.

Another area of interest would be to study the degree of variability among examiners, or interrater reliability, in applying the Listings, which would provide some insight into which listings need to be reconsidered and revised. For example, the same case or set of cases could be given to multiple adjudicators to review consistency in the decisions made.

CORRELATION OF IMPAIRMENTS AND FUNCTIONAL LIMITATIONS

SSA would benefit from research on the relationship among various degrees of anatomical impairment, which can be fairly objectively determined, and the functional limitations of individuals with those impairments. A body of research shows the average exercise limitations of individuals with a particular diagnosis, such as the limitations on the walking capacity of patients with PAD, defined as an ABI less than 0.90. However, little information is available on limitations by degree of severity, that is, an ABI less than 0.50 versus 0.40 versus 0.30, which would be more useful for validating and fine-tuning the criteria in the PAD listing.

In addition, little information is available on the relationship between functional assessment performed with a 10-minute treadmill or exercise bike test and the capacity to work an 8-hour workday. Well-validated and up-to-date information on the metabolic equivalents of task needed for various work-related activities is also needed. Current evidence is dated and limited to a small range of activities (Ainsworth et al., 2000).

TRUE PREVALENCE OF AND TRENDS IN IMPAIRMENTS THAT MEET THE SOCIAL SECURITY DEFINITION OF DISABILITY OR MEET THE LISTINGS

This information is needed for program planning and budget projections, but it would also be useful in validating the Listings. Currently, key information about the performance of the Listings is absent, such as sensitivity and specificity (or type 1 and type 2 errors), positive and negative predictive values, and overall accuracy, because the underlying rates of true disability are not known. SSA has begun and abandoned several efforts to determine the prevalence of disabilities that meet the statutory definition of disability and the validity of the Listings, probably because of the technical difficulties and cost. However, it seems that it ultimately would be cost effective to conduct this research, given the large dollar value of the benefits attached to disability determination decisions.

CONCLUSIONS AND RECOMMENDATION

SSA has a substantial in-house research program and supports some external research, but most of it is related to the Old Age and Survivors Insurance program and retirement behavior and trends rather than the Disability Insurance and Supplemental Security Income programs and disability prevalence and trends. Recently, the agency has expanded its research efforts related to the Listings. To better assist the next round of revisions of the cardiovascular and other listings, SSA should sponsor, both in house and externally, a full and balanced program of research in the four areas listed above.

RECOMMENDATION 16-1. SSA should plan and sponsor a balanced program of research to improve the reliability, validity, and utility of the Listings in four areas: policy implications, programmatic issues, correlation of impairments and impairment severity with functional limitations related to work capacity, and the underlying prevalence of and trends in impairments in the population. This program would also enable SSA to enhance the other steps of the disability determination process.

REFERENCES

Ainsworth, B. E., W. L. Haskell, M. C. Whitt, M. L. Irwin, A. M. Swartz, S. J. Strath, W. L. O'Brien, D. R. Bassett Jr., K. H. Schmitz, P. O. Emplaincourt, D. R. Jacobs Jr., and A. S. Leon. 2000. Compendium of physical activities: An update of activity codes and MET intensities. *Medicine and Science in Sports and Exercise* 32(Suppl):S498–S516.

IOM (Institute of Medicine). 2007. *Improving the Social Security disability decision process*, edited by J. D. Stobo, M. McGeary, and D. K. Barnes. Committee on Improving the Disability Decision Process: SSA's Listing of Impairments and Agency Access to Medical Expertise. Washington, DC: The National Academies Press.

Appendix A

Biographical Sketches of Committee Members and Staff

COMMITTEE MEMBERS

Nanette K. Wenger, M.D., is a professor of medicine in the Division of Cardiology at the Emory University School of Medicine, chief of cardiology at Grady Memorial Hospital, and a consultant to the Emory Heart and Vascular Center. One of her major clinical and research interests is coronary heart disease in women, and she is an expert on heart disease in the elderly and in cardiac rehabilitation. She has served as vice president of the American Heart Association (AHA), governor for Georgia of the American College of Cardiology (ACC), and president of the Georgia Heart Association. Dr. Wenger also has served as a member and frequent chair of more than 500 committees, scientific advisory boards, task forces, and councils of the American Medical Association; ACC; AHA; National Heart, Lung, and Blood Institute (NHLBI); and Society of Geriatric Cardiology. She is a fellow of the AHA, Society of Geriatric Cardiology, American Association of Cardiovascular and Pulmonary Rehabilitation, and American College of Chest Physicians. She is a master of the American College of Physicians and of ACC. Dr. Wenger served as a member of the IOM Committee on Acute Myocardial Infarction. She is a graduate of Hunter College (summa cum laude) and Harvard Medical School. She had her residency training in internal medicine and cardiology fellowship at the Mount Sinai Hospital in New York City, and an additional fellowship in cardiology at the Emory University School of Medicine.

William E. Boden, M.D., is a professor of medicine and preventive medicine at the State University of New York–Buffalo Schools of Medicine and

Public Health. He is director of Cardiovascular Services at Kaleida Health System in western New York and chief of cardiology at Buffalo General and Millard Fillmore Hospitals in Buffalo. Since 1979, Dr. Boden has held university appointments at Brown University, Wayne State University, Tufts New England Medical Center, Boston University, the University of Connecticut, and currently at the State University of New York–Buffalo. His principal research interests include studies in post-myocardial infarction (MI) secondary prevention, acute coronary syndromes and unstable angina, congestive heart failure and dyslipidemia in post-MI, and coronary artery disease (CAD). He has worked extensively in the clinical trials arena of non-Q-wave MI and in assessing the role of calcium antagonists in patients with ischemic heart disease, notably in non-Q-wave MI secondary prevention. Dr. Boden has been involved in clinical research investigator activities as the project director, study chair, and cochair for multicenter clinical trials, and served as a principal investigator, steering committee member, and consultant for numerous clinical research grant activities funded by the Department of Veterans Affairs (VA), the National Institutes of Health (NIH), and industry. He was the study chair and cochairman for the VANQWISH and INTERCEPT trials, respectively. Currently he is the study cochair and lead investigator in the COURAGE trial (the largest randomized trial comparison of percutaneous coronary intervention [PCI] versus optimal medical therapy in stable CAD patients). He is the study cochair of the NIH-funded AIM-HIGH trial evaluating the long-term role of combination dyslipidemic therapy (niacin and statin versus statin) in CAD patients with low HDL cholesterol. Dr. Boden has lectured widely and written more than 350 peer-reviewed publications, original articles, books, chapters, and abstracts. He has been selected as one of the *Best Doctors in America* continuously since 2003. He is a member of several professional cardiology organizations as well as a member of the editorial boards of the *American Journal of Cardiology*, the *Journal of the American College of Cardiology*, and *Clinical Cardiology*. Dr. Boden also serves as an editorial reviewer for the *New England Journal of Medicine*, the *Annals of Internal Medicine*, *Circulation*, the *Journal of the American Medical Association*, the *American Heart Journal*, and the *Archives of Internal Medicine*. He received his M.D. from the State University of New York, Upstate Medical Center, Syracuse. Dr. Boden performed his internal medicine training at Boston University Medical Center and completed his fellowship training in cardiology at Tufts University School of Medicine. He is board certified in internal medicine and in the subspecialty of cardiovascular diseases (CVDs).

Blase A. Carabello, M.D., is a professor of medicine and the vice chair of the Department of Medicine at Baylor College of Medicine. He is currently vice president of Programs and Education for the Heart Valve Society of

America, and he serves as Michael E. DeBakey VA Medical Center's Medical Care Line Executive. He has served as chair of the AHA physiology study section and has more than 200 publications exploring the physiology and cell biology of valvular heart disease and its role in causing congestive heart failure. Dr. Carabello is an author of the joint AHA/ACC 2006 guidelines for the management of valvular heart disease. He attended medical school at Temple University in Philadelphia. He completed his residency in internal medicine at Massachusetts General Hospital–Harvard Medical School and his cardiology fellowship at Peter Bent Brigham Hospital–Harvard Medical School.

Robert M. Carney, Ph.D., is a professor of psychiatry and the director of the Behavioral Medicine Center at the Washington University School of Medicine. He is a licensed psychologist specializing in cognitive behavior therapy for the treatment of depression and anxiety disorders in medical patients. He is a fellow of the Society of Behavioral Medicine and an elected member of the Academy of Behavioral Medicine Research. Dr. Carney has been an active researcher in the area of depression and comorbid medical illness, especially heart disease, for more than 20 years. He was a member of the Aging and Medical Co-morbidity subcommittee for the development of the National Institute of Mental Health's strategic plan for mood disorders. He has also served as a reviewer for research proposals in this area for NIH, the Medical Research Council of Canada, and the Department of Veterans Affairs Scientific Research and Development Committee. Dr. Carney's major research focus is on the relationship of depression to medical morbidity and mortality in patients with coronary heart disease. He was a member of the executive and steering committees for the Enhancing Recovery in Coronary Heart Disease (ENRICHD) clinical trial, designed to determine whether treating depression and improving social support increases survival in patients with a recent MI. He is currently studying the relationship of sleep disorders to cardiac events in depressed cardiovascular heart disease patients, and the relationship of altered autonomic nervous system functioning and mortality in depressed patients with a recent acute myocardial infarction. Dr. Carney has a B.A. in psychology and a Ph.D. in counseling psychology from Washington University in Missouri.

Manuel D. Cerqueira, M.D., is chair of nuclear medicine in the Imaging Institute and a staff cardiologist in the Heart and Vascular Institute at the Cleveland Clinic. He has a special clinical and research interest in using cardiovascular imaging methods to identify patients with CAD and those at high risk for having heart attacks or dying from a cardiac cause. Prior to his appointment to the Cleveland Clinic in 2004, Dr. Cerqueira was chief of cardiology at Georgetown University Medical Center. He also served as a consultant in nuclear cardiology to NIH. During his tenure at Georgetown, he was also director of nuclear cardiology, the Exercise Stress Testing Laboratory, and cardiac rehabilitation. He was a professor in the Departments of Medicine and Radiology at Georgetown and in the Department of Radiology and Medicine at the University of Washington School of Medicine in Seattle. He was also chief of nuclear medicine at the VA Medical Center. Dr. Cerqueira is a grant reviewer for NIH. He works in many capacities with the *Journal of Nuclear Cardiology*, *American Journal of Cardiology*, *American Journal of Roentgenology*, *Journal of the American College of Cardiology*, and *European Journal of Nuclear Medicine*, among others. He is widely published, authoring or coauthoring more than 170 articles, 26 book chapters, and 95 abstracts on issues related to clinical and research findings. A native of Portugal, Dr. Cerqueira did his undergraduate work at Franklin & Marshall College in Lancaster, Pennsylvania, and received his M.D. from New York University School of Medicine. He did an internship and residency in internal medicine at Bellevue Medical Center in New York City, where he became chief resident in internal medicine. He continued his clinical training with a fellowship in cardiology from Yale–New Haven Hospital in Connecticut, and continued on at the hospital, becoming chief resident in nuclear medicine. He is certified in internal medicine, nuclear medicine, CVD, and nuclear cardiology.

Michael H. Criqui, M.D., M.P.H., is a professor and the chief of the Division of Preventive Medicine in the Department of Family and Preventive Medicine, a professor of cardiology in the Department of Medicine, and the director of the Preventive Cardiology Academic Award, all at the University of California–San Diego School of Medicine. He is an active investigator in cardiovascular epidemiology and preventive cardiology, and he has made substantial contributions in the fields of peripheral artery disease, subclinical atherosclerosis, peripheral venous disease, and ethnic differences in CVD. He currently chairs the International Peripheral Arterial Disease and Abdominal Aortic Aneurysm Working Group for the Global Burden of Diseases, Injuries, and Risk Factors Study, sponsored by the World Health Organization. He is senior consultant to the editorial board for the *Journal of the American College of Cardiology*. Honors include election as a distinguished scientist of AHA in 2010; the Distinguished Achievement Award from the Council on Epidemiology and Prevention of AHA in 2008; the Special Recognition Award from the AHA Council on Epidemiology and Prevention in 2004; the Fredrick H. Epstein Memorial Lecture Award from the Working Group on Epidemiology and Prevention of the European Society of Cardiology in 2002; and the Joseph E. Stokes III Preventive Cardiology Award from the American Society for Preventive Cardiology in 2001. He has an M.P.H. in epidemiology from the University of California–Berkeley and an M.D. from the University of California–San Francisco, and he is board certified in general preventive medicine.

Andrew E. Epstein, M.D., is a professor of medicine, Cardiovascular Division, at the University of Pennsylvania, and the chief of the Cardiology Section at the Philadelphia VA Medical Center. He is a fellow of ACC, the Council on Clinical Cardiology of AHA, and the Heart Rhythm Society (HRS). For AHA he has served as chair of its committees on sudden cardiac death and on electrocardiography and arrhythmias. He is currently chair of the ACC/AHA/HRS Guideline Committee for the Implantation of Cardiac Pacemakers and Antiarrhythmic Devices. His teaching awards at the University of Alabama–Birmingham include a "10 Best Teachers" award from the Department of Medicine in 1998 and 2008, the Cobbs-Rutsky Clinical Excellence Award from the Department of Medicine in 2006, and the H. Cecil Coghlan Teaching Excellence Award for the Division of Cardiovascular Disease in 2006. Dr. Epstein's research interests are in the management of atrial and ventricular arrhythmias. He has been involved in numerous clinical trials, and he chaired the recruitment committees for the NIH/NHLBI-sponsored Cardiac Arrhythmia Suppression Trial (CAST), the Antiarrhythmics versus Implantable Defibrillators (AVID) Study, the Atrial Fibrillation Follow-up Investigation of Rhythm Management (AFFIRM) Study, and the Dual Chamber and VVI Implantable Defibrillator (DAVID) Trial. He has authored several hundred papers, abstracts, book chapters, and reviews and has edited two books. He serves on the editorial boards of the *Journal of Cardiovascular Electrophysiology*, the *Journal of Interventional Cardiac Electrophysiology* (as an associate editor), *Heart Rhythm*, *PACE*, and the *American Journal of Cardiology*. He graduated from Amherst College and the University of Rochester School of Medicine and Dentistry. After completing his internship and residency in internal medicine at Washington University/Barnes Hospital, Dr. Epstein moved to the University of Alabama, where he completed his fellowship in cardiovascular medicine and joined the faculty in 1982. He remained there until 2009, when he was recruited to Philadelphia. He is board certified in internal medicine, cardiology, and clinical cardiac electrophysiology.

Erika S. Froelicher, R.N., Ph.D., is a professor at the University of California–San Francisco School of Nursing in the Department of Physiological Nursing, with a collaborative appointment in the Occupational Health Program in the Community Health Systems Department, as well as a joint appointment in epidemiology and biostatistics in the School of Medicine. Her research is in the areas of primary, secondary, and tertiary (rehabilitation) prevention through nursing interventions to reduce CVD risk factors (smoking cessation and relapse prevention, psychosocial risk factors with depression in particular, exercise, blood pressure, lipids, obesity, and relapse prevention) as well as social isolation. She has a strong interest in physiological, psychosocial, and economic issues relevant to her expertise in methods, design, and epidemiology. Dr. Froelicher has a broad perspective because she is trilingual and tricultural and has extensive experience in international health through research consultation, education, and teaching. Dr. Froelicher's recent major research projects included participating in the ENRICHD project at the Collaborative Studies Coordinating Center, Department of Biostatistics, School of Public Health, University of North Carolina–Chapel Hill. She is also involved in the Women's Initiative for Nonsmoking (or WINS), a randomized clinical trial to test the short- and long-term efficacy of a nurse-managed smoking cessation and relapse prevention program for women smokers hospitalized for CVD. Dr. Froelicher has an extensive publication record in nursing and in epidemiology and biostatistics. Her Ph.D. in epidemiology and her M.P.H. are from the University of California–Los Angeles. Her M.A. in nursing is from the University of Washington in Seattle. She has a diploma in nursing from Queen Mary's Hospital in London, with certificates in midwifery from the City of London Maternity Hospital and in psychiatric nursing from Charing Cross Hospital in London.

Gary H. Gibbons, M.D., is a professor of medicine and the director of the Cardiovascular Research Institute at the Morehouse School of Medicine in Atlanta. He directs research in the fields of vascular biology, hypertension, atherosclerosis, and cardiovascular medicine. His program has made important contributions to the understanding of how humoral factors that regulate blood pressure activate molecular pathways that predispose to vascular complications, such as stroke and heart attacks. His laboratory currently focuses on defining the molecular basis of vascular disease by integrating DNA microarray technology and epigenetics with genetically engineered mouse models. In addition, he is collaborating with genetic epidemiologists to define the role of gene–environment interactions as determinants of ethnic disparities in CVD. He is a member of the Institute of Medicine (IOM). Dr. Gibbons received his A.B. in biology from Princeton University and his M.D. from Harvard Medical School.

Mark A. Hlatky, M.D., is a professor of health research and policy and a professor of medicine (cardiovascular medicine) at Stanford University. His major interests are in outcomes research, evidence-based medicine, and cost-effectiveness analysis. He has studied the effects of CVD and therapies on economics, quality of life, and employment outcomes. He has served on the Medicare Evidence Development and Coverage Advisory Committee and the Medical Advisory Panel of the Technology Evaluation Center of the

Blue Cross and Blue Shield Association, as well as on several national committees of ACC, AHA, and NHLBI. He is an associate editor of the *Journal of the American College of Cardiology*. Dr. Hlatky received his M.D. from the University of Pennsylvania and, after residency at the University of Arizona, studied as a Robert Wood Johnson clinical scholar at the University of California–San Francisco. He trained in cardiology at Duke University Medical Center, and then joined the Duke faculty. He has been on the faculty of Stanford University School of Medicine since 1989.

Alice K. Jacobs, M.D., is a professor of medicine at Boston University School of Medicine and the director of the Cardiac Catheterization Laboratory and Interventional Cardiology at Boston Medical Center. She is a recent past president of AHA. She is also involved in local AHA activities and served as the president of the northeast affiliate in 2002–2003. Dr. Jacobs has been a member of several ACC writing groups, establishing training criteria in interventional cardiology, assessing and maintaining competence in interventional cardiology, and updating the ACC/AHA guidelines for the performance of PCI. Dr. Jacobs currently serves as chair of the ACC/AHA Task Force on Practice Guidelines. She was recently elected vice president of the Association of University Cardiologists, and she is a member of the American Board of Internal Medicine Interventional Cardiology Self-Assessment Test Committee and the New York State Cardiac Advisory Committee. Dr. Jacobs' major research interest is in coronary revascularization strategies. Currently, she is leading AHA's Mission: Lifeline, a community-based, national initiative to develop systems of care to improve the quality of care and outcomes of patients with ST-elevation MI. Dr. Jacobs is principal investigator of the MASS COMM trial evaluating the safety and effectiveness of coronary angioplasty performed in community hospitals without onsite cardiac surgery in Massachusetts. She serves on the steering committees of several multicenter trials, including the NHLBI-funded BARI 2-D in the NHLBI Dynamic Registry. She is also interested in heart disease in women and the sex-based differences in the epidemiology, diagnosis, treatment, and prognosis of ischemic heart disease. Dr. Jacobs is board certified in internal medicine, CVD, and interventional cardiology.

Karen S. Kuehl, M.D., M.P.H., is a professor of pediatrics at the George Washington University Medical School. Among her academic appointments, she is the director of the Adult Congenital Heart Disease Program at Children's National Medical Center, a professor of pediatrics at George Washington University Medical School, and a member of the Children's Research Institute in the Center for Health Services and Clinical Research. Among her honors, Dr. Kuehl was recognized as a National Merit Scholar and National Research Fellow and received an Award of Merit for Research, Montgomery

County. In addition to her academic appointments, she is currently a member of the Children's National Health Network Board, and of the Medical Advisory Board of the Adult Congenital Heart Association. Dr. Kuehl earned her B.A. from Swarthmore College, her M.D. from Harvard Medical School, and her M.P.H. from Johns Hopkins University.

Todd D. Miller, M.D., currently serves as a consultant of cardiovascular medicine and the codirector of the nuclear cardiology laboratory at the Mayo Clinic. Since 1999, he has also served as a professor of medicine at the Mayo Clinic College of Medicine. Among his many awards are the Mayo Fellows Association Teacher of the Year and the Mayo Outstanding Teacher of Physical Exam Skills. In addition to serving on the editorial board of the *Journal of Nuclear Cardiology*, Dr. Miller is an editorial board member for the *American Heart Journal.* He has been a reviewer for more than 30 peer-reviewed journals, and is a guest editor for the *Journal of the American College of Cardiology* and *American Heart Journal.* He received his M.D. and completed his residency in internal medicine at the University of Illinois College of Medicine in Chicago.

Lynne W. Stevenson, M.D., is a professor of medicine at Harvard Medical School and the codirector of the Cardiomyopathy and Heart Failure Program at Brigham and Women's Hospital. Her major commitments are to ensure that multiple options are developed and offered in parallel to patients with advanced heart disease, and that there will be continuing entry of new cardiologists dedicated to refining the physiologic basis and art of caring for patients with heart failure. Her early research focused on the central role of reversible congestion in the symptoms, valvular regurgitation, and prognosis of advanced heart failure. Dr. Stevenson has been involved in the conception and culmination of the recent NHLBI REMATCH and ESCAPE trials and the launch in 2006 of the INTERMACS Registry for Mechanical Circulatory Support. She has been the chair of the Heart Failure and Transplant Committee for ACC, a member of the Board of Directors for the International Society for Heart and Lung Transplantation, and a member of the Executive Board of the Clinical Council of AHA. She chaired the Consensus Conference on Mechanical Cardiac Support in 2000, and she serves on the heart failure guideline committees for ACC, AHA, and the Heart Failure Society of America. She has participated on advisory panels for NHLBI on heart failure, cardiorenal connections in heart disease, and the role of future ventricular assist devices; the Centers for Medicare & Medicaid Services; and the Joint Commission. She was selected as an NIH Great Teacher in 2004. She received her M.D. from Stanford University School of Medicine and is certified in internal medicine, with a subcertification in CVD.

CONSULTANT

Howard H. Goldman, M.D., Ph.D., M.P.H., is a professor of psychiatry at the University of Maryland School of Medicine. His expertise is in evaluating mental health services and financing programs and policies. He is the director of the Network on Mental Health Policy Research (The Network), funded by the MacArthur Foundation. The Network is the sponsor of several studies on mental health financing and disability policy. Dr. Goldman is currently a member of the executive committee of the Social Security Administration (SSA) Mental Health Treatment Study, a trial of supported employment and enhanced treatment for 2,000 Social Security Disability Insurance beneficiaries with schizophrenia or a mood disorder who are interested in working. He also served as principal investigator of the study team conducting the Evaluation of the Implementation and Impact of Mental Health and Substance Abuse Parity in the Federal Employees Health Benefits program, sponsored by the federal government. He served as the senior scientific editor of the *Surgeon General's Report on Mental Health* from 1997 to 1999, for which he was awarded the Surgeon General's Medallion. During 2002 and 2003, Dr. Goldman was a consultant to the President's New Freedom Commission on Mental Health. He is the editor of *Psychiatric Services*, a mental health services research and policy journal published monthly by the American Psychiatric Association. He also serves on the editorial boards of several other journals, including the *American Journal of Psychiatry* and the *Journal of Mental Health Policy and Economics*. Dr. Goldman received joint M.D.-M.P.H. degrees from Harvard University, and a Ph.D. in social policy research from the Heller School at Brandeis University. He is a member of the National Academy of Social Insurance, having served on its disability policy panel, and he is an IOM member. He served on IOM's Committee on Medical Evaluation of Veterans for Disability Compensation.

PRINCIPAL STAFF

Frederick (Rick) Erdtmann, M.D., M.P.H., is currently the director of IOM's Board on the Health of Select Populations and the Medical Follow-up Agency. Prior to joining the IOM, he was a career military physician in the U.S. Army. While in the military, he served as chief of several large departments of preventive medicine at U.S. and overseas installations. He also was commander of the military community hospital at Ft. Carson, Colorado, and later served as hospital commander for the Walter Reed Army Medical Center. Dr. Erdtmann had several assignments at the Army Surgeon General's Office, where he worked on military health care policies. The board that Dr. Erdtmann directs was responsible for managing a major study involving SSA's disability decision process and two other VA disability-related studies in the recent past. He received his undergraduate degree from Bucknell University and his M.P.H. from the University of California–Berkeley. He is a graduate of Temple University Medical School and is board certified in preventive medicine.

Michael McGeary is a senior program officer on the Board on the Health of Select Populations, serving as director of the Committee of Medical Experts to Assist Social Security on Disability Issues and the Committee on Social Security Cardiovascular Disability Criteria. He is a political scientist specializing in health, science, and technology policy analysis and program evaluation. Before 2004, he was an independent consultant to government agencies, foundations, and nonprofit organizations in issues of science and technology. Between 1981 and 1995, Mr. McGeary was a senior staff officer at the IOM and the National Academy of Sciences, where he produced more than a dozen major reports on topics such as federal funding of research and development; graduate education and employment of scientists and engineers; and priority setting, funding, and management of the NIH. From 2004 to 2007, he was staff director for IOM committees that recommended improvements in the SSA and VA systems for determining disability. Mr. McGeary is a graduate of Harvard College and has completed all requirements for a doctorate in political science from Massachusetts Institute of Technology except the dissertation.

Susan R. McCutchen, M.A., is a senior program associate on the Board on the Health of Select Populations. She has been on staff at the National Academies since 1981 and has worked in several institutional divisions and with many boards, committees, and panels within those units. The studies in which she has participated have addressed a broad range of subjects and focused on a variety of issues related to science and technology for international development, technology transfer, aeronautics and the U.S. space program, natural disaster mitigation, U.S. education policy and science curricula, needle exchange for the prevention of HIV transmission, the scientific merit of the polygraph, human factors and engineering, research ethics, health hazard evaluation, medical and public health preparedness for catastrophic events, including terrorist nuclear detonations, and disability compensation programs. Ms. McCutchen has assisted in the production of more than 50 publications and was an editor for *A 21st Century System for Evaluating Veterans for Disability Benefits* and for *Assessing Medical Preparedness to Respond to a Terrorist Nuclear Event: Workshop Report.* She has a B.A. in French, with minors in Italian and Spanish, from Ohio's Miami University, and an M.A. in French, with a minor in English, from Kent State University.

Erin E. Wilhelm, M.P.H., is a research associate with the Board on the Health of Select Populations, serving both the Committee on Social Security Cardiovascular Disability Criteria and the Committee on Social Security HIV Disability Criteria. She is a health policy researcher and writer with experience in global health, nutrition, and flood disasters and their impact on mental health and disability issues. Prior to joining the IOM and the National Academies in 2009, Ms. Wilhelm served as a guest researcher at the NIH Fogarty International Center, where she contributed to a literature review and portfolio analysis for the Trans-NIH Working Group on Climate Change and Health. She has served as a publications editor for the Corporate Executive Board, a best practice research firm in Washington, D.C., and as a staff writer for the *St. Petersburg Times* in Florida. Ms. Wilhelm holds an M.P.H. in global health from George Washington University and a dual B.A. in broadcast journalism and political science from the University of South Florida.

Lavita D. Coates-Fogle is a senior program assistant with the Board on the Health of Select Populations and serves the Committee of Medical Experts to Assist Social Security on Disability Issues and the Committee on Social Security Cardiovascular Disability Criteria. Prior to joining the National Academies in 2008, Ms. Coates-Fogle spent 5 years with the Department of Defense, where she served as a program analyst and contributed to the streamlining of administrative processes and procedures. She is a certified event planner and is currently pursuing her undergraduate degree in communications.

Appendix B

Literature Review

A review of the published literature related to disability was conducted to examine current evidence of cardiovascular conditions and employment capability. The primary strategy included database searches using keywords and Medical Subject Headings (MeSH), yielding initial results of 14,642 studies published between 1980 and October 2009. The studies were reviewed, analyzed, and coded according to a tiered category system. A secondary search strategy included a manual review of references cited in key articles as well as searches executed in PubMed using key terms. Final results included 35 relevant studies for detailed review. Topics of discussion among the relevant studies include frequency of returning to work following an acute myocardial infarction, physical disability in populations with peripheral artery disease, and the impact of job strain and depressive symptoms on return to work after acute coronary syndrome.

METHODS

The primary strategy of the literature review was to search four databases: Medline, EMBase, Web of Science, and PsychINFO. Together these databases contain information on research related to medicine, nursing, health care delivery, psychiatry, sociology, and psychology. Search strategies were developed for each database using text and MeSH terms in groups focused on each of the listing-level cardiovascular conditions (chronic heart failure, ischemic heart disease, recurrent arrhythmias, symptomatic congenital heart disease, heart transplant, aneurysm of the aorta and major branches, chronic venous insufficiency, and peripheral artery disease) and seven separate evaluation sets: disability, employment, quality of life, functional capacity, treatment outcomes, severity of impairment, and comorbidities.

Unique terms were identified in each subject area to yield a wide array of results. Strategy parameters included limiting the search to human subjects, the English language, and publication years from 1980 to October 2009. This time period was chosen to ensure the most relevant studies were captured that examined employment capability of populations with cardiovascular conditions. For those evaluation sets reviewing functional capacity, treatment outcomes, and severity of impairment, the parameters were further limited to results published from 2004 to focus on the most recent medical and science literature.

The secondary strategy of the literature review involved reviewing key articles' cited references. Additionally, the PubMed database was searched using Boolean logic with the main term of *cardiovascular* and key terms related to employment, that is, return to work. Studies were published from 1966 to 2009. Other literature supplemented the body of relevant research supporting the committee's research and report writing, resulting from targeted searches performed on an ad hoc basis to answer specific research questions.

PRELIMINARY ANALYSIS AND RESULTS

A tiered category system was developed to refine results. A rigorous review of study titles and abstracts determined which studies met the inclusion criteria. Each study was coded according to the corresponding tier (see Box B-1). The primary search strategy yielded 85 studies in Tier 1; after removing duplicate articles produced from the primary search strategy, the secondary strategy yielded an additional 88 studies, for a total of 173 Tier 1 studies. To refine these results, the parameters were further limited to focus on studies published between 2004 and 2009, producing the final results of the literature review of 35 Tier 1 articles. Table B-1 provides a more detailed review of the final Tier 1 studies.

An additional 674 articles were identified as Tier 2 articles, which were reviewed to potentially inform the broader parameters affecting functional capacity of populations with cardiovascular diseases leading to disability. These parameters include relative quality of life (with specific measurements for health-related quality of life), comorbid conditions, gender comparisons, and assessments of treatments for cardiovascular conditions or associated conditions that may lead to disability or impairment. The committee determined the Tier 2 studies were not immediately relevant to the statement of work, and few of the studies were included in the final report. The remaining studies were categorized as Tier 3 and 4 studies. Tier 3 studies were available to inform background research during report writing as necessary. Tier 4 studies do not meet the inclusion criteria and were not included in the study process.

BOX B-1
Definition of Tiers

Tier 1: Studies on clinical measures of treatment outcomes, diagnostic techniques, or health status indicators as they relate to employment capability (i.e., return to work, employability) for populations with cardiovascular disease diagnoses that may lead to disability

Tier 2: Studies on one or more parameters of disability (e.g., comorbid conditions, quality of life, mortality) as they affect functional capacity for populations with cardiovascular conditions

Tier 3: Studies on disability or employment factors that do not explicitly address, measure, or estimate medical treatment or functional capacity of populations with cardiovascular conditions (i.e., studies on predictors of disease including employment status, job stress, or demographic values such as race, age, or gender)

Tier 4: Studies not related to cardiovascular disease disability and employment

TABLE B-1 Literature Table of Cardiovascular Employment and Disability Articles

Study	Study Type	Time Frame	Sample Size
Abbas, A. E., B. Brodie, G. Stone, D. Cox, A. Berman, S. Brewington, S. Dixon, W. W. O'Neill, and C. L. Grines. 2004. Frequency of returning to work one and six months following percutaneous coronary intervention for acute myocardial infarction. *American Journal of Cardiology* 94(11):1403–1405.	Observational	Unknown	900
Brisson, C., R. Leblanc, R. Bourbonnais, E. Maunsell, G. R. Dagenais, M. Vezina, B. Masse, and E. Kroger. 2005. Psychologic distress in postmyocardial infarction patients who have returned to work. *Psychosomatic Medicine* 67(1):59–63.	Observational	October 1995–November 1997	990
Crossland, D. S., S. P. Jackson, R. Lyall, J. Burn, and J. J. O'Sullivan. 2005. Employment and advice regarding careers for adults with congenital heart disease. *Cardiology in the Young* 15(4):391–395.	Observational	Unknown	299
Earle, A., J. Z. Ayanian, and J. Heymann. 2006. Work resumption after newly diagnosed coronary heart disease: Findings on the importance of paid leave. *Journal of Women's Health* 15(4):430–441.	Observational	1996	289

Methodology	Outcome Measures	Relevant Findings
Telephone survey at 1- and 6-month follow-ups to determine rates of return to work in population of myocardial infarction patients who received percutaneous coronary intervention	Angiography; demographic and clinical characteristics; employment status pre- and post-acute myocardial infarction and percutaneous coronary intervention	51% of the study population returned to work within 1 month of the myocardial infarction. Predictors of early return to work included employment in the United States (study population was international), no history of smoking, and single-vessel coronary disease. At 6 months follow-up, 78% of the population had resumed work.
Psychiatric Symptom Index (French version)	Prevalence of psychologic distress in women and men after return to work post-myocardial infarction	Psychological distress is significantly more prevalent in return to work post-myocardial infarction patients versus general working population.
Questionnaire	Severity of disease; rates of employment; rates of receiving career advice and education	Receiving career advice was associated with return to work and maintaining employment among study participants.
Cardiac survey; employment status; bivariate chi-square and logistic regression analyses	New diagnosis of myocardial infarction or angina in the 2 years prior; health condition/behavior; severity of condition; social support; demographic characteristics	79% of women return to work after myocardial infarction or angina. Women with paid leave are more likely to return to work. Indicators of a severity of health condition (i.e., myocardial infarction or participation in cardiac rehabilitation) reduced the likelihood of return to work. Higher socioeconomic status and more education increased likelihood of employment.

continued

TABLE B-1 Continued

Study	Study Type	Time Frame	Sample Size
Ellis, J. J., K. A. Eagle, E. M. Kline-Rogers, and S. R. Erickson. 2005. Perceived work performance of patients who experienced an acute coronary syndrome event. *Cardiology* 104(3):120–126.	Observational	July 1999–November 2002	158
Ezekowitz, J. A., D. S. Lee, J. V. Tu, A. M. Newman, and F. A. McAlister. 2008. Comparison of one-year outcome (death and rehospitalization) in hospitalized heart failure patients with left ventricular ejection fraction > 50% versus those with ejection fraction < 50%. *American Journal of Cardiology* 102(1):79–83.	Observational	April 1999–March 2001	9,943
Farkas, J., K. Cerne, M. Lainscak, and I. Keber. 2008. Return to work after acute myocardial infarction—Listen to your doctor! *International Journal of Cardiology* 130(1): e14-e16.	Observational	1999–2002	74
Fonarow, G. C., W. G. Stough, W. T. Abraham, N. M. Albert, M. Gheorghiade, B. H. Greenberg, C. M. O'Connor, J. L. Sun, C. W. Yancy, J. B. Young, and OPTIMIZE-HF 2007. Characteristics, treatments, and outcomes of patients with preserved systolic function hospitalized for heart failure—A report from the OPTIMIZE-HF registry. *Journal of the American College of Cardiology* 50(8):768–777.	Observational	Unknown	41,267

Methodology	Outcome Measures	Relevant Findings
Mailed survey to patients discharged from university-affiliated hospital with diagnosis of acute coronary syndrome during a 3-year period	Health status (SF-8, PCS-8, MCS-8, EQ-5D), cardiac function status (Duke Activity Status Index), symptom count, comorbidity index, patient-perceived cardiac disease severity, medication count and compliance, job satisfaction, current employment duration, patient demographics, acute coronary syndrome type	Current employment is associated with higher work performance post acute coronary syndrome event.
Discharge medication compared with outcome measures	Rehospitalization or mortality within 1 year	ACE inhibitors, spironolactone, and statins are associated with better outcomes in patients with heart failure who have been hospitalized.
Questionnaire	Physical, sociodemographic, psychological factors; return to work following myocardial infarction	Controlling for other variables, only physicians' advice was associated with return to work.
Web-based registry; Pearson chi-square test and Wilcoxon test analyses	Preserved systolic function if ejection fraction documented as $\geq 40\%$ or qualitatively normal or mildly impaired; left ventricular systolic dysfunction if ejection fraction $< 40\%$ or moderate/severe left ventricular dysfunction by qualitative assessment	ACC/AHA performance measure application: adherence to measures more frequent with left ventricular systolic dysfunction; influence of pharmacologic therapy: preserved systolic function—no relationship with beta-blocker or ACE inhibitor, left ventricular systolic dysfunction and beta-blocker experienced significantly lower risk all-cause mortality at 60- to 90-day follow-up.

continued

TABLE B-1 Continued

Study	Study Type	Time Frame	Sample Size
Fonarow, G. C., W. T. Abraham, N. M. Albert, W. G. Stough, M. Gheorghiade, B. H. Greenberg, C. M. O'Connor, K. Pieper, J. L. Sun, C. Yancy, and J. B. Young. 2007. Association between performance measures and clinical outcomes for patients hospitalized with heart failure. *Journal of the American Medical Association* 297(1):61–70.	Observational	March 2003–December 2004	5,791
Fukuoka, Y., K. Dracup, M. Takeshima, N. Ishii, M. Makaya, L. Groah, and E. Kyriakidis. 2009. Effect of job strain and depressive symptoms upon returning to work after acute coronary syndrome. *Social Science & Medicine* 68(10):1875–1881.	6-month prospective longitudinal study	January 2004–March 2006	240
Geyer, S., K. Norozi, R. Buchhorn, and A. Wessel. 2009. Chances of employment in women and men after surgery of congenital heart disease: Comparisons between patients and the general population. *Congenital Heart Disease* 4(1):25–33.	Observational	April 2003–January 2004	314
Grady, K. L., P. M. Meyer, D. Dressler, C. White-Williams, A. Kaan, A. Mattea, S. Ormaza, S. Chillcott, A. Loo, B. Todd, M. R. Costanzo, and W. Piccione. 2003. Change in quality of life from after left ventricular assist device implantation to after heart transplantation. *Journal of Heart & Lung Transplantation* 22(11):1254–1267.	Observational	August 1994–August 1999	40

Methodology	Outcome Measures	Relevant Findings
Multivariable and propensity-adjusted analyses to assess process-outcome relationship for each performance measure	Rehospitalization or mortality rates 60 to 90 days post-discharge	Current heart failure performance measures have little relationship with patient mortality and hospitalization in 60–90 days post-discharge.
Follow-up at 3 and 6 months; mailed written questionnaires; BDI-II; Job Content Questionnaire; Duke Activity Status Index	Job strain/characteristics; Beck Depression Inventory II	Even mild depressive symptoms were a strong predictor of delay or failure to return to work.
Examined relationship between disease severity and employment status	Classification by type of surgery (curative, reparative, palliative) as indicator of disease severity; classified by New York Heart Association system	Likelihood of full-time employment decreases as disease severity increased.
Quality of Life Index, Rating Question Form, Heart Failure Symptom Checklist, Sickness Impact Profile, Left Ventricular Assist Device (LVAD) Stressor Scale, Heart Transplant Stressor Scale, Jalowiec Coping Scale	Quality of life at 3 months post-LVAD versus 3 months post-heart transplant	Patients were significantly more satisfied with quality of life after heart transplantation compared with LVAD; mobility, self-care, physical ability, and overall functioning were more improved in transplant group

continued

TABLE B-1 Continued

Study	Study Type	Time Frame	Sample Size
Grady, K. L., D. C. Naftel, J. K. Kirklin, C. White-Williams, J. Kobashigawa, J. Chait, J. B. Young, D. Pelegrin, K. Patton-Schroeder, B. Rybarczyk, J. Daily, W. Piccione Jr., and A. Heroux. 2005. Predictors of physical functional disability at 5 to 6 years after heart transplantation. *Journal of Heart and Lung Transplantation* 24(12):2279–2285.	Observational	Unknown	311
Holper, E. M., J. Blair, F. Selzer, K. M. Detre, A. K. Jacobs, D. O. Williams, H. Vlachos, R. L. Wilensky, P. Coady, D. P. Faxon, Registry Percutaneous Transluminal Coronary Angioplasty, and Investigators Dynamic Registry. 2006. The impact of ejection fraction on outcomes after percutaneous coronary intervention in patients with congestive heart failure: An analysis of the National Heart, Lung, and Blood Institute Percutaneous Transluminal Coronary Angioplasty Registry and Dynamic Registry. *American Heart Journal* 151(1):69–75.	Randomized controlled trial	July 1997–February 1998; February 1999–July 1999; October 2001–March 2002	4,697
Incalzi, R. A., A. Corsonello, C. Pedone, F. Corica, P. Carbonin, and R. Bernabei. 2005. Construct validity of activities of daily living scale: A clue to distinguish the disabling effects of COPD and congestive heart failure. *Chest* 127(3):830–838.	Observational	4 months, (unknown period)	1,271

Methodology	Outcome Measures	Relevant Findings
Sickness Impact Profile, Quality of Life Index, Heart Transplant Symptom Checklist, Jalowiec Coping Scale, Positive and Negative Affect Schedule-Expanded Form, Cardiac Depression Scale, Assessment of Problems with the Heart Transplant Regimen	Differences in physical functional disability at 5 to 6 years post-transplant; clinical data collected from hospital records, clinic charts, and the Cardiac Transplant Research Database	Physical functional disability was low at 5 to 6 years post-transplant; women had more overall physical functional disability; patients with comorbidities had more physical functional disability; and physical functional disability was related to activities of daily living.
Telephone interview by trained nurse assessing symptoms, medication status, and coronary event	Demographic; angiographic and lesion characteristics; patient-specific procedural data, outcomes (ejection fraction values)	Patients with chronic heart failure were older and were more often women and African Americans. They presented with history of prior myocardial infarction and revascularization, diabetes, hypertension, and other severe concomitant noncardiac disease; lower ejection fraction; more extensive coronary artery disease; higher frequency of triple-vessel disease and total occlusions; and higher mean number of significant lesions.
Construct validity for self-reported activities of daily living (ADLs) and instrumental activities of daily living (IADLs); surveys; questionnaires	Functional status prehospital admission compared with assessments of postdischarge; comparing chronic obstructive pulmonary disease (COPD) and diabetes mellitus	COPD is associated with a pattern of disability expressed by loss of select ADL/IADLs; with ADL/IADL cluster similar in two populations with different chronic conditions (e.g., chronic heart failure and diabetes mellitus); and crude lost IADL may not fully represent loss of personal independence.

continued

TABLE B-1 Continued

Study	Study Type	Time Frame	Sample Size
Jalowiec, A., K. L. Grady, and C. White-Williams. 2007. Functional status one year after heart transplant. *Journal of Cardiopulmonary Rehabilitation and Prevention* 27(1):24–32. Erratum in: *Journal of Cardiopulmonary Rehabilitation and Prevention* 2007 27(3):165.	Observational	Unknown	237
Kiessling, A., and P. Henriksson. 2005. Perceived cognitive function in coronary artery disease—An unrecognized predictor of unemployment. *Quality of Life Research* 14(6):1481–1488.	Observational	2 years (unknown period)	169
Kuoppala, J., and A. Lamminpää. 2008. Rehabilitation and work ability: A systematic literature review. *Journal of Rehabilitation Medicine* 40(10):796–804.	Review	N/A	N/A
Lau-Walker, M. O., M. R. Cowie, and M. Roughton. 2009. Coronary heart disease patients' perception of their symptoms and sense of control are associated with their quality of life three years following hospital discharge. *Journal of Clinical Nursing* 18(1):63–71.	Observational	3 years (unknown period)	253
Massie, B. M., J. J. Nelson, M. A. Lukas, B. Greenberg, M. B. Fowler, E. M. Gilbert, W. T. Abraham, S. R. Lottes, J. A. Franciosa, and Cohere Participant Physicians. 2007. Comparison of outcomes and usefulness of carvedilol across a spectrum of left ventricular ejection fractions in patients with heart failure in clinical practice. *American Journal of Cardiology* 99(9):1263–1268.	Observational	1 year (unknown period)	4,280

Methodology	Outcome Measures	Relevant Findings
Sickness Impact Profile; paired t-tests; medical and demographic data on patient questionnaire	Pre- and post-transplant functional scores from Sickness Impact Profile	1-year post-transplant predictors of worse functional status included greater symptom distress, more stressors, neurologic problems, depression, female gender, older age, and lower left ventricular ejection fraction (worse function).
Health-related quality of life questionnaires	Gainful employment and return to work in patients with coronary artery disease	Perceived cognitive function predicts both prevalence of unemployment and early retirement and sick leave due to coronary artery disease.
N/A	N/A	Vocational rehabilitation may help reduce absentee rates; concepts of workplace must be integrated into rehabilitation practices.
Questionnaires	SF-36 (physical and mental summary scores)	Coronary artery disease patients' perception of their symptoms and sense of control at time of discharge was significantly associated with their quality of life 3 years postdischarge.
Comparing beta-blocker carvedilol, characteristics, carvedilol titration, and outcomes of patients according to left ventricular ejection fraction > 40% or < 40%	Patient status and clinical events provided at baseline, end-titration and 6 and 12 months thereafter; clinical events defined as hospitalizations, unscheduled visits	Patients with preserved ejection fraction were more likely to be older, female, and hypertensive; lower left ventricular ejection fraction was associated with worse functional class and more heart failure hospitalizations in the previous year.

continued

TABLE B-1 Continued

Study	Study Type	Time Frame	Sample Size
McBurney, C. R, K. A. Eagle, E. M. Kline-Rogers, J. V. Cooper, D. E. Smith, and S. R. Erickson. 2004. Work-related outcomes after a myocardial infarction. *Pharmacotherapy* 24(11):1515–1523.	Observational	7 months (unknown period)	89
Mital, A., A. Desai, and A. Mital. 2004. Return to work after a coronary event. *Journal of Cardiopulmonary Rehabilitation* 24(6):365–373.	Review	N/A	N/A

Methodology	Outcome Measures	Relevant Findings
Work-Performance Scale of the functional Status Questionnaire; health-related quality of life; Physical Component Summary (PCS-12)	Return to work post-myocardial infarction	Variables associated with not returning to work included past myocardial infarction, coronary artery bypass graft, heart failure, positive stress test, low score on the PCS-12 scale of the SF-12; patients who did not return to work also tended to have more comorbidities and take more prescribed drugs; median WPS scores were higher for patients who had higher ejection fraction at discharge, had not experienced a previous myocardial infarction, underwent a percutaneous revascularization intervention at the time of hospitalization, and had not recently been absent from work; and workers reporting absence from work had lower PCS-12 scores or reported rehospitalization.
N/A	N/A	Patients with coronary artery bypass graft indicate likelihood to return to work based on information other than cardiac findings: education level (higher, more likely), work history (high stress, less likely), gender (men, more likely), age (older, less likely), and psychological factors (depressive mood, less likely).

continued

TABLE B-1 Continued

Study	Study Type	Time Frame	Sample Size
O'Connor, C. M., D. J. Whellan, K. L. Lee, S. J. Keteyian, L. S. Cooper, S. J. Ellis, E. S. Leifer, W. E. Kraus, D. W. Kitzman, J. A. Blumenthal, D. S. Rendall, N. H. Miller, J. L. Fleg, K. A. Schulman, R. S. McKelvie, F. Zannad, I. L. Pina, and HF-ACTION Investigators. 2009. Efficacy and safety of exercise training in patients with chronic heart failure: HF-ACTION randomized controlled trial. *Journal of the American Medical Association* 301(14):1439–1450.	Randomized controlled trial	April 2003–February 2007	2,331
Paris, W., and C. White-Williams. 2005. Social adaptation after cardiothoracic transplantation: A review of the literature. *Journal of Cardiovascular Nursing* 20(Suppl 5): S67–S73.	Review	N/A	N/A
Petrucci, R. J., K. C. Truesdell, A. Carter, N. E. Goldstein, M. M. Russell, D. Dilkes, J. M. Fitzpatrick, C. E. Thomas, M. E. Keenan, L. A. Lazarus, N. D. Chiaravalloti, J. J. Trunzo, J. W. Verjans, E. C. Holmes, L. E. Samuels, and J. Narula. 2006. Cognitive dysfunction in advanced heart failure and prospective cardiac assist device patients. *Annals of Thoracic Surgery* 81(5):1738–1744.	Observational	January 1984–December 2002 (18 years)	252
Phillips, L., T. Harrison, and P. Houck. 2005. Return to work and the person with heart failure. *Heart & Lung* 34(2):79–88.	Review	N/A	N/A

Methodology	Outcome Measures	Relevant Findings
Multicenter randomized controlled trial; aerobic exercise training for patients with chronic heart failure	Rehospitalization; all-cause mortality	There were nonsignificant reductions in outcomes for primary group; authors propose reasons in the discussion; exercise training is associated with significant reductions for both all-cause mortality or hospitalization and cardiovascular mortality or heart failure hospitalization; exercise training was well tolerated and safe.
N/A	N/A	Describes social adaptation for heart, lung, and heart–lung transplant recipients; less than half of recipients who are physically able to work are employed; patients who do not resume working within first year less likely to return to work at all.
New York Heart Association Stage III to IV symptomatic left ventricular ejection fraction < 20% requiring frequent hospitalization for worse heart failure and neuropsychological exam	Memory, motor, and processing speed; neuropsychological exam	Cognitive deficits are common in advanced heart failure and worsen with increasing severity of heart failure.
N/A	N/A	Nurses may be a necessary and important advocate for patients with heart failure. Nurses should be available to assess, provide resources. Additional research is needed for safe transition for heart failure patients to workforce.

continued

TABLE B-1 Continued

Study	Study Type	Time Frame	Sample Size
Poston, R. S., R. Tran, M. Collins, M. Reynolds, I. Connerney, B. Reicher, D. Zimrin, B. P. Griffith, and S. T. Bartlett. 2008. Comparison of economic and patient outcomes with minimally invasive versus traditional off-pump coronary artery bypass grafting techniques. *Annals of Surgery* 248(4):638–646.	Observational	January 2005–June 2007	200
Reynolds, M. W., D. Frame, R. Scheye, M. E. Rose, S. George, J. B. Watson, and M. A. Hlatky. 2004. A systematic review of the economic burden of chronic angina. *American Journal of Managed Care* 10(Suppl 11):S347–S357.	Review	N/A	N/A
Rollman, B. L., B. H. Belnap, M. S. LeMenager, S. Mazumdar, H. C. Schulberg, and C. F. Reynolds III. 2009. The Bypassing the Blues treatment protocol: Stepped collaborative care for treating post-CABG depression. *Psychosomatic Medicine* 71(2):217–230.	Randomized controlled trial	8 months (unknown period)	450
Ruel, M., A. Kulik, B. K. Lam, F. D. Rubens, P. J. Hendry, R. G. Masters, P. Bédard, and T. G. Mesana. 2005. Long-term outcomes of valve replacement with modern prostheses in young adults. *European Journal of Cardiothoracic Surgery* 27(3):425–433.	Observational	1976–2002	500

Methodology	Outcome Measures	Relevant Findings
Examine the efficacy of mini- versus standard-coronary artery bypass graft. Patients prescreened and interviewed 3- and 12-months post major adverse cardiac and cerebrovascular event (MACCE)	Patient satisfaction; post-operative clinical data; demographics	Mini-coronary artery bypass graft shortens patient recovery time, minimizes MACCE risk at 1 year, and shows superior quality and outcome metrics versus standard coronary artery bypass graft; there are higher return to work rates and/or normal activities in a significantly shorter period of time.
N/A	N/A	Chronic angina may require substantial costs caused by frequent hospitalizations and expensive revascularization procedures. Angina also causes substantial workplace productivity loss. Long-term and lasting improvement in work status is difficult to achieve.
300 patients with depressive symptoms post-coronary artery bypass graft (PHQ-9) and 100 nondepressed patients, measured by SF-36 Mental Component Summary score	Mood symptoms, cardiovascular morbidity, employment, health services use, and treatment costs	To be determined.
Primary valve replacement, either aortic or mitral	Mortality, stroke, bleeding events, reoperation, heart failure, other prosthesis-related complications, quality of life	Late outcomes of modern prosthetic valves in young adults remain suboptimal; bioprostheses deserve consideration in the aortic position, as mechanical.

continued

TABLE B-1 Continued

Study	Study Type	Time Frame	Sample Size
Vohra, R. S., P. A. Coughlin, and M. J. Gough. 2007. Occupational capacity following surgical revascularization for lower limb claudication. *European Journal of Vascular and Endovascular Surgery* 34(6):709–713.	Observational	February 2001–February 2005	139
White-Williams, C., A. Jalowiec, and K. Grady. 2005. Who returns to work after heart transplantation? *Journal of Heart & Lung Transplantation* 24(12):2255–2261.	Observational	Data collection ended in 1997	237

Methodology	Outcome Measures	Relevant Findings
Questionnaires	Employment status after procedure (lower limb revascularization)	Two-thirds of potentially employable patients with claudication return to work following surgery. Factors influencing decision to return to work include age, type of procedure, and preoperative occupation.
Work history tool, rating question form, heart transplant stressor scale, quality of life index, Sickness Impact Profile, Jalowiec Coping Scale, social support index, heart transplant symptom checklist, and chart review form; frequency distributions, chi-square, t-tests, and stepwise regression analysis	Work history, quality-of-life outcomes collected at time of enrollment and 1-year post-transplant; functional status measured with the Sickness Impact Profile; Heart Transplant Stressor Scale developed for this study measures perceived stressful nature of issues related to HF and transplant; Quality of Life and Jalowiec Coping Scale measure patient life satisfaction and coping mechanisms	81% of participants maintained employment status post-transplant. Those who did not work prior to transplant did not work post-transplant. Those who worked before surgery maintained employment after surgery. Twenty-one patients returned to work post-transplant, on average resuming work 4.8 months post-surgery. Ejection fraction did not differ significantly among those working and those not working. Those who returned to work were mostly white-collar, business/executive employees; those who did not return to work included mostly sales clerks, technicians, and factory workers.

Appendix C

Review of ACC/AHA Clinical Practice Guidelines

BACKGROUND

The Social Security Administration (SSA) asked the Institute of Medicine (IOM) to analyze the clinical practice guidelines developed by the American College of Cardiology/American Heart Association (ACC/AHA) for their relevance to improving the criteria required to meet the cardiovascular listings.

ACC/AHA Letter

As part of its charge, IOM's Committee on Social Security Cardiovascular Disability Criteria was asked to review the ACC/AHA cardiovascular practice guidelines. The guidelines to be reviewed were named in an ACC/AHA letter to SSA, dated June 16, 2008, that was sent to SSA in response to SSA's Advance Notice of Proposed Rulemaking entitled "Revised Medical Criteria for Evaluating Cardiovascular Disorders," which was published in the *Federal Register* on April 16, 2008 (Table 1 of that issue).

In its letter, ACC/AHA urged SSA to "base its proposals on evidence-based clinical practice guidelines" as it undertook the task of revising the criteria for cardiovascular disease.

SSA's Charge to the Committee

In the committee's statement of work, SSA tasked the committee with analyzing "the AHA and ACC guidelines to determine which, if any, guidelines have the potential to become indicators of disability as defined by SSA," that is, to determine whether the guidelines would be useful in developing listing criteria for evaluating disability. The guidelines identified by ACC/AHA are listed in Box C-1.

ACC Briefing of IOM Committee

James Fasules, M.D., senior vice president, advocacy, American College of Cardiology, participated in the first committee meeting to discuss the role of the ACC/AHA clinical practice guidelines in updating SSA's cardiovascular disability criteria in the Listings. He indicated four potential contributions of the guidelines:

1. Comprehensive review of natural history of disease process;
2. Explicit guidance on activity restrictions and capabilities—a direct bearing on disability;
3. Consistent terminology for conditions and diagnostic and therapeutic services; and
4. Guidance on standard of care for evaluation and treatment.

The guidelines were relied on extensively in the report as the basis for descriptive, diagnostic, and treatment terminology for the diagnostic procedures and tests and recommended treatments that should be expected to be in the average medical record and required or assumed in the listing criteria, and for information about the natural history of each condition. They were also reviewed to see if they provided any guidance on activity limitations and capacity, which relate directly to disability criteria. Few of the guidelines contained this information.

APPROACH TO REVIEWING THE GUIDELINES

IOM staff reviewed the clinical guidelines listed in the ACC/AHA letter and, in addition, the guidelines for valvular heart disease. The clinical guidelines for the diagnosis and management of heart failure in adults had been updated in 2009; they were reviewed in this analysis instead of the earlier one cited in the ACC/AHA letter.

The first step was to search each guideline for any mention of the impact of the heart condition or its treatment on a person's capacity to engage in gainful activity, using terms such as *employment*, *return to work*, or *work capacity*. An electronic copy was scanned for the following terms:

BOX C-1
American College of Cardiology/American Heart Association (ACC/AHA) Guidelines

Heart Failure

2009 Focused Update Incorporated into the ACC/AHA 2005 Guidelines for the Diagnosis and Management of Heart Failure in Adults: A Report of the American College of Cardiology Foundation/American Heart Association Task Force on Practice Guidelines
Note: Updated version of the guideline cited in the appendix to the June 2008 ACC/AHA response letter to the Social Security Administration Advance Notice of Proposed Rulemaking.

Ischemic Heart Disease

2002 Guideline Update for the Management of Patients with Chronic Stable Angina: A Report of the American College of Cardiology/American Heart Association Task Force on Practice Guidelines (Committee to Update the 1999 Guidelines for the Management of Patients with Chronic Stable Angina)

2007 Chronic Angina Focused Update of the ACC/AHA 2002 Guidelines for the Management of Patients with Chronic Stable Angina: A Report of the American College of Cardiology/American Heart Association Task Force on Practice Guidelines Writing Group to Develop the Focused Update of the 2002 Guidelines for the Management of Patients with Chronic Stable Angina
Note: Only recommendations related to secondary prevention in patients with chronic angina were revised.

Peripheral Arterial Disease
ACC/AHA 2005 Guidelines for the Management of Patients with Peripheral Arterial Disease (Lower Extremity, Renal, Mesenteric, and Abdominal Aortic): A Collaborative Report from the American Association for Vascular Surgery/Society for Vascular Surgery, Society for Cardiovascular Angiography and Interventions, Society for Vascular Medicine and Biology, Society of Interventional Radiology, and the ACC/AHA Task Force on Practice Guidelines (Writing Committee to Develop Guidelines for the Management of Patients with Peripheral Arterial Disease)

2010 ACCF/AHA/AATS/ACR/ASA/SCA/SCAI/SIR/STS/SVM Guidelines for the Diagnosis and Management of Patients with Thoracic Aortic Disease: A Report of the American College of Cardiology Foundation/American Heart Association Task Force on Practice Guidelines, American Association for Thoracic Surgery, American College of Radiology, American Stroke Association, Society of Cardiovascular Anesthesiologists, Society for Cardiovascular Angiography and Interventions, Society of Interventional Radiology, Society of Thoracic Surgeons, and Society for Vascular Medicine
Note: This is relevant to the committee's work, although it is not cited in the ACC/AHA letter.

continued

BOX C-1 Continued

Congenital Heart Disease

ACC/AHA 2008 Guidelines for the Management of Adults with Congenital Heart Disease: A Report of the American College of Cardiology/American Heart Association Task Force on Practice Guidelines (Writing Committee to Develop Guidelines on the Management of Adults with Congenital Heart Disease)

Valvular Heart Disease

2008 Focused Update Incorporated into the ACC/AHA 2006 Guidelines for the Management of Patients with Valvular Heart Disease: A Report of the American College of Cardiology/American Heart Association Task Force on Practice Guidelines (Writing Committee to Revise the 1998 Guidelines for the Management of Patients with Valvular Heart Disease)
Note: This is relevant to the committee's work, although it is not cited in the ACC/AHA letter.

Arrhythmias

ACC/AHA/ESC 2006 Guidelines for the Management of Patients with Atrial Fibrillation: A Report of the American College of Cardiology/American Heart Association Task Force on Practice Guidelines and the European Society of Cardiology Committee for Practice Guidelines (Writing Committee to Revise the 2001 Guidelines for the Management of Patients with Atrial Fibrillation)

ACC/AHA/ESC Guidelines for the Management of Patients with Supraventricular Arrhythmias: A Report of the American College of Cardiology/American Heart Association Task Force and the European Society of Cardiology Committee for Practice Guidelines (Writing Committee to Develop Guidelines for the Management of Patients with Supraventricular Arrhythmias)
Note: Issued in 2003.

ACC/AHA/ESC 2006 Guidelines for Management of Patients with Ventricular Arrhythmias and the Prevention of Sudden Cardiac Death: A Report of the American College of Cardiology/American Heart Association Task Force and the European Society of Cardiology Committee for Practice Guidelines (Writing Committee to Develop Guidelines for Management of Patients with Ventricular Arrhythmias and the Prevention of Sudden Cardiac Death), Developed in Collaboration with the European Heart Rhythm Association and the Heart Rhythm Society (HRS)

ACC/AHA/HRS 2008 Guidelines for Device-Based Therapy of Cardiac Rhythm Abnormalities: Report of the American College of Cardiology/American Heart Association Task Force on Practice Guidelines (Writing Committee to Revise the ACC/AHA/NASPE [North American Society of Pacing and Electrophysiology] 2002 Guideline Update for Implantation of Cardiac Pacemakers and Antiarrhythmia Devices), Developed in Collaboration with the American Association for Thoracic Surgery and Society of Thoracic Surgeons

Exercise Testing

ACC/AHA 2002 Guideline Update for Exercise Testing: A Report of the American College of Cardiology/American Heart Association Task Force on Practice Guidelines (Committee on Exercise Testing)

Echocardiography

ACC/AHA/ASE (American Society of Echocardiography) 2003 Guideline Update for the Clinical Application of Echocardiography: A Report of the American College of Cardiology/American Heart Association Task Force on Practice Guidelines (ACC/AHA/ASE Committee to Update the 1997 Guidelines for the Clinical Application of Echocardiography)

- Work (e.g., working, worked, worker);
- Occupation (e.g., occupations, occupational);
- Employ (e.g., employment, employed, employability, employee, employer);
- Unemploy (e.g., unemployment, unemployed);
- Vocation (e.g., vocation, vocational);
- Job;
- Economic; and
- Gainful activity.

Each time one of these words appeared in the text of the clinical guideline, the paragraph in which it appeared was examined to see if and how it referred to the patient situation. The main objective was to see whether any diagnostic or treatment criterion, such as a laboratory test result, an examination finding, a clinical severity score, or a treatment, was associated in the clinical guideline with the existence or severity of employment disability.

The second step was to search each clinical guideline for any mention of the disabling effects of the heart condition or its treatment other than on employment. An electronic copy was scanned for the following words:

- Disab (e.g., disability, disabled, disablement);
- Functional capacity;
- Functional limitation; and
- Functional status.

RESULTS[1]

If any of these words appeared in the text of the clinical guideline, the paragraph in which it appeared was examined to see if and how it referred to the patient situation. For example, if the word *impairment* was used, did it refer to organ function or whole-person function? The main objective was to see if any diagnostic or treatment criteria (e.g., laboratory test results, examination findings, clinical severity scores, or treatment regimens) were associated with the existence or severity of disability or whole-person impairment.

The Guidelines and Disability

Generally, the guidelines contain little information relevant to developing criteria for evaluating degree of disability. They are focused on decision making regarding diagnosis and treatment. None of the guidelines addressed patient disability, employment, or employability as a major topic of discussion. For example, none had a heading or subheading for disability or employment. They rarely indicate the relationship of impairment severity to employment restrictions or even to functional limitations that might affect work capacity. Most frequently, references to disability were in the context of general assertions that the condition in question is a cause of disability, functional limitations, and lower quality of life. For example, the heart failure guidelines say heart failure is a "common, costly, disabling, and potentially fatal disorder" (Hunt et al., 2009:e395). Those guidelines go on to say that dyspnea and fatigue, the "cardinal manifestations" of heart failure, may lead to pulmonary congestion and peripheral edema, abnormalities that can reduce functional capacity and quality of life (Hunt et al., 2009:e397).

Sometimes, there are statements that a specific examination or test would be useful for determining disability but not how. For example,

> The primary value of exercise testing in valvular heart disease is to objectively assess atypical symptoms, exercise capacity, evaluation of LV function during exercise with imaging modalities, and extent of disability, which may have implications for medical, surgical, and social decision making. (Gibbons et al., 2002:40)

Several of the guidelines note that clinical findings, such as hemodynamic variables, that they recommend for diagnostic and prognostic purposes are *not* strongly associated with degree of functional limitation.

---

[1] A complete set of references to disability, employment or work, and functional capacity, limitation, or status in the ACC/AHA guidelines is included in a supplementary online table available at http://www.iom.edu/ssacardiodisability.

> Patients with a very low EF [ejection fraction] . . . may be asymptomatic, whereas patients with preserved [i.e., normal or near normal] LVEF [left ventricular ejection fraction] may have severe disability. The apparent discordance between EF and the degree of functional impairment is not well understood. . . . (Hunt et al., 2009:e397)

> The ABI [ankle-brachial index] correlates only weakly with treadmill-based walking ability for any individual patient. For example, some patients with a low ABI report minimal walking impairment, whereas some with a higher ABI report marked walking impairment. This is due at least in part to the wide range of comorbidities that can coexist with intermittent claudication in patients who have PAD [peripheral artery disease]. (Hirsch et al., 2006:e481)

Even if the guidelines placed more emphasis on disability, little available research correlates degree of impairment severity with disability outcomes, such as the relationship of different percentages of ejection fraction and employment capacity or activity limitations for individuals with heart failure. Most clinical trials look at clinical outcomes, such as mortality, recurrence, and rehospitalizations, and patient registries usually track the same outcomes. The small number of trials that have collected and reported data on employment, such as return to work after myocardial infarction or angioplasty, have found that clinical variables explain only part of the employment-related outcome; these trials did not collect information on the range of nonclinical variables that are needed to explain the employment-related outcome completely. Thus, for example, the *Guidelines for the Management of Patients with Chronic Stable Angina* note the finding in the Bypass Angioplasty Revascularization Investigation study that about 30 percent of patients who undergo angioplasty never return to work, but they do not provide guidance on how to predict which patients will not return to work because they are incapacitated by their coronary heart disease rather than for other reasons (Gibbons et al., 2002).

Some guidelines provide guidance on effective rehabilitation techniques. Effectiveness is generally based on degree of improvement in functional capacity (see next section). None are based specifically on work-related outcomes.

The Guidelines and Functional Capacity

Most of the guidelines discuss assessment of function, usually through treadmill or bicycle exercise tests or, for more disabled patients, the 6-minute walk test. A few make the statement that such tests, such as capacity to walk, are useful for evaluating disability, but none provide guidance on how specific test results predict work capacity.

The guidelines also endorse the New York Heart Association (NYHA) functional classification of symptom severity, widely used to gauge degree of functional limitation from heart failure, and the Canadian Cardiovascular Society (CCS) classification of symptoms and physical limitations from angina, used in the evaluation and treatment of ischemic heart disease. Each classification system has four classes based on the degree of exertion required to elicit symptoms, from no symptoms during ordinary activity (Class 1) to symptoms from any exertion or even at rest (Class 4). The patient's NYHA class is the basis for a number of diagnosis and treatment recommendations in the heart failure guidelines. CCS class is similarly used in the guidelines for management and follow-up of patients with chronic stable angina. NYHA functional class is also a criterion for some indications in the valvular heart disease guidelines (e.g., aortic valve repair, mitral balloon valvotomy, mitral valve repair and replacement) (Bonow et al., 2008). NYHA Class II or III is indicated for implantable cardioverter-defibrillator therapy in the guidelines on ventricular arrhythmias (Class I Recommendation, Level of Evidence: A) and for other indications (Zipes et al., 2006).

The Guidelines and Activity Limitations

The heart failure guidelines say that physical activity should be encouraged in patients with current or prior symptoms of heart failure to avoid deconditioning and exercise intolerance, "although most patients should not participate in heavy labor or exhaustive sports" (Hunt et al., 2009:e412). Guidelines for chronic stable angina similarly encourage normal physical activity, although "patients in special circumstances, for example, those who engage in extremely strenuous activity or have a high-risk occupation, may require special counseling" (Gibbons et al., 2002:63).

Patients on anticoagulants should be advised of activity restrictions, according to the valvular heart disease guidelines. The same guidelines recommend restrictions on participating in competitive sports for patients with symptomatic mitral valve prolapse and certain signs (e.g., moderate left ventricular [LV] enlargement, LV dysfunction, uncontrolled tachyarrhythmias, long-QT interval, unexplained syncope, prior resuscitation from cardiac arrest, or aortic root enlargement is present individually or in combination). Patients with mitral regurgitation "with definite LV enlargement (greater than or equal to 60 mm), pulmonary hypertension, or any degree of LV systolic dysfunction at rest should not participate in any competitive sports" (Bonow et al., 2008:e59).

The guidelines on management of patients with peripheral artery disease contained no activity restrictions (Hirsch et al., 2006). Guidelines for adult congenital heart disease contain a guidance on physical activity and exercise for patients with each type of congenital condition (e.g., atrial septal defect, ventricular septal defect, atrioventricular septal defect, dextro-transposition of the great arteries, tetralogy of Fallot) (Warnes et al., 2008). Guidelines for the diagnosis and management of patients with thoracic aortic disease include a recommendation regarding limitations on employment and lifestyle in patients with thoracic aortic disease (but based on scanty data):

> For patients with a current thoracic aortic aneurysm or dissection, or previously repaired aortic dissection, employment and lifestyle restrictions are reasonable, including the avoidance of strenuous lifting, pushing, or straining that would require a Valsalva maneuver (Class IIa, Recommendation Level of Evidence: C). (Hiratzka et al., 2010:e344)

The thoracic aortic disease guidelines go on to explain more about work:

> In terms of work, patients with thoracic aortic disease generally can function normally in most types of occupations. The exception is any job involving heavy physical and manual labor accompanied by extreme isometric exercise (e.g., lifting heavy boxes in a stockroom, carrying furniture up and down stairs). As with the heavy weight lifting described earlier, this type of unusual sudden stress on the aorta may predispose to a triggering of either aortic rupture or AoD [aortic dissection]. Therefore, when patients have a vocation in which such extreme lifting might be required, it is important to discuss the details of their daily job responsibilities and to prescribe avoidance of activities that might put them at risk. In some cases patients can readily avoid such heavy lifting on the job, but in many cases a letter from a physician explaining the restrictions may be required. (Hiratzka et al., 2010)

REFERENCES

Bonow, R. O., B. A. Carabello, K. Chatterjee, A. C. de Leon Jr., D. P. Faxon, M. D. Freed, W. H. Gaasch, B. W. Lytle, R. A. Nishimura, P. T. O'Gara, R. A. O'Rourke, C. M. Otto, P. M. Shah, and J. S. Shanewise. 2008. 2008 focused update incorporated into the ACC/AHA 2006 guidelines for the management of patients with valvular heart disease: A report of the American College of Cardiology/American Heart Association Task Force on Practice Guidelines (Writing Committee to Revise the 1998 Guidelines for the Management of Patients with Valvular Heart Disease). *Journal of the American College of Cardiology* 52(13):e1–e142. http://www.heartj.com/GuideLines/Valvular%20Heart%20Disease.pdf (accessed August 3, 2010).

Gibbons, R. J., J. Abrams, K. Chatterjee, J. Daley, P. C. Deedwania, J. S. Douglas, T. B. Ferguson Jr., S. D. Fihn, T. D. Fraker Jr., J. M. Gardin, R. A. O'Rourke, R. C. Pasternak, and S. V. Williams. 2002. ACC/AHA 2002 guideline update for the management of patients with chronic stable angina: A report of the American College of Cardiology/American Heart Association Task Force on Practice Guidelines (Committee to Update the 1999 Guidelines for the Management of Patients with Chronic Stable Angina).

http://www.acc.org/qualityandscience/clinical/guidelines/stable/stable_clean.pdf (accessed July 9, 2010).

Hiratzka, L. F., G. L. Bakris, J. A. Beckman, R. M. Bersin, V. F. Carr, D. E. Casey Jr., K. A. Eagle, L. K. Hermann, E. M. Isselbacher, E. A. Kazerooni, N. T. Kouchoukos, B. W. Lytle, D. M. Milewicz, D. L. Reich, S. Sen, J. A. Shinn, L. G. Svensson, and D. M. Williams. 2010. 2010 ACCF/AHA/AATS/ACR/ASA/SCA/SCAI/SIR/STS/ SVM guidelines for the diagnosis and management of patients with thoracic aortic disease: A report of the American College of Cardiology Foundation/American Heart Association Task Force on Practice Guidelines, American Association for Thoracic Surgery, American College of Radiology, American Stroke Association, Society of Cardiovascular Anesthesiologists, Society for Cardiovascular Angiography and Interventions, Society of Interventional Radiology, Society of Thoracic Surgeons, and Society for Vascular Medicine. *Circulation* 121(13): e266–e369. http://circ.ahajournals.org/cgi/reprint/121/13/e266 (accessed July 9, 2010).

Hirsch, A. T., Z. J. Haskal, N. R. Hertzer, C. W. Bakal, M. A. Creager, J. L. Halperin, L. F. Hiratzka, W. R. Murphy, J. W. Olin, J. B. Puschett, K. A. Rosenfield, D. Sacks, J. C. Stanley, L. M. Taylor Jr., C. J. White, J. White, R. A. White, E. M. Antman, S. C. Smith Jr., C. D. Adams, J. L. Anderson, D. P. Faxon, V. Fuster, R. J. Gibbons, S. A. Hunt, A. K. Jacobs, R. Nishimura, J. P. Ornato, R. L. Page, and B. Riegel. 2006. ACC/AHA 2005 practice guidelines for the management of patients with peripheral arterial disease (lower extremity, renal, mesenteric, and abdominal aortic): A collaborative report from the American Association for Vascular Surgery/Society for Vascular Surgery, Society for Cardiovascular Angiography and Interventions, Society for Vascular Medicine and Biology, Society of Interventional Radiology, and the ACC/AHA Task Force on Practice Guidelines (Writing Committee to Develop Guidelines for the Management of Patients with Peripheral Arterial Disease). *Circulation* 113(11):e463–e654. http://circ.ahajournals.org/cgi/reprint/113/11/e463 (accessed July 9, 2010).

Hunt, S. A., W. T. Abraham, M. H. Chin, A. M. Feldman, G. S. Francis, T. G. Ganiats, M. Jessup, M. A. Konstam, D. M. Mancini, K. Michl, J. A. Oates, P. S. Rahko, M. A. Silver, L. W. Stevenson, and C. W. Yancy. 2009. 2009 focused update incorporated into the ACC/AHA 2005 guidelines for the diagnosis and management of heart failure in adults: A report of the American College of Cardiology Foundation/American Heart Association Task Force on Practice Guidelines. *Circulation* 119(14):e391–e479. http://circ.ahajournals.org/cgi/reprint/119/14/e391 (accessed September 9, 2010).

Warnes, C. A., R. G. Williams, T. M. Bashore, J. S. Child, H. M. Connolly, J. A. Dearani, P. del Nido, J. W. Fasules, T. P. Graham Jr., Z. M. Hijazi, S. A. Hunt, M. E. King, M. J. Landzberg, P. D. Miner, M. J. Radford, E. P. Walsh, and G. D. Webb. 2008. ACC/AHA 2008 guidelines for the management of adults with congenital heart disease: A report of the American College of Cardiology/American Heart Association Task Force on Practice Guidelines (Writing Committee to Develop Guidelines on the Management of Adults with Congenital Heart Disease). *Journal of the American College of Cardiology* 52(23):e143–e263. http://content.onlinejacc.org/cgi/reprint/52/23/e143.pdf (accessed July 9, 2010).

Zipes, D. P., A. J. Camm, M. Borggrefe, A. E. Buxton, B. Chaitman, M. Fromer, G. Gregoratos, G. Klein, A. J. Moss, R. J. Myerburg, S. G. Priori, M. A. Quinones, D. M. Roden, M. J. Silka, and C. Tracy. 2006. ACC/AHA/ESC 2006 guidelines for management of patients with ventricular arrhythmias and the prevention of sudden cardiac death: A report of the American College of Cardiology/American Heart Association Task Force and the European Society of Cardiology Committee for Practice Guidelines (Writing Committee to Develop Guidelines for Management of Patients with Ventricular Arrhythmias and the Prevention of Sudden Cardiac Death), developed in collaboration with the European Heart Rhythm Association and the Heart Rhythm Society. *Journal of the American College of Cardiology* 48:e247–e346. http://content.onlinejacc.org/cgi/reprint/48/5/e247.pdf (accessed July 9, 2010).